D0881212

Future Interaction Design

A. Pirhonen, H. Isomäki, C. Roast and
P. Saariluoma (Eds)

Future
Interaction
Design

 Springer

Antti Pirhonen, PhD
Pertti Saariluoma, PhD
Department of Computer Science & Information Systems,
University of Jyväskylä
Finland

Hannakaisa Isomäki, PhD
Department of Research Methodology
University of Lapland
Finland

Chris Roast, PhD
School of Computing and Management Sciences
Sheffield Hallam University
UK

British Library Cataloguing in Publication Data
Future interaction design
   1. Human-computer interaction   2. Computer software —
   Development   3. User interfaces (Computer systems)   4. Design —
   Human factors
   I. Pirhonen, Antti
   005.1'2'019
   ISBN 1852337915

Library of Congress Cataloging-in-Publication Data is available.

ISBN 1-85233-791-5 Springer-Verlag London Berlin Heidelberg
Springer Science+Business Media
springeronline.com

Typesetting: Electronic text files prepared by the editors
Printed and bound at Kyodo Printing Co (S'pore) Pte Ltd
34/3830-543210   Printed on acid-free paper   SPIN 10964088

Contents

Contributors

Liam J. Bannon
  Interaction Design Centre
  University of Limerick
  Ireland
  liam.bannon@ul.ie

José J. Cañas,
  Department of Experimental Psychology
  University of Granada
  Granada
  Spain
  delagado@ugr.es

Andrew Dearden
  Computing Research Centre
  Sheffield Hallam University
  UK
  a.m.dearden@shu.ac.uk

Inmaculada Fajardo
  Faculty of Computer Science
  Basque Country University
  Donostia
  Spain
  acbfabri@si.ehu.es

Anita Greenhill
  Department of Information Systems
  University of Manchester Institute of Science and Technology (UMIST)
  UK
  a.greenhill@umist.ac.uk

Hannakaisa Isomäki
  Department of Research Methodology
  University of Lapland
  Finland
  hisomaki@urova.fi

Panos Markopoulos
  Technische Universiteit Eindhoven
  The Netherlands
  p.markopoulos@tue.nl

John McCarthy
  Department of Applied Psychology
  University College Cork
  Ireland
  john.mccarthy@ucc.ie

Antti Pirhonen
  Department of Computer Science and Information Systems
  University of Jyväskylä
  Finland
  pianta@cc.jyu.fi

Pertti Saariluoma
  Department of Computer Science and Information Systems
  University of Jyväskylä
  Finland
  psa@cc.jyu.fi

Ladislao Salmerón
  Department of Experimental Psychology
  University of Granada
  Spain
  lalo@ugr.es

Michael Thomsen
  Interactive Institute AB
  Kastrup
  Denmark
  michael.thomsen@tii.se

Jayne Wallace
  Art & Design Research Centre
  Sheffield Hallam University
  UK
  jswallac@athena.shu.ac.uk

Peter Wright
  Department of Computer Science
  University of York
  UK
  peter.wright@cs.york.ac.uk

Mary Zajicek
  Department of Computing, School of Technology
  Oxford Brookes University
  UK
  mzajicek@brookes.ac.uk

Introducing the challenges of future interaction design

Human interaction with technological artefacts is a fascinating research domain. We are constantly surrounded by physical objects that are primarily designed for people to use and from which they can benefit. However, with some of those artefacts we, as users, are satisfied, and with others we are not. We make assessments and judgements about the difficulty, pleasantness, appropriateness and effectiveness of the products we interact with in our everyday life. How we use such products is determined by these continual assessments. Although users may not be systematic in their assessment, user dissatisfaction leads to the potential benefits of an artefact not being realised and its misuse, abandonment or even rejection. For instance, if one word processor is found to be easier to use than another it may be preferred, despite both of them offering the same functionality. The increasing adoption, integration and inclusion of technological artefacts in work, leisure and education means that a considerable range of users' needs must be recognised in order for technology to serve its intended purpose. In the case of a preferred word processor, the preference may be defined at an organisational level, and the users may simply have to manage with the technology provided. Hence, it is vital that interface design can follow the possibilities opened up by technology, ensuring that users are able to interact effectively and efficiently with the ever-improving functionality offered by technology.

Interaction design is a serious problem for a growing user population faced with a constantly evolving range of sophisticated technologies and services while also having to take account of the many factors that influence quality for the end-user. Typical questions often addressed include: how can people know what a device offers, how can they access what is offered and how can they relate what is offered most effectively to their immediate or current needs?

In most cases, probably the most important aim of interaction design is to ensure high quality in terms of the planned use of a product. However, it is not difficult to find examples of failure in this endeavour. There might be limited design resources in terms of time and money. There may also be a lack of sufficient relevant knowledge of users' work and activity, or a lack of necessary design creativity. In addition, the final product may in fact be used for a task, or by a person, for whom it is not designed. In the latter case, it is rarely considered the fault of the designer. For instance, the poor acoustics of Finlandia-house in Helsinki is argued not to be the fault of Alvar Aalto (the architect), but rather an administrative problem. The original assignment was to design a conference centre. Once the building was completed, however, it became used as, and referred to, as a concert hall. Thus it was not designed for use as a concert hall, but it was declared as such. In the case of a word processor it may be misused to produce a poster design and not a document – a distinction that many users may not immediately recognise. Hence, interaction design not only has to take account of how technology may support intended use but also potential peripheral uses.

Although such factors are familiar within design in general, they are particularly problematic in the case of interaction design due to the potential complexity of the technologies involved.

The challenges of interaction design are of a special nature when dealing with artefacts with computational power and interconnectivity. In many cases the computations and communications satisfy clearly identifiable needs: for instance, bank account details are encoded and communicated reliably enough to enable users to obtain cash, and control their finances, at arbitrary locations nationally, if not internationally. Interaction design is concerned with ensuring that technology supporting such needs is designed to suit those intended to benefit from it. Therefore, the financial control offered to users via a Web portal, for example, should provide an acceptable method of controlling their finances. (One can imagine the frustrating experience were this not the case, for instance, if users were required, for example, to validate their identity repeatedly throughout an interaction.) The communication and computational power available to designers, and thus made available to users, means far more complex qualities become relevant in developing a good design. For example, users may have to understand how they have configured their financial control facilities and also assess whether the system they use has followed their instructions correctly. In such cases, interaction designers have to consider the emerging needs that arise from the available technology. So, returning to the example of word processing, understanding the precise effect of, say, hierarchical style sheets becomes a necessary non-trivial skill appropriate for preparing large documents.

The potential of technological advances is great and raises further questions about the nature of human device interaction and its design. For instance, if devices are imbued with distributed intelligence and agency, then it is quite possible that their intended benefits are strongly predicated upon valid functioning and behaviour. The activity of configuring, or training, a device becomes one of setting the attributes of a hidden complex computational process embodied in a device. Conventional design techniques from within the field of human-computer interaction cannot easily cope with the challenges that such advanced systems pose. Hence, it is necessary to examine new types of methods, theoretical concepts and theories to be able to effectively ensure valuable interface design in future.

Multidisciplinary reality

One of the most important features of the realistic practice of interaction design is its multidisciplinary nature. Engineers, designers, social scientists and even humanists have to work productively together. This naturally presents challenges since the values, methods and philosophies of each discipline are, by definition, different. Multidisciplinary work requires a focus for productive communication and co-operation that will enable disciplines to understand their relative roles and potential in development. Skills research has shown that high-level skills presuppose a decade of devoted work. This is why it is hardly possible to be a highest-level engineer, designer and psychologist at the same time. A number of alternative foci for communication and co-operation have proved to be successful. These include: (a) establishing a deep understanding of the alternative perspectives and their conceptual integration (this is often based upon a personal mutual trust between individuals); (b) identifying a currency for communication in the form of results or components that can be exchanged; (c) having an explicit design project or product that serves as an explicit and necessary means of mediation and understanding.

Considerable interdisciplinary challenges arise from the complexity of the uses and multiple interests associated with modern technology, in particular the unplanned mixed use of devices, and the integration of different device technologies. For instance, the use of SMS to influence the flow or outcome of interactive television and streaming shows is now common despite this not being an intended feature of either of the initial technologies (mobile messaging and television). Similarly the integration of technologies can challenge the established uses or paradigms of use. For instance, the advancement of digital cameras has changed the process of domestic photography, in that the pictures can now be previewed and deleted without cost and without delay. These unforeseen effects again complicate the process of effective interaction design, since established or preferred activities may be exactly those which technologies modify or disrupt.

Roots of interaction design

For two decades, the paradigm of human-computer interaction (HCI) has provided an appropriate framework for both researchers and practitioners to design, analyse and evaluate the interaction between a human being and computational artefacts. The interdisciplinary nature of the paradigm has not prevented it from developing as a well-established field, drawing upon a number of, largely scientific, disciplines. Methods and techniques have been developed for HCI practitioners each with accepted strengths, weaknesses and appropriateness for specific design problems. Frequently, these traditions have been formed on the basis of reacting to practical needs within interface design arising from technological advances and new application domains. There certainly exist broad principles that can be used in all stages of design. These principles can even be used during the first steps in the creation of a new product concept or interaction concept, but their scope is limited to the current paradigm of HCI. New technologies and the growing awareness of their uses and of user needs require new types of paradigm, capable of integrating traditional empirical and analytic approaches as well as approaches that are novel though applicable to advanced artefacts in a human world.

Modern interaction research must do more than simply extend human-computer interaction. New types of knowledge and skill have to be applied to the increasingly powerful and complex relationship between humans and computers. The prospect of ambient, ubiquitous and proactive computing and associated advances in services and service production necessitate the consideration of wider perspectives within interaction design. The aforementioned example of the concert hall illustrates how many types of design problems can be ones of effective interaction and interaction design.

The opening up of new technological possibilities invites new types of specialists into the field. It is not enough to be an engineer or psychologist with an active interest in interaction. For example, education, sociology, philosophy, art design, marketing, gerontology, demography and culture research can been shown to have a necessary role in addressing the challenging new problems. Furthermore, it is unrealistic for such a collection of disciplines and expertise to be reflected in a unified field. Hence, future interaction studies will be characterised by the diversity of applicable skills and methods between which practitioners have to choose. Indeed, it can be seen in the chapters of this book that there is a tendency towards a new way of organising work and knowledge.

Meeting the future

The chapters of this volume reflect a sample of contemporary research relevant to future interaction. As such, they are diverse in terms of their core fields, paradigms and directions and have little of a common framework for comparison and utilisation. In terms of the practical utilisation of much of this research, the necessary multidisciplinary skills and expertise are currently rare within many organisations. Within organisations only a relatively small number of people are able to synthesise novel concepts from extant research.

The organisation of creativity involves the facilitation of active multi-disciplinary and interdisciplinary communication within project groups; to embody such groups within the managed processes of an organisation.

At the substance level individual groups of practitioners encounter a diverse set of practitioner disciplines at firsthand. As a result they learn to recognise the skills of people from other backgrounds and how they can be mutually beneficial to each other. As mentioned earlier, effective communication is mediated by the specific project on which a group works. Organisational knowledge of the understanding developed in such groups is not immediately available.

In contrast to the operation of small creative project groups, large manufacturers and service providers require manageable product development processes. The effective integration of the substance-level activities that innovate and the organisational-level activities to manage innovation is a difficult problem in many of the new information technology sectors. The sector needs to look further afield to industries in which innovation and creativity have an established role. For instance, the design industries have distinct practices and organisations in which the relevance of creative thought is recognised as central and intrinsic.

Reflecting this growing range of concerns this book provides an initial step in the broadening of perspectives and techniques with which HCI practitioners and interaction researchers need to be conversant. As such, we wish to emphasise new concepts that are likely to contribute to the discipline and prepare it for design problems of the future. Our emphasis is upon the human being as a social, cognitive, emotional, creative and active agent. It is these values rather than the facilitating technology that determine users' needs and successful interaction. This perspective is especially important considering the diversity of potential users that technology is capable of supporting. The diversity of issues and interests can be seen in those adopted by the contributors to this book. It is difficult, if not impossible, to prioritise the perspective of, and benefits offered by, each chapter. Nevertheless, in solving concrete interaction problems the differing approaches could foster a design process for which the common problem of interaction design effectively provides a unifying tacit discourse.

It is important to note that these new paradigm elements have been successful and are established in other fields and domains. Hence, the work described can be seen as genuinely expanding the field of interaction and in doing so also contributing to practice in other domains. The work calls us to step back from many established systems of beliefs and to reinvestigate the problems of interaction. As such, the book illustrates and offers some of the tools that can be used to build the ideas of new interaction research.

The new perspectives and approaches to HCI are presented in this book both as conceptual approaches and more pragmatic examples of practice. The chapter by Peter Wright and John McCarthy presents a holistic approach to examining the notion of subjective human experience as a significant factor in the quality of many interactive systems. The work draws upon pragmatist views of experience that provide a valuable emphasis when we come to consider the less objective influences upon interaction design. Specifically the work illustrates how employing a literary motivated account of experience offers valuable insights into effective design in various real-life projects. Liam Bannon paints a clear picture about the multidisciplinary nature of the future. He focuses on both new technology and the challenges of the new multidimensional concept of the user. He shows how a variety of new design paradigms arises from the analysis of human activity. Anita Greenhill and Hannakaisa Isomäki emphasise the need for multidisciplinary approaches in solving the problems of future interaction design. In their chapter they start to build a multidisciplinary framework which combines standpoints from HCI, information systems and social theory in order to prepare the ground for designs that support identity construction within Web information systems. Specifically the chapter illustrates the social nature of human interactions in virtual spaces. Within the context of design process, Pertti Saariluoma offers a design framework for alternative, and possibly conflicting, theories. The basic approach is meta-scientific and works to outline the design process and its specification. It also argues that we need to have very different explanatory frameworks, if we intend to base our design decisions on empirical facts rather than intuitions. José J. Cañas, Ladislao Salmerón and Inmaculada Fajardo call attention to the limits of traditional cognitive concepts and the basic theoretical language in interaction design. They illustrate how difficult it is to generalise from standard cognitive models to the reality of interaction problems. Antti Pirhonen proposes metaphors as central representational elements, on the basis of which human conceptualisation processes can be understood. He demonstrates how this kind of view of metaphors can be constructively applied in interaction design. At a more pragmatic level, Panos Markopoulos presents his five principles for the design of ubiquitous computer-human interaction. He applies the principles to a social setting case, a connected family. While Markopoulos focuses upon families as a specific user group, Mary Zajicek is concerned about how older adults are taken into account in the design of new technology. Her work is motivated by both demographics and the special characteristics of senior citizens as users. Michael Thomsen shows the kinds of practical problems that must be resolved in developing new artefacts with previously unimagined computational power. The chapter by Jayne Wallace and Andrew Dearden effectively reflects a practitioner-centred view of concerns similar to those of Wright and McCarthy, but focused specifically upon digital jewellery. In this contribution the starting point is that of introducing jewellery design with its wealth of experience in examining the human desires for worn artefacts. Thus Wallace and Dearden begin from the position of a humanist discipline with an established practice. The work goes on to illustrate that approaches to developing a more explicit understanding of design can be applied in this domain, drawing upon analytic accounts of user experience. Such approaches provide a significant initial link between humanist and scientific disciplines.

It is clear that the interdisciplinary character of interaction design is a core feature to be embraced further in future interaction design. Such work raises familiar problems – each discipline is based on its own history and traditions, which constitute their unique paradigms. These paradigms provide a safe and workable conceptual framework within a discipline. However, these qualities are jeopardised when communication between disciplines is necessary. In practice, a strive toward interdisciplinary communication often results in lowering the conceptual level, perhaps rendering it shallow. In the editorial work we have been forced to encourage the contributors to communicate their ideas to people from outside the contributors' own disciplines. The central method by which contributors have made their ideas understandable even outside their own field has been to provide practical, concrete examples rather than trying to articulate the theoretical points by simplifying them for an interdisciplinary audience. We believe that the book has in this way a lot to offer for both those who wish to get an alternative view on interaction design, a view that is constituted within an unfamiliar discipline – and those interested in finding fresh ideas for work within their own discipline.

Acknowledgements

This book is also a final report of the CogEmo-project, which was funded by National Technology Agency of Finland, Nokia Mobile Phones Ltd. and Yomi Solutions Ltd.

We wish to express our gratefulness to Liz Sillence for her profound work with the language revisions of most of the chapters, as well as Liisa Kuparinen for accuracy and diligence in the laborious typesetting and other formatting of this book.

Jyväskylä, April 2004

Antti Pirhonen, Hannakaisa Isomäki, Chris Roast & Pertti Saariluoma

The value of the novel in designing for experience

Peter Wright[1], John McCarthy[2]

[1]Department of Computer Science, University of York
UK
peter.wright@cs.york.ac.uk

[2]Department of Applied Psychology, University College Cork
Ireland
john.mccarthy@ucc.ie

Abstract

If future interaction design is to take designing for experience seriously we must first understand more clearly what we mean by experience. We argue that the science-based disciplines usually associated with human-computer interaction may not be the best place to look for such theoretical foundations and that it may be time for human-computer interaction to look farther afield to the arts and humanities. We have turned towards the pragmatic philosophy of John Dewey and the literary theory and philosophy of Mikhail Bakhtin as our starting point. In this chapter we lean on Bakhtin's analysis of the novel and "felt life" and use this to explore ways in which we can help designers engage with experience. Building on Bakhtin's analysis of creative understanding, we argue for a dialogical analysis of the relationship between designer and user. We conclude with one or two interesting examples of design work that seem to capture the spirit of this approach to design.

1 Designing for experience

As computers become a ubiquitous part of our lives, no longer confined to the workplace, the focus of design and evaluation has turned towards user experience. The concept of user experience has already been influential in the design and evaluation of electronic commerce systems, computer games and other leisure applications, and it is now beginning to have an influence in other areas of HCI. In their recent textbook on interaction design, Preece, Rogers and Sharp (2002) argue that interaction designers should concern themselves with setting not only usability goals for their products but also user experience goals to assess whether the product is, for example, enjoyable, satisfying and motivating. They also point to the multidisciplinary nature of interaction design teams comprising engineers, programmers, graphic artists, writers and so on as a means of ensuring the user experience is given due consideration in the design process.

Despite this commitment to user experience as a design driver, our understanding of experience and how it might be positioned with respect to design, remains underdeveloped in the research and practice of interaction design. In some cases it is used unproductively as a discursive rather than analytical concept. In others, it is reduced to the more familiar problem of usability engineering. In the worst case experience is reduced to something that is controlled by the designer through the interactive device itself. Take, for example, these quotes from a recent book on Web design (Garrett 2002):

The user experience development process is all about ensuring that no aspect of the user's experience with your site happens without your conscious, explicit intent. This means taking into account every possibility of every action the user is likely to take and understanding the user's expectations at every step of the way through that process. (p. 21)

That neat, tidy experience actually results from a whole set of decisions – some small, some large – about how the site looks, how it behaves, and what it allows you to do. (p. 22)

This kind of description of user experience and its relation to design belies a way of thinking about experience which is deeply rooted in traditional cognitivist and behaviourist ways of thinking about human-computer interaction. It presumes a closed world of action, a view of the user as passive and the interface/designer as controlling. Even its approach to Web site look and feel is deeply routed in a scientific and formal conception of aesthetics as a property of the artefact.

Such an approach to user experience does not do justice to the richness of people's lived experience with technology. If we are to take user experience seriously as a way of enriching our understanding human-computer interaction and interaction design we need to begin with a much clearer conception of what we mean by experience.

When someone talks about a personal experience they have had, they tend not to be solely concerned with telling people what they did. Rather their story seeks to talk about why they did it, what it felt like, what it meant to them, its value in their lives and what commitments they have made as a consequence. These are not things with which the human sciences are traditionally comfortable. The realist ontology of science and its objective third-person stance make the study of something as firsthand and particular as felt life difficult. Other disciplines such as art and literary theory are much more comfortable with the personal and with felt life. Dewey's work on art as experience (Dewey 1934) and Bakhtin's work on the philosophy of the act (Bakhtin 1993), for example, shun the abstract theoreticism of both science and formal aesthetics in favour of an account of experience which emphasises the particularity of felt life. So as HCI turns its attention to experience then, perhaps it is time to explore new metaphors from other disciplines in order to find a way of answering these problematic questions.

Our own search for a conception of experience that does full justice to the felt life of interactions with technology leans heavily on pragmatist philosophy (in particular, Dewey (1934)) and literary theory (in particular, Bakhtin (1993)) for an account that places the individual, the aesthetic and the act of sense making at the centre of our conception of experience. McCarthy and Wright (2004) argue that human experience can be usefully viewed as constituted by continuous engagement with the world through acts of sense making at many levels.

Continuous engagement involves an irreducible relationship between self and object, the concerned, feeling person acting and the materials and tools he or she uses. In this pragmatic approach, experience registers life as lived and felt, and as something with the potential to be richly integrated and meaningful. Everyday experience is primarily aesthetic since meaning emerges out of the dynamic relationship between sensual, emotional and intellectual levels of engagement at a particular time and place that bring about a particular quality of experience be it satisfying, enchanting, disappointing or frustrating. In a meaningful and satisfying experience each act relates coherently to the total action and is felt by the experiencer to have a unity or a wholeness that is fulfilling.

This general approach to analysing experience has been usefully applied in a number of interestingly diverse settings. Wright, McCarthy and Meekison (2003) describe how this general approach can be used to develop a framework for analysing users' experiences of e-shopping (see also McCarthy and Wright 2004). E-shopping is one of those applications where usability and user experience come into strong contact. Usability is clearly essential to any e-shopping site, but our approach to user experience with its emphasis on feltlife orients the analysts to issues of trust, sense of self, loyalty and identity. It also extends the analysis beyond the boundaries of any given episode of on-line interaction to a consideration of how the idea of e-shopping at a particular store fits with people's lives. McCarthy, Wright, Wallace and Dearden (2004) have also used the approach to analyse the enchantment of contemporary jewellery and suggest ways the design of digital jewellery might be improved. For example, they argue that the depth of a design is central to the experience of enchantment. They characterise depth in terms of a set of sensibilities, which highlight relational qualities, such as paradox and being-in-play that were present in contemporary non-digital jewellery, but not yet well developed in digital jewellery (see also McCarthy and Wright 2003).

A key feature of our approach to experience emphasised by this case study is that how an individual makes sense of a situation, interaction, episode or artefact is as much about what the individual brings to the experience as it is about what the designer puts there. If we take, for example, the everyday experience of watching a movie, different people may take away different things from watching the same movie. Even the same person watching a movie for a second time may have different feelings about it and understand it differently.

Our experiences are different because we bring different experiences to the movie. We bring experiences of past films into a movie with us, but in addition we also bring our experiences of the day we have just had and the day we expect tomorrow to be. Our expectations, and the quality of the felt experience, are likely to be different when we go to the movies having had a bad day at home or work than when we go after a good day. Moreover, the feeling that we should really be at home preparing for what is likely to be a demanding day tomorrow brings an expectation of a future experience into the present one of watching the movie.

Of course it is sometimes the case that people experience some parts of a movie in very similar ways. For example, many people find the shower scene in Hitchcock's *Psycho* or the random shooting of prisoners in *Schindler's List* chilling even the second time they watch it. Even if we don't experience these scenes in the way the moviemaker intended, we can nevertheless understand how we were expected to experience them.

Boorstin (1990), a script writer, argues that, in order to achieve these effects, the moviemaker must be able to experience the movie in the way he hopes the public will, but in addition must know what it takes on a technical level to help the public construct that experience. They must understand how they want the audience to "see" the movie and must be able to relate this understanding to the technical means of supporting those ways of seeing. As we argue later, there is an important if subtle distinction here: the moviemaker doesn't see the movie in the same way an untrained moviegoer does; his technical knowledge gives him a surplus of knowledge over the moviegoer. But he *understands* the ways in which such a moviegoer *could* see the movie. The moviemaker must be able to *engage with* the moviegoer's ways of seeing. This skill is more than just simulating how the moviegoer will put together the plot. Such an analogy is too cognitivist for what Boorstin is trying to get at. Rather the skill is more like identifying with – or having empathy for – the moviegoer's possible experience. But the moviemaker cannot control how the moviegoer will ultimately make sense of the movie on a personal level or what he or she will get out of it on a particular occasion. This will depend on the moviegoer's particular and unique perspective.

This tight relationship posited by Boorstin between the moviemaker's and moviegoer's way of seeing and the designed artefact which is the film, is central to how we think about the relationship between interaction design and experience. It implies that we cannot design an experience but that, with a sensitive and skilled way of seeing user experience, we might be able to design *for* an experience. From this perspective designed artefacts, be they mobile telephones or Internet shops, are means by which designers can mediate experience but not a means by which they can control it.

Having put forward a substantive conception of what we mean by experience, one which places felt life and sense making at its centre, and having argued that experience cannot be designed, it remains to be seen what it might mean to design for experience. Like our account of experience itself, our account of what it might mean to design for experience leans heavily on ways of thinking about design that emerge from arts and humanities rather than from sciences and engineering.

As Dewey (1934) points out, the realist ontology of the natural sciences is no more useful for understanding design than it is for understanding human experience. The problem lies, according to Dewey, in the fact that the natural sciences are backward looking inasmuch as they seek to describe the way the world is, whereas the problem of design is to create an understanding of the way we might want the world to be. So instead of objective description it is necessary to place creative imagination and ways of seeing at the centre of our approach. In particular, we turn our attention to Bakhtin's suggestion that the novel is the most sophisticated tool available for seeing experience (Bakhtin 1981, 1984, 1986; Morson and Emerson 1990). In doing this our aim is not to provide new methods and techniques. Interaction design is full of methods and techniques. If future interaction design is to make progress, it is not more techniques that are required. Rather what is required is means by which practitioners can critically reflect (Agre 1997) on the methods, tools and techniques they use in order to understand how, why and when they are useful for engaging with experience.

So, while we might argue that Bakhtin's conception of the novel could quite literally be used as another experience design tool, our aim is more substantive than this in two ways. Firstly, it is not Bakhtin's claim that the novel is the best way of seeing human experience that is centrally important; rather it is his way of analysing the novelistic genres as offering qualitatively different ways of seeing experience that can provide us with ways of positioning different interaction design techniques. Secondly, it is Bakhtin's analysis of the process of authoring a novel as well as his approach to analysing the different relationships between characters, authors and plots that provides us with ideas about the relationships among interaction designers, users and designed artefacts.

2 The novel as a way of seeing experience

Bakhtin argued that the novel can be treated as a sophisticated tool for seeing, valuing and expressing human experience, sophisticated in the sense that it is "a style of styles, an orchestration of the diverse languages of everyday life into a heterogeneous sort of a whole" (Morson and Emerson 1990, p. 17). Wayne Booth, in his introduction to *Problems of Dostoevsky's Poetics* (Booth 1984), argues that Bakhtin's deep interest in the power of some novelists to transcend the author's voice and to create a multicentred, multivoiced universe is not a technical or literary-theoretic interest, rather it is:

…part of a lifetime inquiry into profound questions about the entire enterprise of thinking about what human life means. …When novelists imagine characters, they imagine worlds that characters inhabit, worlds that are laden with value. Whenever they reduce those worlds to one, the author's, they give a false report. (Bakhtin 1984, pp. xxiv-xxv)

The novel can have a rich interior as well as exterior life, reflecting one of the qualities of people's experience with computers that we are trying to explore. Moreover great novels seem to operate at both mimetic and diegetic levels, engaging us at precognitive and cognitive levels, creating experiences which are at once sensual, emotional and intellectual. We surely feel what is happening in a novel, and identify and empathise with the characters. But we also bring ideas to the novel and take new ideas away, ones that we discuss with others and that may have changed our selves. Moreover, the novel has the potential to be a multivoiced dialogic – a useful stance for expressing the open and continually changing and developing nature of experience with technology.

But not all novels are alike. Bakhtin distinguished between different styles of novel in terms of the richness with which they present experience and their view on what it is to be human. To understand the novel as a way of seeing the personal and the particular in user experience, we need to step back for a minute to examine Bakhtin's approach to the variety of ways of seeing that is available to us, which he characterised as *genres*.

2.1 Novelistic Genres and the different qualities of experience

For the formalists of Bakhtin's time, genre meant the collection of literary devices that authors use to give a literary work a certain style. But, concerned to keep creativity central and to avoid the implication that aesthetic was somehow a property of the artefact, Bakhtin and his group used the term genre not to refer to different ways of describing the world but rather to different ways of seeing it, where a particular genre gives the author and reader a particular way of looking at experience. Although genre was central to Bakhtin's work on what it is to be human, his ideas on genre changed from time to time throughout his career. However, what remained constant was the idea that one particular genre of novel, which he referred to as the *polyphonic novel*, was the best tool for conceptualising human experience that our cultures have so far developed.

The polyphonic novel has a number of important characteristics. Firstly, its emphasis is on characters rather than plot. In a polyphonic novel, unlike say in an adventure novel, what the characters do is not simply a function of what is going on around them. Characters and their goals and intentions are not determined by their situation. In the polyphonic novel, plot serves more to bring characters together to engage in dialogue than to determine what they must do. Bakhtin described the function of plot in the polyphonic novel thus:

"Its goal is to place a person in various situations that expose and provoke him, to bring people into conflict – in such a way however, that they do not remain in this area of plot-related contact but exceed its bounds. (Bakhtin 1984, pp. 276-277)

Thus plot becomes a way of creating scenes for intense dialogues with unforeseen outcomes. Such dialogues are central to the polyphonic novel. We do not learn of the fate of characters, their personality traits, their intentions or their values by listening to the author talking about them. Rather, they are revealed to us through the dialogue between the characters themselves. Furthermore, the only access we have to the world of the novel is through the eyes of the characters and this includes our access to the characters themselves. We see what some characters do and how other characters make sense of it. Dialogues in a polyphonic novel have, not surprisingly, a dialogical sense of truth. That is, we see the world of the novel from the multiple perspectives of different characters with different values systems, and there is seldom one best way forward. Rather it is the relations between these values systems that drive the novel on. By having this direct access to the characters as centres of value, we develop an understanding of their moment-to-moment concerns and the emotional-volitional nature of their agency. Furthermore, because in a polyphonic novel, characters' actions are not causally determined by plot, a creative response can be drawn out of them without destroying the coherence of the story.

Another important feature of the polyphonic novel is the idea of emergence. In an adventure novel, which Bakhtin took to be a less sophisticated view of experience, the action leaves no trace on the hero. For all the difference it makes to the hero it might as well never have happened. The entire action of the adventure novel takes place in what Bakhtin describes as "an extratemporal hiatus between two moments in biological time" (1981, p. 90). The adventures themselves are often caused by chance events, a shipwreck, an aircraft crash, an unexpected war or a crime. Actual historical time and place are entirely irrelevant to this genre. For a shipwreck one needs a sea and a storm but which sea and when doesn't matter.

In contrast, in the genre of the polyphonic novel, the fullness of time and place colour substantially the hero's possibilities. What a heroine such as Anna Karenina does, thinks and feels is seen in the context of the cultural and social position of women of that period. Perhaps more important is the fact that characters change as a consequence of their experience and we, the readers, do not know from the outset whether the heroine and hero will get together in the end. What happens in between is crucially important in this regard. Unlike James Bond, Anna Karenina is not the same person on the last page as she was on the first page.

Bakhtin uses the term chronotope to describe these different qualities of space-time or what we might think of as the sense of place that different settings have. To quote from Morson and Emerson (1990):

Bakhtin's crucial point is that time and space vary in qualities; different social activities and representations of those activities presume different kinds of time and space. Time and space are therefore not just neutral "mathematical" abstractions.

Morson and Emerson go on to suggest that considering the quality of space and time in a situation leads one to ask questions such as whether the setting simply serves as an unchanging backdrop for human activity but does not change that activity: whether actions are deeply bound to a specific time and place and implausible or meaningless in different settings; whether actors have any initiative, creativity or control over events or whether they simply respond to changes beyond their control in predictable ways; whether individuals grow and develop as they experience or whether they remain unchanged by what they experience. Is there a concept of the personal and private that is distinct from the public and shared? How does past impinge on present and how is future oriented to and envisioned? Such questions asked by Morson and Emerson of the setting for novels, could equally well be asked of the kinds of descriptions of workplaces or other settings for interaction design. Furthermore, whether interaction designers see work as routine and repetitive or full of change and growth should have quite different implications for how a tool to support that work might be designed.

3 Helping designers see experience

The brief introduction to the Bakhtin's analysis of the novelistic genre offered above illustrates why he saw the novel as the best means of seeing human experience. But as well as providing an insight into ways of seeing human experience the metaphor of the polyphonic novel can be used to characterise, critique and explore different approaches to analysing experience for design. These different approaches will be presented as different ways in which designers can engage with user experience. Some approaches use representational tools both as a way of seeing and a way of reporting experience, others require the designer to enter into particular forms of dialogue with users, and still others require the designers to adopt a particular sensibility or mindset when they design.

3.1 Engaging designers through narrative

At the heart of the novelistic genre is the idea of narrative, so perhaps the best way to engage designers is by writing narratives that make visible people's personal experience with computers. Strange though such a proposition might sound, in some sense at least, that is central to a number of user-centred design approaches.

3.1.1 The ethnographic vignette

Over the last twenty years, HCI has come to recognise the potential contribution to design that can be made by ethnographic workplace studies. Interpretive ethnographic analysis with its commitment to culturally shared meanings has always had a flirtatious relationship with experience. Geertz (1986) wrote, for example, that without experience, or something like it "cultural analyses seem to float several feet above their human ground" (Geertz 1986, p. 374). If culture is not to be used in a meaningless manner, separate from people fearing, hoping, imagining, revolting and consoling, "it must engage some sort of felt life, which might as well be called experience" (Geertz 1986, p. 374). Examples of this ethnographic engagement with felt life can be found in Bruner and Turner's *The Anthropology of Experience* (Bruner and Turner 1986).

In workplace studies, narrative vignettes, short pen pictures of people in a setting, have been used to capture the felt experience of working in a particular place or setting. For example, Julian Orr's (1996) description of the work of photocopier repairers includes vignettes of work in the field, structured as stories. For example:

First Vignette-A breakfast meeting.
I drive across the valley to meet the members of the CST (or subteam) for breakfast at a chain restaurant in as small city on the east side. Silicon valley is clear this morning... (Orr 1996, p. 15)

Vignettes are also used in Hutchins' (1995) opening chapter of *Cognition in the Wild* entitled "Welcome on board" where he tells the story of an incident in which a naval vessel loses steerage as it comes into port at San Diego; and Wenger (1998) provides vignettes such as "Welcome to claims processing!" (Wenger 1998, p. 18) in which he describes the life of insurance claims officers.

While ethnographic vignettes have proved a useful tool for communicating something of the felt life of people working with technology, they are essentially descriptive tools. Anderson (1994) goes further and argues that not only can narrative be a useful way of describing experience but also that a narrative sensibility features centrally in the way in which ethnographers should think about their analysis. He argues that literary techniques such as metaphor, metonym and synecdoche are crucial tools for the analytic ethnographer, where the aim is not merely to describe the way things are but to provide new insight through comparison and analogy. Taylor and Harper's (2002) description of mobile phone messaging as *gift giving* is a good technological example of this. Here parallels are drawn between the text messaging of modern-day teenagers and the ritualised gift giving amongst members of pre industrial societies as studied by anthropologists.

Through the tool of narrative these ethnographers attempt to give the reader a first-hand feel of what it is like in the workplace they are studying. But many of these approaches, while embodying something of the novelistic genre in their use of narrative and literary techniques in their writing do not exploit the full expressive power of the novelistic genre as Bakhtin understood it. For the most part ethnographers abstract from the unique and particular felt life perspective of individual characters towards more culturally shared and constituted meanings. This abstraction removes the sense of plurality, dialogue and the tensions between self and community that Bakhtin sought to characterise in the polyphonic novel.

3.1.2 Character and scenario-based design

Scenario-based design is another HCI work analysis method that adopts a narrative approach. It tries to capture "users" and their activity as a story, with which designers and users can envision possible design innovations. Carroll (1995) illustrates how scenarios contain all of the traditional elements of narrative. Good scenarios describe a setting, the agents or actors, their goals and purposes and the things they do. But Nielsen (2002) points out that while the kind of scenarios typically created for scenario-based design are narrative, they tend to emphasise plot over character and dialogue. So, for example, while typical scenario descriptions provide a rich account of what happens and what "the user" is trying to do, they tend not to describe users' motivations, personality traits, values, and attitudes. Nielsen argues that this limits the value of design scenarios. If the designer-reader cannot engage with the characters and cannot understand their background, personality, intentions and motives, how can they explore how that person might respond to new situations and new technologies? Nielsen contrasts the plot-driven approach of scenario-based design with the character-driven approach of film script writing. She comes to similar conclusions about the importance of character over plot for dialogue as we found in Bakhtin's account of the polyphonic novel. Horton (1999), one of Nielsen's sources, uses Bakhtin's theories to argue that character needs to be seen as a process of becoming, as multiple voices interacting at different times and as part of a discourse that belongs to an unfinalised culture and its many voices. Horton also places an emphasis on time and place as essential to understanding a character. To quote from Nielsen:

The character includes both personal (inner) and inter-personal (social, public, professional) elements. All characters have inner needs and goals as well as interpersonal desires and professional ambitions that help characterise them and impose their own requirements, restrictions and privileges. When character, circumstance and chance cross there is a possibility for many voices to speak. (Nielsen 2002, p. 103)

Nielsen's position is echoed in Cooper's (1999) recent writing. He argues strongly for design based on "personae" rather than "users". In Cooper's approach more than Nielsen's, there is a striving to get behind abstractions down to unique characters with individual histories, thoughts and feelings. Sometimes however, both Nielsen's and Cooper's characters seem to us to be unconvincing. They seem somehow two-dimensional and lacking in depth compared to the complex and often ambiguous characters of Bakhtin's polyphonic novels. This may simply reflect something of the skill of great novel writers compared to those who write design scenarios. But Blythe (2004) describes an alternative approach to character generation that relies less on the character writing skills of the scenario designer. His approach is based on the idea of pastiche. In this approach, characters are not created from scratch, rather they are taken from already existing novels, movies and plays, and used as the characters in scenarios involving new technology. So for example, Miss Marple from the Agatha Christie novels, Wilson from Orwell's *1984* and Alex in Burgess' *A Clockwork Orange* were used by Blythe to explore the use of wearable cameras as an aid to crime prevention. Here the emphasis is on using the characters to critique the plausibility and desirability of various possible technological futures.

3.1.3 Technology biographies

Nielsen, Cooper and others have focused on narrative as a means of analysing and describing people's experiences. But according to Jerome Bruner (1990), narrative also plays a central role in how individuals understand their *own* experiences. Bruner argues that people make sense of their activities and the activities of others in terms of unfolding events that have story-like structures and offer explanations of activity in terms of agency, needs, desires, commitments and concerns. This folk psychological vocabulary serves as a means of explaining our activities and the activities of others in a coherent way. A historical perspective is part of such a narrative account. Bruner also demonstrates how autobiographies – the stories that people tell about themselves – can be used to analyse why a person does what he or she does, how she accounts for the behaviour of others in her life and how these understandings change over time.

In their *technology biographies* technique, Blythe, Monk and Park (2002) have exploited the narrative character of human sense making to analyse people's understandings of – and relationships with – technology in their lives. As part of their ethnographic studies of people's domestic lives, they asked their informants to tell them stories about the technology in their homes and their personal histories with it. These stories provided valuable insights into how the individuals valued technology and how it related to their sense of place and their sense of themselves. Blythe et al. were able to use these insights to think creatively about new technological possibilities.

Elsewhere we have presented analyses of experience with technology that resembles Blythe, Monk and Park's approach. McCarthy and Wright (2004) use personal autobiography to understand on-line shopping experiences, and Wright and McCarthy (2003) use an individual's personal account of his career as a line pilot as a starting point for understanding the creative and ethical experience of procedure following.

3.2 Engaging designers through dialogue

The use of autobiography, personal stories, character-based scenarios and other narrative techniques are different ways in which designers can engage with user experience. Few if any of these approaches have exploited the full potential of the polyphonic novel, the ideas of dialogue, emergence and the different qualities of agency and time that Bakhtin alluded to in his analysis of the novelistic genre. So there is potential for further development. But perhaps more important, the emphasis in these approaches is on the novel as a way of *representing* experience to designers in durable ways that can be used as a resource for design. But potentially this is a rather indirect form of engagement with experience. Other approaches such as participatory design encourage designers to interact more directly with users in order to understand how best to support their activity. But Bakhtin's analysis of the novelistic genre with its particular emphasis on becoming and emergence also provides a useful metaphor for this kind of direct engagement with experience. Bakhtin was keen to understand the potential for change in any situation, the ability to creatively respond and to create something new out of what is given. He argues that in order to engage with others' experiences in a way that can bring about real change one must enter into dialogue with those others. And according to Bakhtin's analysis of the polyphonic novel, at the heart of successful dialogue is something he called *creative understanding* born of a particular kind of relation among author, character and reader as separate centres of value.

3.2.1 Creative understanding

Bakhtin argued against the idea that one could understand another culture or activity system merely by entering the culture and merging with it by seeing the world through the eyes of that culture while at the same time forgetting one's own. To achieve creative understanding one needs more:

Creative understanding does not renounce itself, its own place in time, its own culture; and it forgets nothing. In order to understand, it is immensely important for the person who understands to be *located outside* the object of his or her creative understanding – in time in space, in culture. For one cannot even really see one's own exterior and comprehend it as a whole, and no mirrors or photographs can help, our real exterior can be seen and understood only by other people, because they are located outside us in space and because they are *others.* (Bakhtin 1986, p. 7)

For Bakhtin any *other* (person or culture) has meaning and potential, which they themselves cannot see. Only by coming into dialogue with another who is different or outside can such potential be revealed. It is only through this outsideness that one can see the potential in that culture in ways that the culture itself cannot see. In Bakhtin's dialogical world such creative understanding works both ways. Both the cultures studied and the analysts studying can learn things about their own culture that they did not know before.

3.2.2 Prerequisites for a dialogical approach to design

In a design context, each designer and user brings to the design activity an outsideness, in Bakhtin's terms. Each user is "their own expert" in the activity whether this activity is ambulance control or electronic shopping. Users have a unique position with respect to that activity which is more than just their formal knowledge of the domain or the training they have received; it is also their experiences of the activity in the web of other experiences that is their life.

While the designers may not be their own experts in the user domain, they are "their own experts" when it comes to design and possible applications of technology. This is more than their formal training or their skills in engineering technical systems. It is also their experiences of the many other users, settings, design problems, technical solutions and visions of possible futures this has engendered. Designer and user then each have a surplus of meaning, which is the prerequisite for a dialogue involving creative understanding. But both designer and user also require something Bakhtin refers to as *addressive* surplus. This is an attitude towards each other that allows them to ask the kinds of questions that provide the stimulus for new understandings:

The addressive surplus is the surplus of the good listener, one capable of "live entering" (vzhivanie). It requires "an active (not a duplicating) understanding, a willingness to listen." (Bakhtin 1984, p. 299)

   Without trying to finalise the other or define him once and for all, one uses one's "outsideness" and experience to ask the right sort of questions. Recognising the other's capacity for change, one provokes or invites him to reveal and outgrow himself. (Morson and Emerson 1990, p. 242)

Without an addressive surplus one cannot use one's own unique perspective; one cannot bring about change in a character.

3.2.3 Participatory design as dialogue

The kind of sensibilities that Bakhtin captures in his ideas of creative understanding and addressive surplus provide useful ways to critique the contribution of different methods of participatory design. For example, Beyer and Holtzblatt (1998) suggest in their Contextual Design approach, that designer-analysts should adopt the role of apprentice when interviewing users. But this is too one-sided for creative understanding. There is an implication that the designer through this process will come see the world as do the users and therefore be able to come to a design solution on their behalf. While seeing the world as users do is important, users must also come to see the world as the designer does, only in this way can the potential of each be used to develop real shared understanding of possible futures. The idea of dialogue expressed by Bakhtin's concept of creative understanding goes beyond the observation that user and designer have different bodies of knowledge on which to draw. It extends the idea that they are different centres of value, with different attitudes, different concerns and different motivations. It is in that kind of dialogical space that potential can emerge and a creative response can be forged.

Creative understanding also requires something that Bakhtin identified as a prerequisite for the polyphonic novel, the ability of the author to exist on the same plane as the character. Often implicit in an engineering approach to design is the idea that designers somehow stand above the activity of users. They observe and talk about users and represent their activities in ways with which it will be useful for themselves and other designers to work. Here users are subjects of analysis, not participants. The reflexive character of observation is not part of this way of seeing; rather designers take an objective, scientific stance, seek an accurate record of what it is users do and use it as a basis for design innovation that assumes everything else will remain the same. This way of seeing experience assumes a chronotope that is more like the adventure novel than the novel of emergence. In short, designers take up an authoritative position with respect to users, where activities, individuals and artefacts are finalised, outcomes determined in advance and perfect control exercised over what the other is required to do. In contrast, creative understanding and addressive surplus require designers to enter into dialogue as differently placed equals with the expectation that both designers and users will learn and change their ideas as a result of the dialogue and thus experience genuine surprise.

3.2.4 Design representations as resources for dialogue

The way in which representations are used in a dialogical approach to design is different from the way they are used in a monological engineering approach (McCarthy 2001). Many requirements engineering notations, such as UML use cases and interaction diagrams (Fowler 1997), and even some more user-centred representations such as scenarios (Carroll 1995), rich descriptions (Patching 1990) and contextual design work models (Beyer and Holtzblatt 1998), tend to present to users a finished image of themselves and their activities. Such finalisation, if presented authoritatively and without the kind of addressive surplus that creates a feeling of temporariness, tends to close off dialogue. Human experience resists finalisation and, through addressive surplus, always draws out a creative response from those finalised. That's why, in some critical sense, requirements are always incomplete. This is not a result of some human failure to capture the true and complete picture. It is because there is no complete picture to be captured, no thing to be captured at all, rather some thing constructed and created. Thus the representation of users and their activities must include the sense of openness that encourages users to give voice to creative response, and that creative response must not be stifled by the author adapting an authoritative position.

McCarthy (1998) argues that the kind of representations that create dimensions rather than categories readily mediate dialogue. Dimensions can be used to position different kinds of activity or practice relative to each other but they also encourage their users to change relationships and juxtapositions freely, to playfully engage with possibilities. Such representations also tend towards ambiguity (Gaver et al. 2003), a useful attribute for engaging with the plurality of user experience. A representation that supports dialogue does not invite a single veridical interpretation but allows for different and even conflicting readings to be inscribed alongside or on top of one another, thus expressing a dialogical sense of truth. Such a sense of truth is also facilitated by the use of multiple representations and a variety of representational styles. McCarthy et al. (1997) identify several dimensions for viewing the relationship between work activities and accountability in sociotechnical systems. These dimensions included implicit-explicit, locally negotiated-globally imposed, stable-transient and so on. They use these dimensions to create a simple set of graphs to facilitate dialogue about the relationships between accountability and work activities for a number of different work settings.

This approach is also apparent in Wright, McCarthy and Meekison's (2003) framework for analysing user experience. This is another tool that is both sparse and ambiguous and that accommodates a plurality of representations. The aspects of experience and the processes of sense making incorporated into the framework are deliberately left underspecified, and the way in which people use the framework is not proceduralised. Rather, underlying concepts and stories of how other people have used the framework are given. These can then be appropriated in a way that gives voice to the particular concerns of particular designers and users.

3.2.5 Rethinking the boundary between designer and user

Our account has so far presumed that there is a clear distinction between designer and user and that there is a clear distinction between the activity of design and the activity of use. By analogy in the world of the novel we have assumed a clear distinction between author and reader and between the act of authoring and the act of reading. But, for Bakhtin, the distinction between authoring a novel and reading it was to some large extent an artificial one. For him, all utterances and texts are made with the expectation of a particular response and carry an evaluative weight. Moreover, utterances are made in the knowledge of the many ways in which the words and gestures comprising an utterance have been used on past occasions. So an utterance is neither neutral nor unitary with respect to its meaning. In this view, an utterance carries the meanings of many different authors and thus the potential for many different interpretations – and as writing is embedded in reading so reading becomes a kind of writing.

In a similar way, Bakhtin argues that the process of authoring a new novel involves the author reading existing novels and genres. But because of his or her unique position of surplus, an author can use the genre's potential in the particular context of the project, by seeing the new meanings that emerge from the text given his unique position. Bakhtin argues that all great works have this surplus or potential meaning that the writer senses and her own writing is guided not by whether it encodes her intended meaning but rather by the richness of the possible meanings it might have for others in unknown contexts.

To put the point paradoxically but precisely, authors intend their works to mean more than their *intended* meanings. They deliberately endow their works not only with specified meanings they could paraphrase, but also with "intentional potentials" for future meanings in unforeseen circumstances. (Bakhtin 1981, p. 421, according to Morson and Emerson 1990, p. 286)

Sensitive readings of a work can make some of these potentials manifest so that the work grows in meaning. This point is not only central to Bakhtin's theory of literature but to his whole philosophy:

Thus what Bakhtin maintains about great works he also maintains about individuals and entire cultures. Both contain potential they could not specify. Or as Bakhtin sometimes puts the point, potentials are why great works, individuals and cultures are "noncoincident" with themselves, why they always have a loophole, and why, no matter how fully they are described, they have not been *exhaustively* described. Just as individuals always have a "surplus of humanness" (Bakhtin 1981, p. 37), great works and cultures have a surplus of unexploited potentials. Potentials, non-coincidence, and the surplus make all three unfinalizable and able to render untrue any definition of them. (Morson and Emerson 1990, p. 287)

While these potentials exist in the work, they are drawn out by the surplus of vision that a reader has with respect to the work and the genre. There is a symmetry between author and reader – the one using surplus to create potential, the other using difference to see potential. This symmetry has led some to refer to the "reader as writer" (Shusterman 2000), and others to refer to the process as the co-creation of meaning (Morson and Emerson 1990). The point here is that it is only in the dialogical interaction between reader and writer that utterances have any sense. The obvious analogy with relationships between designers and users leads to an interpretation of design-in-use that is more creative and constructive than conventional interpretations.

3.2.6 Design-in-use as a creative response

It has frequently been observed that when new technology is introduced into a situation, users tinker with and adapt it to meet their specific needs (Norman 1988; Bannon and Bodker 1991; Greenbaum and Kyng 1991; Béguin 2003). There is a parallel here with the reader of the novel actively seeking new meanings in a work. We have also previously reported examples of a pilot creatively modifying and ultimately designing his own version of a quick reference handbook (Wright and McCarthy 2003), and ambulance controllers designing a supplementary representation to record order of arrival at the station (McCarthy and Wright 2004). The novel ways that users find to adapt technology can be a source of genuine surprise to designers and delight to both designers and users when they lead to an enriched quality of experience. But in some situations they can also be a source of concern when, for example, the unexpected ways in which technology gets used violate design assumptions about the safety of that technology (Wright et al. 2000). This phenomenon, which has been referred to as design-in-use, has been seen by some as a response to bad design and a call for more user-centred approaches (Norman 1988). By others it has been seen as an inevitable consequence of the openness of human activity and as an argument against normative approaches to design (Vicente 1999). A more constructive and inconclusive interpretation is possible.

In the context of Bakhtin's dialogical analysis of reader and writer, design-in-use is less surprising and problematic. New technology after all is just another temporary finalisation drawing a creative response. Viewed dialogically then, a representation of work, a requirements specification, a prototype and even the fully working system are just different forms of finalisation each in their turn evoking a creative response and leading to new temporary finalisation. In this context, Béguin (2003) sees design-in-use as a process of mutual learning and development. He makes a distinction between the designed artefact and its appropriation into the use context, by differently placed others. Appropriation involves giving the artefact meaning as a tool and changing the activity to accommodate it. Design-in-use then, is an emergent feature of this process. It is not just a response to bad design, it is what is involved in appropriating a new artefact into one's life (Wright et al. 2003).

3.3 Engagement through dialogical imagination

We began this chapter with the claim that one can't design an experience but one can design *for* experience. Bakhtin's ideas on creativity and surplus and the importance of mutual outsideness provide the rationale for this claim and the idea of design-in-use provides empirical support for it. The main implication we have drawn thus far is that in order to design for experience, designers need appropriate ways of engaging with user experience. They need to enter into a dialogue of creative understanding with users and they need appropriate representations to support such dialogue. But this way of talking about design makes the assumption that designers know who their users are and can get access to them. It also assumes that there is a known context of use that can serve as the focus for dialogue about possible design solutions. These assumptions are implicit in most approaches to user-centred design. But what if these preconditions don't hold? What if we don't know what activity we want to support; what if we don't know who our users might be? Can the novel provide us with a metaphor for a radically different kind of user-centred design?

In our opening arguments, we suggested that Hollywood moviemakers don't so much engage with the audience in order to determine what they want, rather through the accumulated skills of a lifetime of moviemaking and watching they come to a deep understanding of their audience. Similarly, an author of a novel does not dedicate many hours to user surveys and market research; like the moviemaker he has a sense of his audience based on a lifetime of reading and writing for them. What both moviemaker and novelist must do, however, is anchor what they produce in forms with which the audience and reader can work. Both moviemaker and novelist are adept at understanding the respective genres of their art: the suspense movie, the action movie, the thriller novel, the historical novel and so on. They are also versed in different works in these genres, and the works of different filmmakers and novelists. They also have some knowledge of how audiences have responded both to the genre and the individual work. Once they have the seeds of an idea for a new work then they can work with this knowledge to create something new, something that is grounded in the familiar but also something that makes a new contribution. As Bakhtin points out, for truly great novels and also arguably for truly great movies, the author will build in a surplus of possible meanings and interpretations. This can be done through techniques that leave open the possibilities for different interpretations of how a story might have ended or how characters might have been worked out differently.

In the world of user-centred system design it might be considered something of a blasphemy to suggest that we design interactive artefacts without getting feedback from users. And clearly there are aspects of the design of an interactive artefact that are quite different from both a novel and a movie. Not the least of these are the difficulties that designers have in appropriately supporting the actual means of interaction – the realm of traditional usability engineering. But if we take seriously the idea that a properly positioned designer can exploit the potential hidden in genres of interaction, we are led to conjecture that we can design from the imagination to engage the imagination. Such artefacts might be quite simple but combine in interesting ways with familiar ways of interacting.

We offer two examples of interactive systems that appear to us at least to exemplify the idea of creative potential and imaginative engagement, but there are many others (see, for example, Blythe et al. 2003).

3.3.1 Pen Pets

O'Mahony and Robinson (2003) described an augmented reality application called Pen Pets. Pen Pets was designed in the Department of Electronics at the University of York. It focuses on no activity at all. It was not designed in response to a user requirements study or a user needs analysis. It was not designed for a particular type of user or user group. It was not even designed with a particular kind of user experience in mind.

The prototype involved a video camera attached to a multimedia projector positioned vertically above a table surface made of whiteboard material. The multimedia projector and camera were connected to a PC. The design includes a number of software agents that project an image onto the whiteboard surface that exhibits very simple behaviour. For example, one of the agents was capable only of forward movement and detecting a boundary (e.g., the edge of the whiteboard or a line drawn on the whiteboard). If it detected a boundary it would simply turn left and continue forwards until it met another boundary, in which case it would turn left and continue its forward movement. The agent obtained this information from the video camera, which was capable of detecting lines and edges as well as the position of the projected image. By coordinating these pieces of information the software could determine whether a collision had taken place.

As described so far the prototype is not particularly interesting. However, a user could interact with the system by drawing lines on the whiteboard with a board marker, and when the image hit the line it would turn left and follow it. By erasing parts of lines a user could create doorways through which the agent passed. A user could also trap the image in a box or circle and send it off in a specific direction by intersecting its path with an appropriate line. One of the most surprising and enchanting behaviours of the agent and one that was not intentionally designed by O'Mahony and Robinson was the way in which users could catch and lift up the agent. A piece of paper could be slipped under the agent and lifted from the surface of the whiteboard. The agent was "lifted" with the paper. The agent now detected the edge of the paper as a boundary and the image would not "jump off" the paper back onto the board until it was lowered carefully down. In this way the image could be picked up and moved to different parts of the whiteboard. With a bit of practice this same effect could be achieved not with a piece of paper but with a user's bare hands, giving the impression that they were picking up and holding the image. Other curved three-dimensional objects could be used to capture the image. For example, placing a teapot under the image would condemn it to forever roam up, down and around the outer surface of the pot, never regaining the whiteboard.

For us, the prototype was *enchanting* (McCarthy and Wright 2003) – an illustration of imaginative design which incorporated ambiguity, depth and potential, which only become visible through the sense-making engagement of users. There was no activity analysis, no user requirements and no functional specification. Instead what O'Mahony and Robinson had done was work creatively with some basic capabilities: the ability to track a projected image using a video camera, the ability to detect drawn lines and edges and the ability to write a program to move a simple image around a flat surface. These basics had been woven together to produce something quite surprising not just in its unexpected behaviour but also in its ability to engage users. Of course, on reflection one can imagine a number of applications for such a device as a children's game, for example, or as some kind of educational tool, but in the sense that misses the point. The prototype was engaging in and of itself, and interacting with it was an enchanting experience.

3.3.2 The influencing machine

Phoebe Sengers is another designer who has explored designing for creative potential in a number of her works (Sengers 2003). As part of the SAFIRA project she has been involved in the design of the *Influencing Machine*. The Influencing Machine is not designed to support users' tasks; it is not a tool. Rather the aim of it is to allow both designer and user to explore what it might mean for machines to have emotions. Users do not so much interact with the Influencing Machine as enter it through a door. They see digital images of children's drawings and hear a soundscape. These are intended to evoke an emotional or sensual response. In the middle of the room there is a wooden mailbox in which they can place certain postcards or art reproductions. By placing something in the mailbox, the users can change the mood of the images and the soundscape. Users explore a postcard or a work of art and reflect on what it means to them emotionally and then insert it into the machine to find out what it means to the machine. Early evaluations of the Influencing Machine show that users are enchanted by the machine, interacting with it for up to twenty minutes and debating whether and how a computer can be said to have emotions (Sengers 2003).

The Influencing Machine is an interesting example of designing for aesthetic experience with an intellectual challenge too. It is designed to engage the imagination of users but it does so in a dialogical way by inviting each user to compare his or her own emotional meanings and values to that of the machine: engagement through dialogical imagination.

These examples serve to illustrate how designers can work with what in one sense are simple materials to produce truly innovative interactive experiences. They also show how, with a sensibility for user experience rather than tasks and goals, designers can produce interactive potential, which when appropriated by individuals can lead to new ways of experiencing and imagining.

4 Conclusions

Borrowing from the arts and exploring the idea of design as narrative, storytelling, conversation or even dialogue is not new. Many authors, including some whose work we have described in this chapter, have used the metaphor of conversation or at least storytelling. Brenda Laurel (1993) has also used ideas from the dramatic arts and aesthetics as her starting point for an analysis of computers as theatre. What we have tried to do here, however, is to use Bakhtin's ideas on the novel not to provide another alternative metaphor but rather to provide some understanding of what is at the heart of such views and to show how these ideas can be used practically to relate and re-evaluate familiar conceptions. We have also attempted to provide practical ideas about what a dialogical approach to design would look like, by rethinking what could constitute scenarios for design, offering ideas about dialogical representations and illustrating how others have implemented a dialogical approach. We have also offered examples of how it is possible to design enchanting products through the playful engagement of imagination.

Phil Agre (1997), in his book *Computation and Human Experience*, demonstrates how the metaphors, models or paradigms we use when conceptualising and theorising bring some phenomena to the centre and put others at the margins. Whereas those in the centre are easy to understand and explain, dealing with those at the margins is always relatively problematic. In a traditional way of looking at human-computer interaction, for example, placing *behaviour*, *performance* or *task* centre makes *felt experience* relatively difficult to deal with. Within HCI research the concept of experience will be problematic while cognitivist rationalistic conceptions of humanity are central to our way of looking at experience.

Future interaction design if it is to take user experience seriously must look farther afield to the humanities and the arts to find a pragmatically useful conception of experience. Furthermore we argue, this is not just a question of recruiting graphic artists into design teams: it is a question of revising the very way of looking at the "human" in human-computer interaction. Using the novel as a metaphor for seeing experience provides one way of placing prosaic experience and felt life at the centre of our thinking about human experience. In so doing we hope we have shown how otherwise problematic or even invisible phenomena such as person, creativity, freedom, initiative and design-in-use become more approachable within a design discipline.

References

Agre P (1997) Computation and Human Experience. CUP, Cambridge

Anderson RJ (1994) Representation and requirements: The value of ethnography in system design. Human-Computer Interaction 9:151-182

Bakhtin M (1981) Epic and the Novel. In: Holquist M (ed) The dialogic imagination: Four Essays by M.M. Bakhtin. University of Texas Press, Austin, pp 3-40

Bakhtin M (1984) Problems of Dostoevsky's Poetics. University of Minnesota Press, Minneapolis

Bakhtin M (1986) Speech Genres and Other Late Essays. University of Texas Press, Austin, TX

Bakhtin M (1993) Toward a Philosophy of the Act. University of Texas Press, Austin, TX

Bannon L, Bodker S (1991) Beyond the interface: encountering artefacts in use. In: Carroll JM (ed) Designing Interaction: Psychology at the Human-Computer Interface. Cambridge University Press, Cambridge, pp 228-253

Béguin P (2003) Design as a mutual learning processe between users and designers. Interacting with Computers 5(5):709-730

Beyer H, Holtzblatt K (1998) Contextual Design: Defining Customer-Centered systems. Morgan Kaufman, San Francisco

Blythe M (2004) Pastiche scenarios: Fiction as a resource for design. Submitted to International Journal of Human-Computer Studies

Blythe M, Monk A, Park J (2002) Technology biographies: Field study techniques for home use product development. Proceedings of the Conference on Human Factors in Computing Systems CHI 2003, Extended Abstracts. ACM Press, pp 658-659

Blythe M, Monk A, Overbeeke C, Wright P (eds) (2003) Funology: From Usability to User Enjoyment. Kluwer, Dordrecht

Boorstin J (1990) Making Movies Work: Thinking Like a Filmmaker. Salman-James Press, Los Angeles

Booth W (1984) Introduction. In: Bakhtin M (1984) Problems of Dostoevsky's Poetics. University of Minnesota Press, Minneapolis

Bruner EM, Turner V (eds) (1986) The Anthropology of Experience. University of Illinois Press, Urbana

Bruner J (1990) Acts of Meaning. Mass, Harvard University Press, Cambridge

Carroll J (ed) (1995) Scenario-Based Design: Envisioning Work and Technology in System Development. John Wiley and Sons

Cooper A (1999) The Inmates are Running the Asylum: Why High Tech Products Drive us Crazy and How to Restore Sanity. Sams

Dewey J (1934) Art as Experience. Pedigree, NY

Fowler M (1997) UML Distilled. Addison-Wesley, Harlow

Garrett JJ (2002) The Elements of User Experience: User-Centred Design for the Web. New Riders Publishers, Indianapolis

Gaver WW, Beaver J, Benford S (2003) Designing design: Ambiguity as a resource for design. Proceedings of the Conference on Human Factors in Computing Systems CHI 2003. ACM Press, pp 233-240

Geertz C (1986) Making experiences, authoring selves. In: Bruner EM, Turner V (eds) The Anthropology of Experience. Urbana, University of Illinois Press, pp 373-380

Greenbaum J, Kyng M (1991) Design at Work: Cooperative Design for Computer Systems. Lawrence Erlbaum, Hillsdale, NJ

Horton A (1999) Writing the Character Centred Screenplay. University of California Press, Los Angeles

Hutchins E (1995) Cognition in the Wild. MIT Press, Cambridge Mass

Laurel B (1993) Computers as Theatre, 2nd edn. Addison Wesley

McCarthy J (1998) The viability of modelling socially organised activity. In: Markopoulos P, Johnson P (eds) Design, Specification and Verification of Interactive Systems '98. Springer, Austria, pp 9-23

McCarthy J (2001) The paradox of understanding work for design. International Journal of Human-Computer Studies 53(1):197-217

McCarthy J, Wright P (2003) The enchantments of technology. In: Blythe M, Monk A, Wright P, Overbeeke C (eds) Funology: From Usability to user enjoyment. Kluwer, Dordrecht

McCarthy J, Wright P (2004) Technology As Experience. MIT Press, Cambridge, MA

McCarthy J, Wright P, Healey PGT, Harrison MD (1997) Accountability of work activity in high-consequence work systems: human error in context. International Journal of Human-Computer Studies 47(6):735-766

McCarthy J, Wright P, Wallace J, Dearden A (2004) The experience of enchantment in human-computer interaction. Submitted to CHI'2004 Fringe Papers, The ACM conference on human factors in computing systems. ACM Press

Morson GS, Emerson C (1990) Mikhail Bakhtin: Creation of a Prosaics. Stanford University Press, Stanford, CA

Nielsen L (2002) From user to character: An investigation into user descriptions in scenarios. Proceedings of DIS2002 Designing Interactive Systems. ACM Press, New York, pp 99-104

Norman D (1988) The Psychology of Everyday Things. Basic Books, New York

O'Mahony S, Robinson JA (2003) A physical environment for virtual animals. Proceedings of the Conference on Human Factors in Computing Systems CHI 2003, Extended Abstracts. ACM Press, pp 622-623

Orr J (1996) Talking About Machines: An Ethnography of a Modern Job. Cornell University Press, Ithaca, NY

Patching D (1990) Practical Soft systems analysis. Pitmann, London

Preece J, Rogers Y, Sharp H (2002) Interaction Design: Beyond Human-Computer Interaction. Wiley, New York

Sengers P (2003) The engineering of experience. In: Blythe M, Monk A, Overbeeke C, Wright P (eds) Funology: From Usability to User Enjoyment. Kluwer, Dordrecht, pp 19-29

Shusterman R (2000) Pragmatist Aesthetics: Living Beauty, Rethinking Art, 2nd edn. Rowman and Littlefield, Boston

Taylor AS, Harper R (2002) Age-old practices in the new world: A study of gift-giving between teenage mobile phone users. Proceedings of the Conference on Human Factors in Computing Systems, CHI'2002. ACM Press

Vicente KJ (1999) Cognitive Work Analysis: Toward Safe, Productive and Healthy Computer-Based Work. Lawrence Erlbaum Associates, Hillsdale, NJ

Wenger E (1998) Communities of Practice: Learning, Meaning and Identity. CUP, Cambridge

Wright P, Dearden AM, Fields B (2000) Allocation of Function: Perspectives from studies of work practice. International Journal of Human-Computer Studies 52(2):335-355

Wright P, McCarthy J (2003) A dialogical analysis of cockpit operating procedures. In: Hollnagel E (ed) Handbook of Cognitive Task Analysis. Lawrence Erlbaum Associates, Hillsdale, NJ

Wright P, McCarthy J, Meekison L (2003) Making sense of experience. In: Blythe M, Monk A, Overbeeke C, Wright P (eds) Funology: From Usability to User Enjoyment. Kluwer, Dordrecht, pp 43-53

A human-centred perspective on interaction design

Liam J. Bannon

Interaction Design Centre, University of Limerick
Ireland
liam.bannon@ul.ie

Abstract

This chapter outlines a "human-centred" perspective on the design of novel interactive artefacts and environments. The approach builds on a variety of human and social science traditions that focus on understanding human activity, all of which seek to provide useful and pertinent observations on human action in the world. While technology may play an important role in these human activities, often the use of the technology is as an intrinsic mediating influence, rather than being the goal of the activity. The relevance of this approach to technology development is that it provides a distinct perspective that encompasses many of the key issues being faced by (ubiquitous) technology designers today – issues such as awareness, context, interaction, engagement and emotion. All of these aspects concern the activities of human actors in a (variety of) setting(s). The chapter then outlines a major research programme being conducted within our research unit which provides an exemplar of the human-centred interaction design research programme that we are advocating, which we believe could significantly shift the way in which we design, develop and evaluate novel technological artefacts and environments.

1 Introduction

This chapter provides an outline of a "human-centred" approach to computing, more specifically in the area of interaction design. While one might argue that a label such as "human-centred" is rather vacuous – after all, what is the alternative, "system-centred"? – I believe that the increasing use of the term does imply a shift in perspective in the field of computing and information systems, just as twenty years ago, the term "user-centred design" signified a shift in perspective. Back then, we had the emergence of a new field of human-computer interaction (HCI), which began to systematically investigate the ways in which people interact with computer systems, and developed concepts and methods for the design of more usable interfaces to systems. Now, while the field of HCI has become a mainstream activity, with HCI courses an integral part of standard computing curricula, the emergence of human-centred computing signifies a deeper paradigm shift, if we can use this somewhat over-hyped word. The paradigm shift is one that signifies a more fundamental change in our approach to understanding the field of computing. It is one that shifts attention away from the question, "What can be automated?" – the traditional way of stating what computing is about – to one which views computing as a human activity (Naur 1985), where the human activities of design, development and use of software systems are a fundamental aspect of the computing discipline.

Ideas expressed in such emerging areas as the "new informatics", and "interaction design" are, in my opinion, examples of shifts in perspective, in the information systems and human-computer interaction communities, respectively, towards a more holistic view of human-systems interaction that begins to privilege the human, social and cultural aspects of computing. Many people have been involved in the move to shift the focus of computing – and informatics more generally – away from a purely technical approach, to one that considers the human activities of design and use of information systems as being of central concern. Many of these people have historically come from the Nordic countries – people such as the late Kristen Nygaard, who argued for a perspective on systems development that included the social and political, as well as the technical: people like Peter Naur, whose compilation of papers was published under the title *Computing: A Human Activity*, which showed deep insight into the human side of programming and systems development and people like Christiane Floyd, from Germany, who provides evidence of different paradigms in software engineering. In the United States, the late Rob Kling spent many years as an advocate of a more open computer science discipline, which he labeled "Social Informatics". Other influential figures whose insights have, in my opinion, contributed to the emergence of this new perspective include Bo Dahlbom, with his paper on "The New Informatics", Peter Denning, in his arguments for a new kind of computing profession, Denis Tsichritzis, critiquing much old-fashioned "computer" science as being akin to "electric motor" science, and Peter Wegner, arguing that the concept of interaction is more powerful than that of algorithms.

The argument here is not that the above-mentioned researchers share a distinct and well-articulated perspective, but rather they have all contributed to the critique of the "normal science" view of computing and computer science over the past quarter of a century. They raise foundational issues for the field of *computing per se*. And it is just such critiques of computing that have led to the slow emergence of what is sometimes termed "human-centred" computing. This essay is not the place to provide a detailed and densely argued case for the evolution of this new perspective. However, I would argue that the reasons for this shift in perspective are many and varied, with some impetus coming from the very nature of the new technologies themselves, for example, ubiquitous computing. In this chapter, I will focus on outlining how this emerging human-centred computing perspective might influence the field of Interaction Design. I will mainly use personal material to make my points, both from earlier papers I have written, from work done at our own Interaction Design Centre (IDC) in Limerick, and from our planned research programme in human-centred interaction design over the next few years.

1.1 Background context

As the computer migrates from the desktop into everyday objects and our living environments, a host of new challenges are being posed to our hardware and software engineers (Norman 1998). Just as the notion of usability – making products and services that people can really *use* – has finally become generally accepted in computing circles, with courses on human-computer interaction and design of graphical user interfaces (GUIs) a mandatory requirement for computing students, we discover that a new revolution is on the way – ubiquitous computing – and that this has huge implications for how we develop ICT applications and infrastructures, going well beyond screen design (See Weiser 1991 for a prescient description of the revolution).

Linking design and use has been one of the major achievements in the fields of HCI and participative design over the past fifteen years. However, now we must once again develop a new frame for understanding the design of computer products and services that are the basis of our ICT-enabled economy. Understandings of computer use built on the GUI interface, and the standard desktop PC, are no longer valid. Hand-held mobile devices with "small" interfaces, for example, require us to devise novel interaction strategies other than those of direct manipulation (Shneiderman 1983) that have become so commonplace. The kinds of challenges that our ICT engineers and scientists need to address are quite far-reaching and mark a qualitative break with the thinking about people and computers that has gone before. Computational devices are no longer simply functional items for accomplishing tasks, but become part of the environment, or even wearable. Design questions far beyond screen layout come to the fore.

From the viewpoint of the user[1], consumer or more correctly, citizen, the world is changing in a variety of ways. While for some purposes, developments in mobile technology and "smart" objects and appliances (Gershenfeld 1999) do indeed offer improved quality of service, they can also create novel frustrations and increase stress levels as people try to adapt to our wired (or wireless) world. We thus need a better understanding of how people live in the world – a world populated with artefacts – rather than simply focus on how people use specific tools to accomplish specific tasks. This has been characterised as a shift from understanding *use* of artefacts to understanding their *presence* in our everyday lives (Hallnäs and Redström 2002). More generally, Winograd (1997) notes: "*Successful interaction design requires a shift from seeing the machinery to seeing the lives of the people using it.*" Issues surrounding *user experience* as distinct

---

[1] The term "user" is problematic, as people do not simply "use" the technology to accomplish specific tasks.

from *user performance* are being highlighted (Wright et al. 2003), and issues of *desirability* of products and services, not simply *utility* (cf. Blythe et al. 2003).

At the IDC at the University of Limerick, we have been pioneering research and education in the areas of user-centred design, participative design and computer-supported collaborative work in Ireland. All of these themes concern themselves with focusing on user needs and concerns when designing good technology. This work has included both conceptual and methodological work, as well as extensive empirical studies, observing people in the workplace, videotaping them as they use technologies, building novel interaction platforms and evaluating the performance of various human-technology interfaces. We have worked with air traffic controllers using complex radar workstations, with ordinary citizens getting to grips with their PC, with children on exploring possibilities for new kinds of communication devices through paper mockups and storytelling and with dancers examining the uses of new kinds of sensors in dance floors. In the course of the last year, the IDC has developed a research agenda involving theoretical, methodological and empirical issues in interaction design that can be viewed as an agenda for a human-centred interaction design research project. In the second section of this chapter I wish to outline some of the features of this project – called Shared Worlds[2]. (Appendix 1 provides a brief overview of the IDC research group, and a few illustrations of our design research. Further information is available from our Web site.)

2 An example of a human-centred interaction design agenda – Shared Worlds: The design, development, deployment and evaluation of novel interactive artefacts and environments in public shared spaces based on a human activity conceptual model

2.1 Theoretical issues

The theoretical aspects of interaction design need further exploration and analysis. Currently, ICT development in support of ubiquitous computing relies on either a minimal understanding of human cognition, emotion and action in the world, or else employs the dominant information-processing model of the human. While this cognitive model has its uses, it has severe limitations as a basis for developing innovative and engaging ubiquitous technology environments. This approach tends to treat human beings as isolated entities, neglecting the social and cultural conditions for their existence, including their evolutionary development of tools. In our work, we are exploring alternative paradigms for understanding human cognition and emotion that offer some promise for transcending these difficulties. We are examining a number of different conceptual frameworks in an effort to

---

[2] This project has been funded by Science Foundation Ireland for the next four years.

provide fresh perspectives on interaction design. We are working with the activity-theoretical paradigm that takes humans acting through mediating artefacts (tools, instruments) to accomplish an objective as the basic unit of analysis. Thus the separation of humans from their mediating tools is avoided (Bannon and Kaptelinin 2000). The information-processing model treats cognition and emotion as rather separate phenomena, and until very recently, neglected the emotions almost completely. Our approach avoids the separation of cognition and emotion as occurs in information-processing accounts, but provides an encompassing explanatory framework for "affective design" (see Aboulafia et al. 2004). This work is important, given the increasing interest in understanding human engagement and experience with technologies, as evidenced by the research on "affective computing" (Picard 1997). We aim to expand our understanding of the human experience of artefacts, from a phenomenological perspective. Applying phenomenological methodology (and hermeneutics) to design was suggested by Winograd and Flores (1986), whose work has had a significant influence on the development of recent "human-centred" approaches to computing. Moran and Anderson (1990) have proposed as a specific paradigm for design, the Workaday World, which "puts the technology in proper perspective", the perspective of the life world (*lebenswelt*) of people working. This paradigm, also motivated by phenomenology, draws on the works of such figures as Husserl, Habermas, Heidegger, Schutz and Luckmann. The notion of "life world" is defined as the sphere of practical activity and commonsense reasoning (derived from Husserl). It is a description, from the view of a particular "actor", which captures the experience of that actor, involving three aspects: technology, social relationship and work practice. Ehn's notion of "work-oriented design" (1988) within the participative design tradition also draws on this phenomenological account. Ehn argues that a Heideggerian approach to design creates a new understanding of the process of designing computer artefacts that "helps focus on the importance of everydayness of use as fundamental to design". The Scandinavian work on participatory design in systems development – from the late '70s onwards has had a significant influence in "opening up" the computing and more general information systems fields to aspects of human activities relating to the design and use of technology. More recently, one can view the increased interest in "experience design" as yet another attempt to shift the focus from the narrow technological features of the system towards the resulting effect created in the "user" through use of the system. Indeed, the way in which the term "user" is now itself being the subject of examination or framing is just one small example of how terms that were once unproblematic, and indeed, the mainstay of the HCI discipline, are today seen as "problem" terms. They are seen as perpetuating a view of "user-system interaction" that sees people as simple "users" of technology, a perspective that connotes the person as an appendage of the machine, defined in terms of the machine, rather than vice versa.

We will be collaborating with John McCarthy (see the chapter in this book by Wright and McCarthy) of University College, Cork, among others, on this issue of human experience of artefacts over the lifetime of the project. McCarthy's recent work in conceptualising aesthetic and experiential perspectives on technology and teasing out the implications for theories of design and work practice in the context of interactive systems lies close to the interests of the IDC (McCarthy and Wright 2003). There is a growing recognition that as technology becomes more pervasive in our lives – no longer associated mainly with work but also with play, home and leisure – technical and functional characterisations are insufficient. Although there is a growing recognition of the salience of experience in areas such as electronic commerce and other aspects of the Web, there have been few sustained attempts to conceptualise experience in the context of technology. This exploratory work will attempt to draw together Dewey's (1925, 1934) aesthetic and Bakhtin's (1981) dialogical account of experience as the basis for an account of technology as an engaged participant in experience. We are too used to thinking of artefacts such as computers and mobile phones as objects, or even as tools to be used, to "naturally" see them as full participants in the dialogue of experience. In order to appreciate technology as experience, we need to change our way of seeing such that person and technology are both subject and object in experience. We believe that this conceptual framework can contribute significantly in our work on the public experience of ubiquitous computing environments, helping in both the design and evaluation of our prototypes and larger-scale exhibitions.

Our research is predicated on understanding human activity in the world, rather than on understanding abstract, atomised "minds". Recent approaches in HCI which stress the embodied nature of human thinking are thus of relevance to our conceptual framework (e.g., Dourish 2001). Our theoretical paradigm points to human activity as a central concern, thus broadening the field of HCI (Bannon 1985, 1991; Bannon and Bødker 1991; Bannon and Kaptelinin 2000). This perspective provides a clear role for integrating technological artefacts and environments as mediators of human activities. It provides a frame for conceptualising human activities both at the interpersonal level, in terms of accomplishing individual goals, and at the behavioural level, in terms of human action in public spaces. This framework thus allows us to motivate our technological innovations and interventions in public spaces. Our interest in understanding human activities mediated by technology has a long history, with early work focusing on individual activities (e.g., Bannon et al. 1983), other work focusing on computer-mediated collaboration and communication (Bannon 1986; Bannon and Schmidt 1991; Schmidt and Bannon 1992; Bannon and Kuutti 2002) and more recent work examining behavioural aspects of human activities in public spaces (e.g., Ciolfi and Bannon 2002). The relevance of this paradigm for implementing successful ubiquitous computing environments is beginning to be recognised, with a growth of interest in the area of activity-centred computing, as distinct from application-centred, or document-centred, computing paradigms (e.g., Christensen and Bardram 2002). We see the articulation of this activity-based frame for ubiquitous computing as being a major objective of the project, along with our exploration of the concept of experience in interaction design, which we hope will lead to the broadening of the human-computer interaction field.

2.2 Methodological issues

Our research in Shared Worlds involves a strong component of participative practices, and our iterative design methodology, with a strong focus on the use of scenarios and early prototyping, supports this approach. We will be exploring a number of methods by which we can engage with user communities and with various practitioners in the software and industrial design communities, through the use of our Interaction Design Studio (IDS) spaces (see below), where scenarios can be enacted, and early prototypes tested, before moving out to the field for further testing.

While there has been considerable development of evaluation methods for interactive systems over the past several years (e.g., Nielsen 1993), most of these methods are only of use after a system is built. We are much more interested in developing methods that can assist in the early stages of interaction design, in trying to understand human needs and in supporting an open communication between users and developers from the concept design stage through to scenario development and testing of mock-ups. Again, there has been significant work done within the Scandinavian tradition of participatory design, and with which we are familiar (see, e.g., Greenbaum and Kyng 1991). The purpose of this strand of work is to explore both traditional and novel interaction design methods, and particularly related to the context of public spaces, the domain on which Shared Worlds focuses. Also, an appropriate use of methods can facilitate communication within and consolidation of our multidisciplinary research team, bringing together people with different skills and expertise to discuss together user data, mock-ups, video prototypes etc.

In the Shared Worlds project, we wish to work with a variety of methods, from more controlled laboratory usability studies through to more scenario-based methods. We have thoroughly used both groups of methods in the past (significantly in the context of our work with museums and galleries), and we wish to further reflect on their combinations and synergies towards the development of interactive shared spaces. We wish to involve user communities in the design process, through the use of simulations, use of video-diaries, role-playing, interactive game playing and enactment of possibilities. Some of this work can best be done in a studio/workshop-type setting, while other aspects of the research need to be performed in the local settings for which we are designing.

We are developing an Interaction Design Studio space (IDS) that will comprise space and equipment to conduct controlled lab-type studies focusing on time, movement and gesture, as well as a more open "studio" type space, similar to what Buur and Bødker call a Design Co-Laboratory (2000). This flexible and reconfigurable studio space will allow us to ground our scenarios, make mock-ups of various forms, from paper and cardboard, through to solid physical materials, and actual "smart" prototype objects and even settings (e.g., a room-sized ambient environment) where people can experience using and being with our design creations. It would be an ideal space for prototyping installations that are grounded in the environment and cannot be effectively simulated "out of context", for example, on a screen-based interface. The Design Co-Laboratory allows for the display and use of various objects and exhibits that would constitute the core of our main installations. The rationale for such a space is well articulated in Buur and Bødker (2000), namely, the difficulty of importing "use contexts" into a traditional usability lab setting, where the focus is on evaluation, rather than exploration. The IDS will provide a setting where designers, researchers and users can discuss, explore and enact scenarios, gaining concrete experiences of use through "hands-on" activities and semi-immersive experiences. The studio/workshop becomes a meeting space for our multidisciplinary team, and a learning space for all concerned, where issues of location, space and time in future work and domestic environments can all be explored. We believe that, as well as developing novel methods for user-designer communication, there is a need in the field for a more substantive investigation of the strengths and limitations of the myriad of methods that have been described and used in both the social sciences as well as in design contexts. The work of Aldersey-Williams (1999) and colleagues in the EU I3 Presence project in this regard is of interest. They collected a large number of design methods that are being used by people, briefly described them, and then examined some of the features of each of these methods, such as their cost, expertise required to use them, the time they take and the number of people needed to deploy them. We assisted in that method collection process, and in the Shared Worlds Project we will deepen and extend this work as currently the individual method descriptions are of varying depth and quality. We will particularly focus on such methods used in other projects concerned with public and shared spaces, and on the modalities of their use. As this is a relatively recent strand of research, the use of these methods in such contexts has not yet been analysed and evaluated.

The third aspect of our work on methods involves the development of field research techniques, as it is essential for the Shared Worlds Project that the designers move into the spaces and locations of the user community, rather than have the community come to the research or design space. In several of our HCI and CSCW studies, we already go "on location" and use videos to document work processes and conduct interviews with people on-site etc. We are keen to again consolidate some of the knowledge and experience we and others have gained in this area, and also to develop a mobile "lab" where we can move into one of the public spaces we will be analysing and deploy various kinds of devices and prototypes and analyse reactions and use patterns. Also, we wish to introduce an innovative "multidisciplinary" phase of field studies to run through the first six months of the Project, where members of the research team from the technical, socioscientific and design strands will jointly investigate the public spaces of interest for the Project, and then compare their perspectives towards the development of a thorough picture of all the features of the spaces, ranging from the peculiarities of user behaviour and social interaction, to the requirements in terms of safety, accessibility etc.

2.3 Technology exploration

The IDC has been involved in a number of studies developing and testing novel interaction devices. In our previous work, in projects such as LiteFoot, Z-tiles, SOS etc., we have created, investigated and explored novel Physical Interaction Devices (PIDs) for ubiquitous and pervasive applications. Apart from challenges in terms of physics, electronics and computing, our previous work has also required us to reflect on existing design and evaluation methods as we have attempted to orient our technical work to an activity-centred interaction perspective.

Initially in Shared Worlds, we are using our existing PIDs to develop "probes" for use in public environments. We are also experimenting with novel devices for spatial tracking and location-sensing. The results from the probes will inform us about how to further adapt these devices and associated application software and media. Based on our scenario development, we will review what kinds of additional functionality might be required. All devices will be evaluated both in our Interaction Design Studio Space and in the public settings. Most of today's computing and communication equipment still relies on buttons, mice and visual (sometimes touch) displays, although handwriting and voice input is being used in niche areas. Existing devices only facilitate a relatively small repertoire of human action and perception, hence limiting our ways of interacting with, and through, these devices. This problem applies both to stationary and "built-in" facilities as well as portable and mobile devices. What is needed in the field of future interaction design are systems that can pick up more of our actions, in a controlled and contextualized way, and that can deliver seamless information and services in a variety of formats and multiple sensory modalities that are suitable to individuals, tasks and contexts. New and richer physical interaction technology needs to be flexible and adaptable, as human needs and abilities vary over time, in different contexts etc. With an increasing number of information processing appliances being used by people – at work, in the home, on-the-move – there is a need for these devices to be self-organising and self-configuring. It requires a significant degree of interoperability. The devices must also be designed for intermittent use, with graceful degradation of functionality, where applicable. We have already explored some of these issues in earlier projects, for example, Fernström et al. (2002) and McElligott et al. (2002a,b). This is a very rich problem area that links our work across the project, as we know that the topic of "breakdowns" in human activities is of crucial importance.

Our work encompasses both the development of smart objects as well as the embedding of these objects in larger-scale room-sized assemblies of artefacts. We refer to these objects and environments as Computationally Enhanced Environments (CEEs) and Computationally-Enhanced Artefacts (CEAs). CEEs need to "know" how they are configured and that humans are present and sometimes require support from the environment. Interfaces directly between humans and such environments could be termed *macro-interfaces*. Computationally enhanced artefacts, which are sometimes present in CEEs, need to "know" where they are, and how they are being handled by humans, to facilitate interaction with a CEE itself as well as mediating between humans and a CEE.

Interfaces on CEAs are inherently small and could be called *micro-interfaces*. In this work we also need to address multimodality, that is, how to induce seamless and integrated user experiences in more than one sense modality. Visual, auditory and haptic interfaces need to be explored both in isolation and combination, to ensure a rich and valid user experience. We intend to research, develop and explore how a coherent user experience can be created in CEEs with a variety of CEAs in use. For example, there have to be multiple ways to access functionality, with or without a CEE or CEA, and this difference has to be made natural. We also aim to explore the richness of human gesture. How can a CEA recognise if it is used, for example, for pointing? How can CEEs dynamically adapt to the richness in human gesture, locomotion etc.? We should note that our perspective on smart objects does not imply that the objects model human thinking or emotional states, as in some of the Ambient Intelligence research agendas, but simply that they have some minimal capacity for awareness and self-reflection. We believe that the more ambitious attempts at having these objects or environments attempt to model the user are misguided. We prefer to explore ways in which we can support natural intelligences (people!) through our computationally enhanced artefacts.

While new technology allows for pervasive interconnectivity and "always-on" capability, our work may place constraints on how we activate this technological capacity. So, for example, availability of data is not necessarily bidirectional. Support for privacy and an understanding of ethical issues will need to be included from the outset. One major area for investigation is how we design for less than optimal conditions in a densely interconnected computational environment. What happens when there are interruptions in power supply, or when wireless signals are weak or corrupted? How do we build in schemes that allow complex systems to gracefully degrade, and to make apparent to people living in this environment that this is indeed the case? This is a very rich problem area that links our work across the Shared Worlds project strands, as we know that the topic of breakdowns is of importance conceptually, in terms of creating learning situations for people, and we can explore such breakdowns and people's reactions to them in our co-design studio, and ultimately, "on location".

In our research we frame technological development within the context of human activity scenarios, for working, learning and living, from the outset of the design, rather than attempt to "fit" the technology into the social world as an afterthought. Thus, we will explore how ubiquitous technology can improve access – to services, markets, products and other people – for people with various kinds of abilities. We will show how to develop scenarios where cheap computational power and miniaturisation does not necessarily lead to a surveillance society, where people are constantly being monitored, tracked and archived. We will explore cheap, affordable and sustainable technologies that make a difference to people's lives. There is an alternative view of an information society that creates a technologically advanced environment that is under the control of people and not the other way around. Our scenarios do not assume that the future of technology lies in humanoid robots, or "intelligent" artificial machines. Rather, we believe that we can make novel and useful digital artefacts and media without needing to ascertain people's intentions, or to model them. There are powerful theoretical arguments that would support this stance, which is rather unique at this time among scientific research centres engaged in pervasive computing. That said, we do have a strong commitment to pushing the boundaries on what we can do with new technologies, creating new devices and software with novel performance characteristics.

3 Concluding remarks

We believe that the Shared Worlds research programme (described above) will make a significant contribution to interaction design research. Our design ideas have been influenced by several core themes that we attempt to incorporate into our design thinking. These include:

- *Human Activity* – as a fundamental aspect of human being in the world
- *Materiality of Objects* – the central role of material artefacts in human culture
- *Engagement* – the need to excite, motivate and enhance the user experience
- *Interaction* – human play with objects being seen as a narrative activity, not as simple action-reaction (mouse event - action pairs)
- *Multimodality* – incorporating several sensory modalities – visual, tactual, kinaesthetic, sonic, auditory
- *Sociality* – creating artefacts or assemblies of artefacts that allow for collaborative activity
- *Augmentation* – viewing the computer as a medium or tool for human actions, not as an intelligent butler or agent that attempts to model us.

Information and communications technology are part of the infrastructure for the new economy. However, once one has provided the bandwidth, the issue becomes what kind of content is being carried; what will consumers pay for; how do we package and deliver content and services of use to the citizen? Living with a plethora of "intelligent gadgets", or within an "ambient intelligence" space, where our fridges talk to our mobiles or to us, is unlikely to provide us with much new functionality or satisfaction unless our emerging "knowledge society" (underpinned by ubiquitous technology) embodies a deep appreciation of the social world, and of everyday life in that world. Concepts such as e-learning and m-learning (mobile learning) need to be unpacked, subjected to scrutiny, and explored in a variety of scenarios that examine the real meaning of such concepts. Thus we plan to explore the possibilities of mobility and real and virtual community from a variety of perspectives, and reexamine these concepts through artistic exploration, novel design scenarios and public demonstration and feedback sessions. The history of technology is littered with inventions that failed due to lack of public acceptance. Our focus is on human activities, and on the way they may be enhanced, supported and transcended with, by and through novel interactive forms.

Much of the research work being done at the IDC may be viewed as "blue skies" research – funded by an EU programme targeting future and emerging technologies, for example. Thus it is not focused on immediate commercial concerns, but we do discuss our work with commercial organisations, and indeed have links with a number of companies interested in spin-offs from our design explorations. Of course, there is a large gap between showing "proof-of-concept", and having an impact on industrial practice, but we are confident that the paths we are exploring have relevance for organisations involved in interaction design and technological innovation today. We believe that the ideas, methods and technical innovations that we are exploring today will become part of the stock-in-trade of everyday practice in interaction design in the years ahead. In Europe, we have a strong philosophical, psychological, sociological and anthropological research tradition that should be able to make a significant contribution to the articulation of more realistic scenarios for life in the future than those derived purely from technological fetishism or commercially inspired fashions. Building on this rich understanding and thick description of people's lives and activities, we can then attempt to create convivial technologies that may indeed enhance people's quality of life.

Acknowledgements

I wish to thank all members of the IDC, past and present, and our students on the Interactive Media course, for contributing to our vision and accomplishments over the years. I would also like to thank all our research sponsors – Science Foundation Ireland, European Commission, Enterprise Ireland, Higher Education Authority etc. Thanks to Kieran Ferris for help with the illustrations.

References

Aboulafia A, Bannon L (2004) Understanding Affect in Design: An outline conceptual framework. Theoretical Issues in Ergnomics Science 5(1):4-15
Adams P, Bannon L (2003) CUBO: building blocks as graspable interfaces for children's interactive television. UL IDC Technical Report No. 03-12-02
Aldersey-Williams H, Bound J, Coleman R (eds) (1999) The Methods Lab: User Research for Design. Design for Ageing Network, Royal College of Art, London
Bakhtin M (1981) Discourse in the novel. In: Holquist M (ed) The Dialogic Imagination: Four Essays by M.M. Bakhtin. University of Texas Press, Austin, TX, pp 259-422
Bannon L (1985) Extending the design boundaries of human-computer interaction. Institute for Cognitive Science, University of California, San Diego. ICS Technical Report 8505. (Extracts from this report appear as 3 Chapters in Norman DA, Draper SW (eds) (1986) User Centered System Design: New Perspectives on Human-Computer Interaction. (Lawrence Erlbaum Associates, Hillsdale, NJ)

Bannon L (1986) Computer-Mediated Communication. In: Norman DA, Draper SW (eds) User Centered System Design: New Perspectives on Human-Computer Interaction. (Lawrence Erlbaum Associates, Hillsdale, NJ)

Bannon L (1991) From Human Factors to Human Actors: The role of psychology and human-computer interaction studies in systems design. Book Chapter in: Greenbaum J, Kyng M (eds) Design at Work: Cooperative Design of Computer Systems. Lawrence Erlbaum Associates, Hillsdale, NJ, pp 25-44

Bannon L, Bødker S (1991) Beyond the Interface: Encountering Artifacts in Use. In: Carroll J (ed) Designing Interaction: Psychology at the human-computer interface. Cambridge University Press, Cambridge, pp 227-253

Bannon L, Kaptelinin V (2000) From Human-Computer Interaction to Computer-Mediated Activity. In: Stephanidis C (ed) User Interfaces for All: Concepts, Methods, and Tools. Lawrence Erlbaum, Mahwah, NJ, pp 183-202

Bannon L, Kuutti K (2002) Shifting Perspectives on Organizational Memory: From Storage to Active Remembering. In: Little S, Quintas P, Ray T (eds) Managing Knowledge: An Essential Reader. Open University/ Sage Publications, London, pp 190-210

Bannon L, Schmidt K (1991) CSCW: Four Characters in Search of a Context. In: Bowers J, Benford S (eds) Studies in Computer Supported Cooperative Work: Theory, Practice and Design. North-Holland, pp 3-16

Bannon L, Cypher A, Greenspan S, Monty M (1983) Evaluation and Analysis of User's Activity Organization. In: Janda A (ed) Proceedings of the ACM CHI'1983 Conference on Human Factors in Computing Systems. ACM, New York, pp 54-57

Blythe M, Overbeeke K, Monk A, Wright P (eds) (2003) Funology: From Usability to Enjoyment. Academic Publishers, Kluwer, Dordrecht

Buur J, Bødker S (2000) From usability lab to "design collaboratorium": Reframing usability practice. In: Proceedings, ACM Design of Interactive Systems Conference, DIS 2000

Christensen HH, Bardram JE (2002) Supporting Human Activities – Exploring Activity-Centrered Computing. In: Boriello G, Holmquist LE (eds) 4th International Conference on Ubiquitous Computing (UbiComp 2002), Goteborg, Sweden. (Lecture Notes in Computer Science 2498. Springer, Berlin.) pp 107-116

Ciolfi L, Bannon L (2002) Designing interactive museum exhibits: Enhancing visitor curiosity through augmented artefacts. Proceedings of ECCE11, European Conference on Cognitive Ergonomics. Catania, Italy, pp 311-317

Dewey J (1925) Experience and Nature. Open Court, LaSalle, IL

Dewey J (1934) Art as Experience. Pedigree, New York

Ehn P (1988) Work-Oriented Design of Computer Artifacts. Lawrence Erlbaum, Hillsdale, NJ

Dourish P (2001) Where the Action Is: The Foundations of Embodied Interaction. MIT Press, Cambridge, MA

Fernström M, McElligott L, Dillon M, McGettrick C (2002) PuSH-Overture – Extending the Playability of the Traditional Musical Instrument. Proceedings of the International Computer Music Conference ICMC-2002. Gothenburg, Sweden

Ferris K, Bannon L (2002) "A load of ould Boxology..." Proceedings of ACM Conference on Designing Interactive Systems (DIS2002). British Museum, London, pp 41-49

Ferris K, Bannon L, Ciolfi L, Gallagher P, Hall T, Lennon M (2004) Shaping Experiences in the Hunt Museum: A design dase study accepted for publication in the Proc. of ACM Conference on the Design for Interactive Systems, DIS 2004, Cambridge, MA

Gershenfeld N (1999) When Things Start to Think. Henry Holt, New York

Greenbaum J, Kyng M (eds) (1991) Design at Work: Cooperative Design of Computer Systems. Lawrence Erlbaum Associates, Hillsdale, NJ

Hallnäs L, Redström J (2002) From Use to Presence: On the Expressions and Aesthetics of Everyday Computational Things. ACM Transactions on Computer-Human Interaction 9(2):106-124

McCarthy J, Wright P (2003) The Enchantments of Technology. In: Blythe M, Overbeeke K, Monk A, Wright P (eds) Funology: From Usability to Enjoyment. Kluwer, Dordrecht, pp 81-90

McElligott L, Dillon M, Dixon E (2002a) PegLegs in Music – Processing the Effort Generated by Levels of Expressive Gesturing in Music. Proceedings of the international conference on New Interfaces for Musical Expression NIME-02. MediaLab Europe, Dublin

McElligott L, Fernstrom M, Dillon M, Richardson B, Leydon K (2002b) "ForSe FIElds" force sensors for interactive environments. Proceedings of 4th International Conference on Ubiquitous Computing (UbiComp 2002). Sweden, pp 168-175. http://www.idc.ul.ie/ztiles

Moran T, Anderson R (1990) The workaday world as a paradigm for CSCW design. Proceedings, ACM Conference on CSCW. Los Angeles, California, pp 381-393

Naur P (1985) Programming as theory building. Microprocessing and Microprogramming 15(5):253-261

Nielsen J (1993) Usability Engineering. Academic Press, London

Norman D (1998) The Invisible Computer. MIT Press, Cambridge, MA

Picard RW (1997) Affective computing. MIT Press, Cambridge, MA

Rocchesso D, Fontana F (eds) (2003) The Sounding Object. Mondo Estremo, Firenze, Italy. http://www.soundingobject.org

Schmidt K, Bannon L (1992) Taking CSCW seriously: Supporting articulation work. Computer Supported Cooperative Work – an International Journal 1(1-2):7-40

Shneiderman B (1983) Direct manipulation: A step beyond programming languages. IEEE Computer 16(8):57-69l

Weiser M (1991) The computer for the 21st Century. Scientific American 265(3):94-104

Winograd T (1997) The design of interaction. In: Denning P, Metcalfe R (eds) Beyond Calculation: The Next Fifty Years of Computing. Copernicus, Springer-Verlag, New York, pp 149-161

Winograd T, Flores F (1986) Understanding Computers and Cognition. A New Foundation for Design. Ablex, Norwood

Wright P, McCarthy J, Meekison L (2003) Making sense of experience. In: Blythe M, Overbeeke K, Monk A, Wright P (eds) Funology: From Usability to Enjoyment. Kluwer, Dordrecht, pp 43-53

Appendix 1: The UL Interaction Design Centre

The University of Limerick Interaction Design Centre (IDC) is an interdisciplinary research group in the Department of Computer Science and Information Systems focused on the design, use and evaluation of information and communications technologies. The focus is on human-centred design, with a strong interest in collaborative settings, exploring the design and use of novel interactive and communicative artefacts to support human activities. Work in the IDC covers a wide spectrum, from the design and evaluation of new media installations and interfaces to field studies of technology in use in different settings. Members of the group have a range of competencies and disciplinary backgrounds, including software engineering, electronics, psychology, ethnography, ergonomics, communication, media studies, information systems, art, industrial and graphic design. This range of skills and disciplines is selectively brought to bear on issues of user needs assessment, exploratory investigations, storyboarding, the design of novel interactive surfaces, analysis of user interaction patterns and examination of technologies in varied settings of use. Our research covers the fields of Human-Computer Interaction (HCI), Usability, Web Design, Multimedia, User-Centered and Participative Design, Computer Supported Cooperative Work (CSCW), Interaction Design and Experience Design. What keeps the Centre focused is an overall concern with the fit among human, social and cultural concerns and new technologies, where primacy is given to human needs, and technologies are, where possible, investigated in workaday and everyday settings.

The IDC has been in existence for seven years and comprises 25+ members – faculty, research staff and students, visitors, and administrative and technical support personnel, although our core faculty comprises just two people, Liam Bannon as Director and Mikael Fernström, lecturer, inventor, software wizard and comrade-in-arms, as Manager. The Centre has been involved for several years in a variety of European research projects, more recently in two research projects connected to the European Information Society Technology (IST) Future and Emerging Technologies Programme on the "Disappearing Computer": SHAPE (Situating Hybrid Assemblies in Public Environments) and SOb (The Sounding Object). The Centre also has obtained significant funding for new projects on multimodal interaction, and on the investigation of new technological platforms and multimedia tools to support plant operator activities. We have also originated and developed a one-year graduate curriculum in Interactive Media. This has been a hugely time-consuming, but rewarding exercise. Several of the graduates of this programme have moved into the IDC in a research capacity, adding to the multidisciplinary skill base of the Centre. Many of the graduating projects explicitly address themes such as gaming, innovative educational products and interactive TV. We provide a few illustrations of our work, with references, below. For an update, check out our Web site at http://www.idc.ul.ie.

EU SHAPE project

Fig. 1. A view of the Room of Opinion (left) and The Study Room (right) in the EU SHAPE Hunt Exhibition "Re-Tracing the Past" in June 2003

This project has been exploring the design, development and use of novel interactive artefacts and environments in public spaces. The "Re-Tracing the Past: Objects, Stories, Mysteries…" exhibition in June 2003 at the Hunt Museum in Limerick was an innovative approach to the design of interactive installations for art and cultural heritage. The focus was on the museum objects, and visitor opinions on them, not on the technology. We worked in close collaboration with the museum staff, and performed extensive studies on the way visitors approach and make sense of particular exhibits in the museum in order to produce appropriate design ideas that placed the museum artefacts and visitor opinions in the spotlight. Partners in the SHAPE project together with the University of Limerick are: the Royal Institute of Technology (Sweden), the University of Nottingham (UK) and King's College, London (UK) (Ferris et al. 2004).

Fig. 2. Museum visitors listening to visitor opinions on the Radio and exploring items at the Interactive Desk

EU SOb project

In our work on human-computer interaction design with auditory representations in the Sounding Object (www.soundingobject.org) project, we have concentrated on auditory interfaces for ubiquitous computing. The Sounding Object project explored new methods for physically inspired modelling for sound synthesis. We also worked towards *cartoonification* of sound models (i.e., simplifying the models while retaining perceptual invariants). The *cartoonification* increased both computational efficiency and perceptual sharpness of the sound models. The models were implemented in Pure Data or *pd* (www.pure-data.org) and tested in a number of ways ranging from perceptual experiments to artistic performance. Compared to ordinary sound files, sound objects provide "live" sound models parametrically controlled in real-time. Being able to parametrically control sound models in real-time can also, potentially, help to make sonifications less annoying. Pre-recorded sound files, in an auditory interface always sound exactly the same but with sound objects we can vary properties of the sounds, for example, mapping the size of objects or the effort of actions, so that small objects or actions make small sounds and large objects or actions make large sounds.

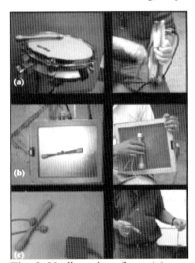

Fig. 3. Vodhran interfaces (a) Clavia drum, (b) Radio Baton and (c) Polhemus Fastrack

As part of the Sounding Object project we created several interfaces and demonstrations of these ideas. One of these was the *Vodhran*, a sound manipulation interface based on a traditional Irish percussion instrument called the *bodhran*. To implement a virtual bodhran, the *Vodhran*, we used three devices that differ in control and interaction possibilities – a drumpad, a radio-based controller and a magnetic tracker system (see Figure 3). Each device connects to a computer running *pd* with the impact model developed within the project. Another interface we developed for the project, was the *Sonic Browser*, a tool that allowed for interactive visualisation and sonification of a sound collection. In the starfield visualisation display (one of several displays) in the *Sonic Browser* shown in Figure 4, each visual object represents a sound. Users can arbitrarily map the location, color, size and geometry of each visual object to properties of the represented objects. They can hear all sounds covered by an *aura* simultaneously, spatialised in a stereo space around the aura's center. The *Sonic Browser* allows users to interactively access large collections of sounds using multiple visualisation displays and dynamic filtering to rapidly pick, group and choose sounds. Further information on the project can be found on-line at http://www.soundobject.org. A book containing the experiments, interfaces, demonstrations and results as well as discussions has also been published (Rocchesso and Fontana 2003).

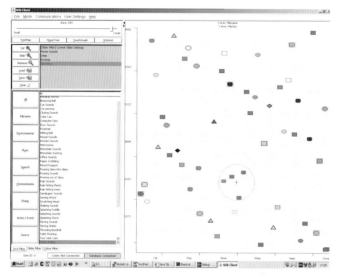

Fig. 4. Sonic Browser tool with *aura* shown as circle and crosshair

Z-Tiles

Over the last few years, a number of projects have been undertaken both in
Limerick at the Interaction Design Centre and farther afield in such places as the
MIT MediaLab in Boston, to develop pressure or force-sensitive floor spaces
which can be used for a variety of purposes. The latest endeavour to develop such
a floorspace is a collaborative effort between the IDC in Limerick and MediaLab
Europe (MLE) in Dublin. The performance surface is composed of smaller
sensory units, which can be used together *en masse* to form a complete floorspace.
As the units are completely modular, the floorspace could be easily disassembled
for transport from one place to another, and the floorspace could also be shaped to
fill the contours of the area in which it is to be used.

The individual units contain twenty pressure sensors each and are known as Z-
Tiles, hence the name of the project, because they sense movement in the Z-plane
by way of pressure changes. Their shape is such that they interlock with one
another so that, when placed together in a floor, each tile will connect tightly with
its neighbours and prevent any movement of the floor itself. The tight connections
also allow information from the sensor readings to be passed from tile to tile
through the floor so that only one data connection is required to gather pressure
information from a large area of tiles, as opposed to having one connection for
each individual tile. (McElligott et al. 2002b)

Fig. 5. Views of Z-Tiles

SOS: Self-Organising Sensors

Human activity involves movement on scales from the macroscopic to the microscopic, and this makes motion capture for electronically "responsive" environments a challenge. One technical aspect of this challenge is the placement and organisation of motion sensors:

Should sensors be grouped densely to accommodate nuances in human motion?
Should they be spread widely to accommodate macroscopic motion?
If sensors are distributed densely and widely how can computational "costs" be minimised?

Self-organising network algorithms hold the potential to facilitate deployment and maintenance of sensor systems for "interactive surfaces". The Self Organising Sensor project addresses issues of sensor system scalability through development of a network architecture for pressure-sensing floor tiles. The effort builds on prior experience with the Z-Tiles project described above and generalises to support different sensors and surface orientations.

Masters in Interactive Media projects

As the IDC has developed, we became increasingly concerned that we needed to introduce our ideas to students in a more structured form than simply having people work in our centre. Starting from a position of computers as media, then good interactive software design should benefit from an understanding of the general design process, and not simply a focus on technical specifications. There is a need to introduce issues such as storyboarding, scripting, animation, video editing, sensor design and application, use of music and some appreciation of issues in TV and film production in order to allow students to understand the design of truly interactive systems. In 1999 we launched a Masters degree in Interactive Media at the University of Limerick. An example of two projects conducted by students from this course is given below.

The cardboard box garden

This project, by Kieran Ferris, involved the design of an augmented children's play environment centred on that most ubiquitous and simple of objects, the cardboard box. Shifting the focus of attention from the GUI to familiar objects, and the child's interactions around and through these augmented objects, results in the computer becoming a facilitator of exploration and learning. The purpose of the exercise was to show how computer technology can be used in innovative ways to stimulate discovery, play and adventure among children. (Ferris and Bannon 2002)

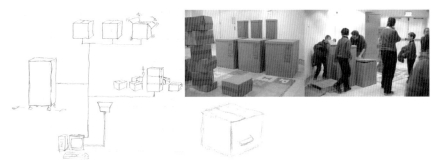

Fig. 6. Outline schematic, view of cardboard box garden and visitors playing with the boxes

CUBO: Building blocks as graspable interfaces for children's interactive television

The Cubo system, developed by Paul Adams, gives children a physical interface that encourages them to actively explore possibilities for constructing narratives for television programmes The aim is to change the child's experience of television through their active participation in the programme. By manipulating building blocks on a playmat, children can actively participate in television programmes and gain control over content. This allows them to explore, play and express themselves by constructing their own narratives. (Adams and Bannon 2003)

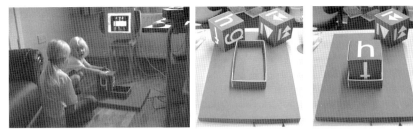

Fig. 7. Children using blocks to control TV programme, and views of blocks – outside and inside active floor area

Further information on the projects done by UL Interactive Media students is available on the Web sites: http://www.csis.ul.ie/imedia/dawn, http://www.csis.ul.ie/imedia/dawn02 and http://www.csis.ul.ie/imedia/dawn03.

Incorporating self into web information system design

Anita Greenhill[1], Hannakaisa Isomäki[2]

[1]Department of Information Systems, University of Manchester Institute of Science and Technology (UMIST)
UK
a.greenhill@umist.ac.uk

[2]Department of Research Methodology, University of Lapland
Finland
hisomaki@urova.fi

Abstract

Identity construction in computer-mediated environments as in "real life" environments, is influenced by existent social processes. In these virtual environments the computer screen mediates specific experiences of localised physicality; however these computer mediated experiences do not alter the overall sense of being for the individual. To interact with the Web Information System in virtual space the individuals do not leave the essence of themselves on one side of the screen to acquire a new layer of meanings and self-ascription within the virtual space. Identity construction is similarly a complex process in cyberspace as it is in real life. In this chapter we will present a post-structural discussion arguing that electronic identity enables a deconstruction of the mind/body dichotomy. We argue that when individuals interact with a Web information system, in virtual space, they do not leave the essence of themselves on one side of the screen to acquire a new layer of meaning and self-ascription within the virtual space that the system occupies. Further, issues of design are considered in regard to systems development that aim at supporting computer-mediated identity construction.

1 Introduction

Recent developments within information and communication technologies (ICT) provide information systems designers with the potential to build systems for various purposes. The emergence of global Information Systems (IS) incorporating ubiquitous computing and wearable computers supported by wireless technologies and distributed interfaces has led to a number of original views of IS (e.g., Paulos and Canny 1997; Stanton 2001). The ever-expanding applications of ICT increasingly pervade human life, changing the nature of information systems, especially with respect to the human being. IS cannot exclusively be understood along the boundaries and operations of organisations. In this way increased technological change imposes new demands on the development of information systems.

The incorporation of on-line technology into human activity has occurred primarily in the name of user-friendliness or human-centred design (Standing and Vasudavan 2000). Therefore, it is necessary to think about and design information systems within a social context. An overview of IS design methods reveals that there is little designer input with respect to the "social mode of being" (Isomäki 2002). Such input is a requirement for adequate human-centred design. Indeed the notion of user is often socially thin within IS research (Lamb and Kling 2003). Eason (2001) argues that recent research shows that IS design – despite significant progress in the adoption of human-centred methods – remains technocentric and organisational outcomes are often unplanned and unwanted. Current design predictions about the development of virtual organisations are likely to be oversimplistic. The appropriate use of methods to assess organisational options and design sociotechnical systems is necessary if emerging forms of technology, such as Web information systems, are to be effectively deployed.

In this chapter we argue that understanding the human social mode of being – the self – is a necessary requirement for the contemporary design of information systems. Discussion surrounding the philosophical discourse of the self, consciousness and reality presents a multiplicity of options from which HCI development could be extended. Existing notions of identity formation reveal that the establishment of individual character is achieved when a stable immutable sense of self occurs whether it is rooted in social class, gender or race (Butler 1990). Giddens (1991, p. 244) similarly defines "self-identity" as "the self as reflexively understood in terms of his or her biography". The following argument situates identity construction within the notion of social constructionism. It assumes that all forms of knowledge exist in relation to the influence of social and cultural factors. This denotes that individuals' self-perceptions and identity construction are related to the socially defined reality (Berger and Luckmann 1966). As a consequence, the construction of self-identity and the identification of others in relation to our own self is itself a series of dynamic and ever-changing processes. As Simon (1991) states: "Social life has entered the computer age."

No longer is the computer merely a tool for personal and professional productivity. Linked via a modem to other computers – a simple and relatively inexpensive arrangement – the keyboard and monitor have become an arena for personal "networking". We argue that the Web as a communications mediator and social space is an important growing cultural reference point where the human-computer interface plays a central role in shaping the interaction between people as well as between people and computers. Design that takes into account the consequences of computer interfaces to the construction of self-identity, emphasising the subjective experiences of individuals involved, is indeed a necessity if contemporary IS development aims at high-quality systems. Indeed it has long been known that when developing Web information systems for social organisations the functionality of those organisations cannot be considered to be a systematic property at all but rather a relation between the IS and the social use of that system (see, e.g., Mumford 1983). The most important issue to note is that social action in computer-mediated environments as in real life environments is influenced by existent social processes. These include the construction of self-identity and the identification of others in relation to our own self, which are enacted in human communicative action. When people interact with each other, either in a virtual space or face-to-face, they evoke and sustain social processes particular to the situation in question (Greenhill 1999). Within these continuously evolving communicative interactions users' self-identities are formed. Therefore, IS designers should be both able to recognise the recurrent formation of social interactions, particularly identity construction, and also be provided with ISD methodologies that promote the social usability of Web information systems.

It is important to emphasise at this point that notions of identity in relation to social constructionism acknowledges the "subjective" position in relation to exploring the self or being. In contrast, the "humanist" notion of the self tells us that human nature determines identity and as human beings we are the authors of all that we think and see around us, including the knowledge that structures the world. As Easthope and McGowan (1992) explain, "Within this framework, the human individual is conceived as a unified centre of control from which meaning emanates". The social contructionist position in contrast replaces human nature as the determiner of meaning with self-awareness and subjective concepts such as history, society and culture. In this way it is not human nature but the subjectivity or self-aware individual which plays an active role in determining the factors relevant to the construction of individual identity. Social construction as a philosophical position is based on Heidegger's writings (Zimmerman 1993). Zimmerman (1993) explains shared action as "a way of being which constitutes a shared agreement in our practices about what entities can show up and, likewise humans are not entities but the clearing in which entities appear". As Berger and Luckmann (1966, pp. 55, 56) state "Social order is not part of 'the nature of thing', it cannot be derived from the 'laws of nature'. Social order exists only as a product of human activity". Importantly, however, Berger and Luckmann (1966, pp. 55, 56) contextualise this understanding and argue that "Human being is impossible in a closed sphere of quiescent interiority. Human being must ongoingly externalise itself in activity". These foundational assumptions are threefold. Firstly it is assumed that we know the world only as we perceive it. Secondly it is assumed that our perceptions are based on learned interpretations and that these learned interpretations are social. Finally, it is assumed that we learn and acquire meaning from, and among, persons in social interaction. Hence the main vehicle for conveying social meaning is through symbols, cultural myths, the structure and practice of our institutions and our rules for similar action. These vehicles of meaning together construct our worldview, our sense of ourselves, our identity and purpose as well as our ideologies. Further to this our selves, our societies and our institutions are in a continual state of change through interaction.

All these assumptions stress the social construction of reality. Therefore if we extend these concepts to the interaction between people and the computer and the Web then understanding the social construction is derived as an active process. It is important to stress that there is a huge variation in the application of the social constructionist theory ranging from the relatively conservative applications in sociological studies exploring issues of social process and policy making (Green 1999; Welch 2003) through to the radical applications such as gender studies (Taysom 1998; Morris 1999; Edwards and Imrie 2003). The focus of the discussion of this chapter, however, is the subjective experiences of individuals in electronically crafted space (such as computer networks and the Web); and exploring the design consequences of identity construction in these environments. We aim to broaden IS research and practice intellectually and give rise to new design ideas, which may yield IS as social systems only technically implemented.

2 Computer mediated identity as with that of real life is socially constructed

Many contemporary information system studies explore the Internet or an Intranet's operations and remind their readers that an integral element of these systems is the new, technologically enabled space within which these systems are contained (Berg and Kreiner 1992; Hensing et al. 1994; Lamb 1996; Pawlowski et al. 2000; Greenhill 2001; Eschenfelder and Sawyer 2001). However, it is rare that information systems, irrespective of their provenance, are acknowledged as contributing to the user's construction of identity. The "presence" of users as a component of the system within technologically enabled spaces means that identity is experienced through the technological mediation of the screen. This is a homogenising influence, which emphasises particular methods of interaction over others and, in turn, has an impact upon the interpretation and ascription[1] of identities that can be "virtually" achieved via the information system.

The construction of computer-mediated identity is not without difficulty. The process is caught between the interposed detachment of the screen and the immersive qualities found "in" virtual space. The articulation of the interactive relationship between the machine and the user in this environment is of "exoticness"[2]. The interaction brings with it an experience of distancing, where the interchange is anchored by the screen (cf. Argyle 1969, p. 75). This is a

---

[1] *Ascription* – that certain qualities of an individual – status, occupation or income, for example, are given by the position into which those individuals are born or over which they have no control, rather than by their own achievement. (Abercrombie et al. 1988, p. 13)

[2] *Exoticness* – being or from or characteristic of another place or part of the world; "alien customs", "exotic plants in a greenhouse", "exotic cuisine". For further insight on this notion see Said (1979).

simulacrum[3] in which layers of meaning electronically overlay, and interlay the presence of the interactive space. It is argued (Spender 1995), that this exotic configuration provides a disassociation from real life experience, which, in turn, enables a rethinking of the social influences that contribute to how individuals construct their identities. The human/machine polarisations claims made for this space imitate the heavily trodden terrain of the mind/body dichotomy. Poststructural theory argues that these dualistic reductions contribute to the reproduction of hegemonic power relations.

2.1 Proxemics and identity

As a facet of such reductions the construction of computer-mediated identity occurs when people interact with others through a computer interface that replaces the proxemics found with face-to-face communication. Proxemics according to its founder, Edward T. Hall, is the study of humankind's "perception and use of space" (Hall 1966, p. 83). The prime directive of proxemic space is that we may not come and go everywhere as we please. There are cultural rules and biological boundaries – explicit as well as implicit and subtle limits to observe – everywhere (Givens 2003). In many instances in information systems development it is the impact of addressing or altering proxemics that is the primary objective when converting existing information systems from real life occupation to the virtual platform. Nonetheless for the user, an understanding, familiarity and interpretation of an identity is dynamically constructed regardless of the platform. For the user identity is often negotiated around an altered set of dichotomised cultural cues as a result of the lack of the conventional reference points to previous identities. However it is possible that with careful consideration and recognition the dualisms of mind/body, public/private and others could be diminished, if not totally dissolved, within the context of a Web information system embracing virtual space (McRae 1996, p. 245). A shift in the manner through which identity is referenced within the Web information system could assist in constructing the system as a social space, albeit one defined through the social worlds of real life (Richardson 1989, pp. 5, 8).

2.2 Spatialising interaction

The significance of spatial arrangements within Web information systems and in the construction and contextualising of identity is evident when examining, for example, the formation of public and private identities. For example Somers states:

---

[3] *Simulacrum* – "The simulacrum is never that which conceals the truth – it is the truth which conceals that there is none. The simulacrum is true". Ecclesiastes cited in Baudrillard (1988), p.166. For an explanation of simulacrum see Baudrillard (1994).

Narrative identities are constituted by a person's temporally and spatially variable place in culturally constructed stories composed of (breakable) rules, (variable) practices, binding (and unbinding) institutions, and the multiple plots of family, nation or economic life. More importantly, however, narratives are not incorporated into the self in any direct way; rather, they are mediated through the enormous spectrum of social and political institutions and practices that constitute our social world. (Somers 1994, p. 635)

The manner in which spatial phenomena are variously experienced as consumer, kin, worker, audience member, sexual being, citizen and as an "other" similarly indicates the shifting frameworks by which we are understood and presented to those around us. These shifting relationships suggest that the experience of the social within the computer-mediated space of a Web information system can be considered as familiar interaction but one that is experienced in the location of reordered significance. For example, culturally shared knowledge, such as media events, physical location, physical sensation and sexual innuendo, are also interchanged by the users in computer-mediated space and consequently strengthen group interactions. On the other hand, as places founded upon the full range of cultural and social imperatives provided by the machinations of advanced capitalism, it is clear that many existing suppositions regarding human communication and interaction persist within Web information systems. The points of departure, if any exist, from other social spaces and their analysis is found in the extent to which real life social structures can be claimed to have become untenable or irrelevant in these types of information systems. These are arguably replaced by formations that can be claimed as new. More reasonably, these "new" social structures are the result of shifted emphasis of the social into unusual or unexpected orders.

Various disparate visions of virtual space and the Web are manifested in descriptions such as the techno-utopian boosterism of Nicholas Negroponte (1995), the celebratory new-ageism of Douglas Rushkoff (1994), the jaded dystopia found by Clifford Stoll (1995) or the masculinist jungle described by Dale Spender (1995). There is a need, however, to treat with caution these, and any, descriptions of virtual space, which attempt to describe a range of observed phenomena and experiences as universal expectations.

2.3 Situating the user in computer design

Interaction and communication must eventually occur between people, although this interaction can be indefinitely deferred across time and space. Entering virtual space through a Web information system as with other computer-mediated experiences de-emphasises the corporeal cues to identity (Gumpert and Drucker 1994, pp. 169, 170). Unlike communications media such as the television, the radio and the telephone, which rely upon visual, aural or oral information to assist in the construction of identity, the World Wide Web of 2002 remains a generally textual and anonymous arena for communication and interaction. Identity or identities, then, can be heavily constructed in this space through one's own volition, without the direct influence of cultural assumptions and social stereotypes made by "others" from a physical presence. This situation does not, however, disentangle or dissolve the range of power relations, which inform our movement through Web-mediated spaces (Kendall 1996, p. 213). In Web information systems interaction cues are still sought in order to define the relationship between the user and the system and now in many cases between the user and other users.

The most apparent user identity is the network identity. This is carried through all computer-mediated exchanges. The only piece of information directly conveyed by the network identity that has any real life meaning is the physical location of the computer handling the exchanges of each participant. When a user utilises the Web information system, the communication is conducted via the keyboard. The user can generally only be identified by his user id code. These codes, however, provide few clues regarding the individual's identity, beyond his point of entry, the time he entered and exited and a trail of what he did within the system. Technical experts argue that the specific identity construction of the user is of little interest or use in more conventional information systems, oriented towards efficient high-speed information processing (Isomäki 2002). Social libertarians would also argue against Web information systems being able to attain information about the personal identity of the user. When considering the user's position, however, the lack of cues currently available to help navigate human-to-human interaction via the computer can be described as stark, barren and even alienating. From the user's perspective it could reasonably be argued that it is time to humanise the computer-mediated experience. That rather than controlling the experience and presenting it as a predominantly mental experience where the body is left on the other side of the screen, a more deliberate, physical space should be activated. In this way the user could consciously leave behind traces of her own identity and physically ground the experience.

2.4 Enabling identity formation in design

An obvious and positive example of the attempts being made to establish identity in virtual space exists in the gendering of electronic space beyond the assumptions regarding one's personal name. In many interactive and virtual environments the individual is requested to ascribe themselves a name, and in effect, an identity. In this way the person can label themselves anything ranging from Erik Bloodaxe, the male hacker and editor of *2 600*, to Saint Jude, the outspoken on-line technofeminist, who utilises an ambiguously gendered (and curiously theologised) name, to the use of a favourite media character. The result is a "fantastic" association of one's personal identity with the well-known images and social attributes of a famous person. Despite the paucity of this received information, these cues enable the participants in chat groups to choose who to interact with and who to avoid. These personal acts of self-identity are empowering in the mind/body dichotomy as the ascription of physical cues can reverse the domination of machine in the interactive space making it a more humanised experience.

Seeking cues regarding the identity of "others" beyond a server's network address is a major activity of many chat groups. This generally involves trying to ascertain the gender, age and, sometimes, the ethnicity or education of the participants via a direct request. It is conceivable that a simple and if necessary automated process could be set up within a Web information system. This would enable the system users to construct their own computer-mediated identity from which they could work or even simply interface with the system. These parameters of identity and the gathering of this information corresponds, perhaps unsurprisingly, to many of the focal concerns of everyday sociological inquiry and serves to develop a range of social and power relations in virtual space which mirrors our more conventional experience (Gisler 1997, p. 219).

Drawing on the popularity and success of chat groups and virtual communities examples of the importance of identity construction can and should be integrated into the ethos of Web information systems construction. By providing, within the information system, identity cues the user can interact with other participants in a meaningful way. An interactive Web information system in this way can assist the user in identifying other users who share a common interest, therefore enabling unification of a community that is founded upon voluntary participation and common interest. The Web pages, manuals and information files associated with each Web information system produce a different context for the range of interaction and constructs that the user may experience, which, in turn, offer different reflection grounds for the user's identity construction. Individuals are often perceived as being physically excluded from computer-mediated communication. Here we argue that once access to computer mediated space is obtained and its usefulness perceived, then the processes by which identity is constructed can be a source of empowerment for Web information systems users.

The Web is a medium that can assist in the breakdown or at least call into question the existence of essentialist and structuralist dichotomies. These include those associated with the mind and body, human and machine, masculine and feminine, public and private and reality and illusion. The technological determinist claims made for virtual space can also be countered within this reading. As an alternate suggestion to the claims that virtual space is predefined to serve a mental experience, we argue that the extent and forms of existing identity construction experienced on-line indicate the extent to which the contemporary configurations of real life have an impact upon virtual space. These considerations reject the inevitability of virtual space and the Web as a domain already defined by machine-oriented functionality. Instead the domain is one in which the processes of defining identity are, and may necessarily always be, shifting and continually reconstructed at both individual and institutional levels of interaction. Similarly, the expectation that personal identity in computer-mediated interaction is an almost inevitable outcome of obtaining access is also empowering as it enables any opinion or philosophy to become an aspect of the social construction of the Web information system and networked interaction *in toto*.

2.5 Altering the mind/body dichotomy in computing

The importance of the use of the mind/body dichotomy in maintaining structural inequalities is profoundly evident. As long as the user's identity is seen as being inconsequential to the Web information system, particularly under the premise of efficiency, effectiveness and efficacy, then the body and an association of physicality to computer-mediated experiences will continue to be marginalised in information systems construction. A hierarchical order of mental hegemony will be maintained for as long as it is assumed that mental attributes are advantageous to the acquisition of knowledge and that therefore the mind should be addressed over physical characteristics such as social cues and identity (Farganis 1986, p. 157). We have asserted that virtual space and the expansion of information systems development into Web information systems development allows a rethinking of the mind/body dichotomy because the processes of identity formation and sociality move beyond existing simple ascriptions. The ability to identify one's self in virtual space and on the Web forces a reconsideration of the authority and legitimacy of the notion that the mind and body are separate things. The complex interplay of sociality that exists between people is similar, at a generalised level, within this space and those spaces of real life. The difference of virtual space is evidenced in the differing parameters applied to the construction of identity. The existing notions of identity construction that are associated with real life have been mutually extended, reprioritised and re-crafted. Even in the most extreme situations, popular representations of the mind melded with machine – the cyborg – do not reflect the experience of computer-mediated identity construction and therefore should not be exported into the computer-mediated experience of a Web information system.

3 Implications for design

Information systems developers and designers must acknowledge that the basis of electronic identity is founded upon the spatial context in which it is articulated. In order to develop systems that allow the incorporation of self into the design and thus support computer-mediated identity construction Web information systems designers should acquire appropriate means of systems development and design. A careful consideration of the manner through which identity is referenced within the Web information system could assist in constructing the system as a social space. These considerations should be made continuously during the different phases of Web information systems development, that is, planning, design, implementation and maintenance. The phases are cyclical and intertwining (e.g. Beynon-Davies et al. 1999), but planning is regarded as the most crucial phase for the success of information systems (e.g., Marakas and Elam 1998).

Information systems planning refers to the initiation and requirements analysis actions including client contacts and the definition of user requirements. During this phase the greatest degree of interaction occurs between the users and the designers (Marakas and Elam 1998). In order to accomplish requirements analysis (i.e., define the system's context of use), the designers need to understand all the many associated technical and human issues. Goguen (1996), for instance, regards culture, organisational structure, legal and economic constraints, users' work practices and marketing strategies as essential issues for such definitions. Ramey et al. (1996) describe a practice-oriented application of ethnography in studying users as members of a distinct subculture, which involves the group with different intrinsic qualities. The phases of the approach aim at extracting the actions, goals of actions and the values that animate them from a "stream of behaviour". Iteratively sampling behaviour and confirming its interpretation with the future users can define guidelines for social cues that support identity construction. These parameters of identity and the gathering of this information corresponds often to many of the focal concerns of everyday sociological inquiry. They serve to develop a range of social and power relations in virtual space, which reflects our more conventional experience. In all instances of planning it should be emphasised that the most crucial social elements that need to be taken into account are power and control (e.g., Klein and Hirschheim 1993). Social constructivist and poststructural approaches to interpreting social life through, for example, deconstruction are particularly suited to the examination of computer-mediated identity, and should be drawn upon more readily in developing systems for social interaction and identity construction.

Design denotes procedures where the user requirements are refined and turned into specifications and finally software. In addition to converting the results of requirements analysis into specifications, an essential task in the design phase is the design of a user interface. Winograd (1995), as well as Preece (1994), have stated that the properties of a user interface should meet with people's social, cognitive and aesthetic needs in addition to meeting their technical requirements. Stephanidis (2001) specifies that, within new ubiquitous technological environments, the design of human-computer interaction should focus, in addition to social and cultural features, on individuals' perceptual, cognitive and emotional space. In Web information systems interaction cues are sought in order to define the relationship between the user and the system and now in many cases between different users. Seeking cues regarding the identity of "others" beyond a server's network address is a major activity of many chat groups. By providing identity cues within the information system, the user can interact with other participants in a meaningful way. In this way an interactive Web information system, utilising techniques of social navigation, for example, can help the user to identify other users who share a common interest, therefore enabling unification of a community that is founded upon voluntary participation and common interest. In this way the user could consciously leave behind traces of her own identity and physically ground the experience. A particular nuance that involves tracing social cues is the sensitive, personal and emotional content of the cues, which require sophisticated ways of concrete design alternatives.

Implementation consists of final system testing, data conversion and user training. In addition, implementation refers to the institutionalisation of the system when being designed and realised. Maintenance refers to the operating, maintaining and evaluating actions of the system. These phases, depicted above, may include iteration both between the phases and within them. Vidgen (1997) stresses the emergent nature of requirements in that they tend to evolve during systems development when the current and future requirements are pondered. When designing for identity construction the iterative nature of systems development becomes a crucial success factor; identity is something that is constructed over a period of time and can constantly be updated or changed completely. The existent cues of identity construction that are associated with real life are mutually extended, reprioritised and recreated during the use of IS. New strategies for change management during development are required in order to manage the emergent and constantly updating virtual space.

As noted before, entering virtual space through a Web information system as with other computer-mediated experiences de-emphasises the corporeal cues to identity. Individuals actively and creatively sample available cultural symbols, myths and rituals as they produce their identities. Designers should pay attention to the way they turn their user requirements into specifications and finally software design with respect to the system's policies for membership, access (universal/restricted), registration, codes of conduct, trust, privacy and free speech (Preece 2000). In addition to other appropriate means, such as methods and tools, developers need a holistic view of humans in order to design for identity construction. However, as argued above, the complex interplay of sociality that exists between people is similar, at a generalised level, within this space and those spaces of real life. The difference of virtual space is evident in the differing cues applied to the construction of identity. A holistic form of thought is comprised of conceptualisations that regard human cognitive, volitive, emotional, social and cultural features as inherent in people, incorporated in technology and emerging within the interactions of humans and IS. These human features emerge in this form of thought as behavioural affordances indicating a human basis for the construction of electronic identity, and thus, should be taken into account when aiming to design high-quality IS emphasising high-grade usability.

References

Abercrombie N, Hill S, Turner B (1988) Sociology dictionary. Penguin Books, London, p 13

Argyle M (1969) Social Interaction. Methuen, London

Baudrillard J (1988) Jean Baudrillard Selected Writings. Poster M (ed), Stanford University Press, Stanford, p 166

Baudrillard J (1994) Simulacra and Simulations. Glaser SF (trans.), Arbor A, The University of Michigan Press

Berg PO, Kreiner K (1992) Corporate architecture: Turning physical settings into symbolic resources. In: Gagliardi P (ed) Symbols and Artifacts: Views of the Corporate Landscape. Walter De Gruyter, Berlin

Berger P, Luckmann T (1966) The Social Construction of Reality. Penguin Books, Harmondsworth

Beynon-Davies P, Carne C, Mackay H, Tudhope D (1999) Rapid application development (RAD): An empirical review. European Journal of Information Systems 8:211-223

Butler J (1990) Gender Trouble: Feminism and the Subversion of Identity. Routledge, London

Eason K (2001) Changing perspectives on the organizational consequences of information technology. Behaviour & Information Technology 20(5):323-328

Easthope A, McGowan K (1992) A Critical and Cultural Theory Reader. Open University Press, Buckingham

Edwards C, Imrie R (2003) Disability and bodies as bearers of value. Sociology 37(2):239-256

Eschenfelder KR, Sawyer S (2001) Web information systems management: Proactive or Reactive Emergence. The International Federation for Information Processing (IFIP) Technical Component 8 Working Group 8.2 Working Conference on Realigning Research and Practice in Information Systems Development: The Social and Organisational Perspective. Boise, ID

Farganis S (1986) Feminism and the reconstruction of social science. In: Jaggar A, Bordo S (eds) Gender/ Body/ Knowledge. Rutgers University Press, New Brunswick

Giddens A (1991) Modernity and Self-Identity. Self and Society in the Late Modern Age. Polity Press, Cambridge, UK

Gisler P (1997) Does gender still matter? Bodily functions in cyberspace: A feminist approach. In: Grundy AF, Köhler D, Oechtering V, Petersen U (eds) Women, Work and Computerization: Spinning a Web from Past to Future. Proceedings of the sixth International IFIP - Conference. Bonn: May 24-27, pp 219-220

Givens DB (2003) Proximics. From http://members.aol.com/doder1/proxemi1.htm

Goguen J (1996) Formality and informality in requirements engineering techniques for requirements elicitation. Proceedings of the Fourth International conference on Requirements Engineering. IEEE Computer SocietyPress, CA, pp 102-108

Green S (1999) A plague on the panopticon. Information, Communication & Society 2(1):26-44

Greenhill A (1999) Blurring the boundaries: Disentangling the implications of virtual space. The International Federation for Information Processing Working Group 8.2 and 8.6 Joint Working Conference on Information Systems: Current Issues and Future Changes. Omnipress, Helsinki, Finland

Greenhill A (2001) Using Space to Explore the Development of a Web Information System. Doctoral Thesis, Griffith University, Brisbane

Gumpert G, Drucker S (1994) Public space and urban life: Challenges in the communication landscape. Journal of Communication 44(4):169-77

Hall ET (1966) The Hidden Dimension. Doubleday, Garden City, N.Y.

Hensing T, Larsen B, Malmborg L, Pries-Heje J, Rasmussen T, Tjornov S (1994) Using VR interface techniques for visualization of information mountains. Seventeenth Information systems Research seminar In Scandinavia (IRIS 17), Syote, Sweden. University of Oulu

Isomäki H (2002) The Prevailing Conceptions of the Human Being in Information Systems Development: Systems Designers' Reflections. Doctoral Thesis, University of Tampere, Dept. of Computer and Information Sciences, Tampere: Finland. (A-2002-6)

Kendall L (1996) MUDer? I Hardly Know 'Er! Adventures of a Feminist MUDer. In: Cherney L, Weise ER (eds) Wired_Women. Seal Press, Seattle

Klein HK, Hirschheim RA (1993) The application of neo-humanist principles in information systems development. In: Avison DE, Kendall TE, DeGross JJ (eds) Human, Organizational, and Social Dimensions of Information Systems Development. Elsevier, Amsterdam, pp 263-280

Lamb R (1996) Interorganizational relationships and online information resources. 29th Annual Hawaii International Conference on System Sciences (HICSS), Honolulu, Hawaii

Lamb R, Kling R (2003) Reconceptualizing users as social actors in information systems research. MIS Quarterly 27(2):197-229

Marakas GM, Elam JJ (1998) Semantic structuring in analyst acquisition and representation of facts in requirements analysis. Information Systems Research 9(1):37-63

McRae S (1996) Coming Apart at the Seams: Sex, Text and the Virtual Body. In: Cherney L, Weise ER (eds) Wired_Women. Seal Press, Seattle

Morris B (1999) Context and interpretation: Reflections on Nyau rituals in Malawi. In: Dilley R (ed) The Problem of Context. Berghahn Books, New York, pp 145-166

Mumford E (1983) Designing Human Systems – The ETHICS method. Manchester Business School, Manchester

Negroponte N (1995) Being Digital. Vintage Books, New York

Paulos E, Canny J (1997) Ubiquitous tele-embodiment: Applications and implications. International Journal of Human-Computer Studies 46(6):861-877

Pawlowski SD, Robey D, Raven A (2000) Supporting shared information systems: Boundary objects, communities and brokering. Twenty-first International Conference on Information Systems (ICIS), Brisbane, Australia

Preece J (1994) Human-Computer Interaction. Addison-Wesley, Harlow, England

Preece J (2000) Online Communities: Designing Usability, Supporting Sociability. Wiley, Chichester

Ramey J, Rowberg AH, Robinson C (1996) Adaptation of an ethnographic method for investigation of the task domain in diagnostic radiology. In: Wixon D, Ramey J (eds) Field Methods Casebook for Software Design. John Wiley & Sons, New York, pp 1-195

Richardson M (1989) The artefacts as abbreviated act: A social interpretation of material culture. In: Hodder I (ed) The Meaning of Things: Material Culture and Symbolic Expression. Harper Collins Academic, London

Rushkoff D (1994) Media Virus. Random House, Sydney

Said E (1979) Orientalism. Vintage Books, New York

Simon HA (1991) Models of My Life. Basic Books, New York

Somers M (1994) The narrative constitution of identity: a relational and network approach. Theory and Society 23:605-49

Spender D (1995) Nattering on the Net; Women, Power and Cyberspace. Spinifex Press, North Melbourne

Standing C, Vasudavan T (2000) Effective Internet cooerce business models in the travel agency sector. The Fourth Pacific Asia Conference on Information Systems (PACIS), Hong Kong

Stanton NA (2001) Introduction: Ubiquitous computing: Anytime, anyplace, anywhere? International Journal of Human-Computer Interaction 13(2):107-111

Stephanidis C (2001) Human-computer interaction in the age of the disappearing computer. In: Avouris N, Fakotakis N (eds) Advances in Human-Computer Interaction. L. Proceedings of the PC HCI 2001, Athens, Greece, pp 15-22

Stoll C (1995) Silicon Snake Oil. Macmillan, London

Taysom S (1998) Mountain bike zeitgeist: Implications for a politics of the corporal subject. In: Greenhill A, Fletcher G, De La Fuente E (eds) Rethinking the Social. Griffith University, Brisbane, pp 27-32

Vidgen R (1997) Stakeholder analysis, soft systems and eliciting requirements. Information Systems Journal 7:21-46

Welch M (2003) Ironies of social control and the criminalization of immigrants. Crime, Law and Social Change 39(4):319-338

Winograd T (1995) From programming environments to environments for designing. Communications of ACM 38(6):65-74

Zimmerman ME (1993) Heidegger, Buddhism and Deep Ecology. The Cambridge Companion to Heidegger. Guignon C, Cambridge University Press, Cambridge, UK

Explanatory frameworks for interaction design

Pertti Saariluoma

Department of Computer Science and Information Systems
University of Jyväskylä
Finland
psa@cc.jyu.fi

Abstract

Explanatory design means the practice by which design solutions are evidence-based. This practice has been the norm in engineering design, relying as it does on the laws of science, but much less attention has been paid to the necessity of abandoning intuitive practices in designing for the human element within technological systems. One reason for this may have been the variety of explanatory bases within psychology. There is no single psychological framework for explaining human behaviour; instead different types of problems must be solved by using very different types of explanatory frameworks and theory language. Cognitive capacity, emotions and mental contents may serve as examples of very different explanatory frameworks. Developing a theory of explanatory interaction design needs to be based on an improved understanding of the differences between explanatory frameworks.

1 Introduction

We may have two basic stances towards design. Firstly, we may base our design on intuitions. For example, design may imitate earlier examples of working solutions with no attempt to understand the rational principles behind the construction. For many centuries architectural design, for example, has been based on well-tested traditions with no attention being paid to deeper considerations such as engineering calculations (Saariluoma 2003; Saariluoma and Maarttola 2003). The outcome has not necessarily been poor, and such intuitively planned houses have been used for centuries. Nevertheless, this kind of intuitive design thinking is no longer cost efficient and it does not meet modern safety demands. This is why it has been necessary to replace intuitive tradition with a more scientific design approach (Carroll 1997; Saariluoma and Maarttola 2003; Simon 1969).

Design, where design decisions are based on scientific evidence, can be called explanatory or evidence-based. The ultimate goal of scientific activity is to enable people to answer "why" and "how" questions. In fact, all the how-questions should be based on why-questions and vice versa. Questions such as "Why were investors unable to pick the correct numbers when reading their spreadsheet, or why did they select incorrect rows in a spreadsheet?" lead automatically to questions like "How could we improve the interaction with the spreadsheets?" These kinds of questions are typical and presuppose explanatory thinking (Hempel 1965).

In scientific explaining, one relies on scientific knowledge about the matter under scrutiny. This means that one looks for scientific laws and empirical findings, which could support the selected solutions. If such principles cannot be found, it is necessary either to make empirical analyses or to search for an alternative solution. One must have good and argued reasons for design decisions.

Explanatory design is a standard approach today when designing industrial artefacts. Historically, designers have been concerned with houses, bridges, milling machines and other engineering constructions. Hence, design ideals or rationales (i.e., the norms of design activity), have been shaped following experience collected on the basis of such design processes. Design has in very authoritative texts been seen as filling predefined requirements and rationales following the laws of nature (e.g., Pahl and Beitz 1989).

If we think about traditional industrial objects such as bikes, tents, shoes, power lines and even television and radio sets then the design stance has been traditionally based on the laws of nature. The user requirements for such designs are relatively simple and straightforward. It is important that a bridge stays standing and that people and cars can travel over it. There is no need to cope with complex interaction problems. Of course, engineering design is still, in the main, concerned with the laws of nature. However, new technology raises new types of problems and designers need a new range of skills to solve them.

The information and communication technological revolution has changed the human's role in interacting with artefacts. People operating with IT artefacts must be able to command complex information systems (Nickerson and Landauer 1997). These systems basically work with signs and symbols, which are rather arbitrarily connected to their references. Designers are encountering new problems such as how to eliminate the risk associated with human information processing systems (Reason 1990). Interactions with different artefacts carry with them different levels of complexity. Walking up the staircase is not a difficult task but programming a computer requires that the user keeps in mind programming commands and complex interrelated sets of symbols. In the future, these kinds of complex interactions will become increasingly more diverse. Therefore, it is essential to change our vision of design.

The revision has been ongoing for some time. Perhaps the first high-level programming languages started this movement. Instead of adapting the human mind to machines, designers started to design machines following the principles of the human mind. Programming languages such as COBOL, FORTRAN and Basic did not aid computing as such but they did make it easier for the human memory to interact with computers. Programming in binary made sense for the computer but the low level of discrimination and memorability had made it practically impossible for the user.

Ever since the early period, the need to take into account the human mind and the principles it follows has increased. Computers and computing devices have become consumer products, hidden computing devices with new forms of interaction are becoming more common and devices such as mobile phones presuppose an increasingly similar interaction mode with computers. Therefore, in future interaction design it will be essential to incorporate scientific information about the human mind into the design process. People need, use and buy artefacts and for these reasons alone the mind should be equally important to technology in formulating design rationales.

The increasing role of psychological and other knowledge about human mentality in interaction design makes it necessary to think more systematically about the nature of the design processes implementing knowledge about the mind. How could we best implement human knowledge into design constructions? How can we use knowledge about the principles of mentality to resolve design problems? To answer such questions we have to consider the foundations of design activities.

2 The necessity of explanatory interaction design

Design is a process in which we construct plans for complex objects. It is a process of individual and group reflection during which numerous individual problem-solving processes take place. In modern constructions such as houses or airplanes thousands to millions of parts must find their place and functional relations to each other (Saariluoma 1990, 2002, 2003; Saariluoma and Maarttola 2003). One of the core problems is, how should human mental activity be harmonised with the available technological possibilities?

Design is thinking, deciding and solving problems (Simon 1969). Normally it is carried out by a number of designers, a project, in which individual problem-solving processes are serving the whole. They are integrated by the project management. There are numerous problem-solving operations of all kinds taking place sequentially and successively. In each stage, numerous decisions must be made about what to do and how to do it. These decisions are naturally an essential component of any design process. If just one serious mistake is made then the whole process is endangered.

A very good illustration of design risks is provided by the set of tanker accidents in the sixties. Several supertankers blew up. An investigation discovered that the design of the tankers had allowed for the development of small pockets of gas in their tanks. Oil itself is not very flammable but when the tanks were empty, they had small pockets of gas, which could explode when the tanks were washed. Even a small spark caused by a nylon shirt or a nylon rope could make them explode. A minimal detail in a huge whole was incorrectly designed and the outcome was an expensive series of accidents (Perrow 1999).

One may think that this example is unnecessarily dramatic. It is very unusual for such an event to take place. However, it is good to keep the example in mind and it serves as a reminder that the PC interface is not the only kind of modern interface in existence. Professional interfaces must be designed for complex systems such as aircrafts, paper mills, cars, nuclear power stations and tankers. In addition, much of the computation is hidden from people, whose activities may depend on it. Consequently, there is no reason to underestimate the design risks in future interaction design.

Decreasing design risks in future computing presupposes that the fundaments of all designs are sufficiently well safeguarded against possible failures. A solution to these problems is to ensure that all the design solutions have rational foundations. Instead of intuitions they must be based on the best scientific knowledge we have about the human mind. It is not sufficient to rely on intuitions and introspections; instead there must be good grounds to decide between the design problems. Problems, which may entail serious risks, in particular, must be backed by scientific information about human behaviour. All the decisions must be evidence-based.

Interaction design concerns human interaction with technical environments. Naturally, explanatory design presupposes under such restrictions both an understanding of the technology and of the principles of the human mind. Psychology, sociology and other fields of human research must be integrated with the knowledge we have about the possibilities that technology has for realising human goals and needs.

However, before such integration is possible, it is good to have a look at the structure of modern psychology. This means that we have to have a clear empirical and theoretical idea about the relevant psychological processes in designing interaction environments and activities. This kind of psychology can be called user psychology. User psychology differs from usability testing in that it focuses on relevant knowledge about the user and implements this prior to design. (Oulasvirta and Saariluoma 2004; Niemelä 2003; Saariluoma and Sajaniemi 1989, 1994)

Investigating interaction from the user's psychological point of view it is possible to shake some dogmatic ideas about the simplicity of the mind. One might think that it opens a single and unified discourse, which can be used to investigate and resolve problems of interaction design. Instead it provides several very different platforms. Indeed, we must ask whether liking and disliking a piece of technology is a similar problem type to being able to use that piece of technology smoothly.

3 Explanatory frameworks

Explanatory design must be based on the idea that the right problems are associated with the right kind of scientific knowledge. There are always alternative ways of explaining human behaviour and it is not a trivial question to ask what kind of problems can be resolved on what kind of explanatory grounds. If a child has reading difficulties, it is quite possible that the difficulties are neural in origin, but this is not necessarily so. A mistaken analysis of the situation may eventually lead to a poor outcome.

Interaction design naturally has numerous dimensions. Some of them can be physiological such as stress; some such as consistency of dialog can instead be connected to mental contents. This means that it is important to look at the field systematically. If there are some problems which can be handled by means of physiological research and arguments and others, to which physiological grounds cannot be applied, it is necessary to find a conceptual way of unifying the right problems with the right system of scientific knowledge. Such conceptual construction is called an explanatory framework.

An explanatory framework means a system in which problems and required scientific knowledge are associated with solutions (Saariluoma 2002, 2003).

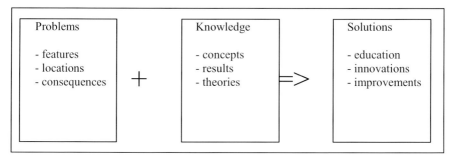

Fig. 1. Schematic structure of explanatory frameworks

An explanatory framework is a discourse in which one can use a unified system of scientific knowledge to explain and resolve some relevant problem.

This kind of framework allows the application of correct information to resolve definite problems. Both the problems and the frameworks vary. Nevertheless, there are not too many frameworks in psychology and this is why they allow the systematisation of design planning. It is possible to evaluate in advance what type of explanatory framework must be used to resolve different kinds of problems.

To make the notion of explanatory framework more precise it is possible to eventually reduce the main explanatory frameworks down to two. They are biological and content-based explanations. These two cannot be eliminated or reduced. Capacity explanation, for example, can be reduced to biological systems (cf. Saariluoma 1990, 1995). However, it would be very impractical to use only two explanatory grounds to discuss all problems. This is why it is better to use a more versatile system of language games in psychological explaining.

Indeed, it is best to see explanatory frameworks as language games (cf. Wittgenstein 1953). This means that there is a set of problems, which can be solved by means of capacity language. Its concepts and meanings are relatively accurate and unified. However, the language makes sense only in capacity-based explanatory contexts. Capacity language is meaningless when we talk about problems typical to content-based problems (Saariluoma 1997).

Some of the most important explanatory frameworks shall now be described. These are not the only possible explanatory frameworks, but they enable us to cope with many typical interaction problems. These frameworks are capacity, emotions and mental contents. One could also discuss physiological and personality or social group-based explanations, but the frameworks presented here are certainly sufficient to demonstrate the nature of explanatory interaction design.

4 Capacity

Human performance is limited in several senses. People can only perceive a limited spectrum of physical energy and only hear around 10 to 20 000 Hz frequencies of sound. The visual angle is around 180 degrees but the sharpest information pickup is within one to three degrees (e.g., Goldstein 1996). Depending on the circumstances one can make only limited background-foreground discriminations and the systems of discriminative cues may vary substantially.

Somewhat different types of limitations are met in attention. Attention is a system, which selects the target or figure out of the background (Pashler 1998; Styles 1997). There are always millions of possible ways to segment perceptual reality and often numerous different messages reach our ears. Attention selects those messages, which are important. In this way, it allows the human mind to focus on important things.

The capacity of selection is normally one unit at a time (Broadbent 1958). It is possible to switch attention from one target to another relatively swiftly and thus follow two or more competing messages at a time (Pashler 1998). However, this kind of performance has its costs and is very risky. Consequently, it is argued that the capacity of human attention is around one unit (Broadbent 1958; Norman 1969).

There are several mechanisms which allow people to circumvent the immediate attentional limits under certain conditions. Task switching, which was described above is one such mechanism (Pashler 1998). Another important mechanism is automatisation (Shiffrin 1988; Underwood and Everatt 1996). If people repeatedly carry out the same task in similar circumstances the speed and efficiency begin to improve. The activities require less cognitive load and they are basically effortless. Often the performance is not conscious. For these reasons, it is possible to carry out automatic tasks simultaneously with a more controlled main task. In fact, our performance is normally composed of a mixture of automatic and controlled parts. However, the existence of automatisation does not change the fact that human attentional capacity is limited. It only allows us to circumvent the limits.

Attention can ultimately be seen as a process of information collection. During the attentive process, target information is defined, and after that it is perceptually completed. Any target object has numerous dimensions such as location, form, color, kind, close environment, movement, size etc. An attention task presupposes that at least one of the required dimensions is open or unfamiliar to the attending person and that there exists at least one criterion on which the target or targets can be discriminated from the background objects. Attentional learning naturally means that people get information, which helps them either to segregate the target from the background or to identify it or to predict its location. This kind of holistic interpretation of attention can be called apperceptive attention.

An additional form of capacity limitation is working memory. We cannot hold more than four to seven independent units in our minds at the same time (Atkinson and Shiffrin 1968). This seriously limits, for example, human thought processes (Anderson et al. 1984; Covan 2000; Johnson-Laird 1983). It is not possible to build up a very complex representation of new items and this is why something is easily forgotten.

It has also been very well demonstrated that working memory has subsystems and that the capacity of these subsystems is also limited (Baddeley 1986; Baddeley and Hitch 1974; Logie 1995). Visuospatial and auditory subsystems cannot carry out two simultaneous tasks effectively in same modality. Though the systems are to some degree safeguarded against interference inference caused by secondary tasks on the other module, within-module interference is a serious problem.

There are cognitive mechanisms, which enable people to chunk information (Covan 2000; Miller 1956). Miller's (1956) famous limit concerned the number of chunks of information but made no comment on the size of the chunks. It is possible to have huge chunks of information (Ericsson and Kintsch 1995). Blindfolded chess players keep in their minds thousands of piece locations and taxi drivers know the street maps of huge cities off by heart (Kalakoski and Saariluoma 2001; Saariluoma 1991; Saariluoma and Kalakoski 1997, 1998). It is also well known that people store information in long-term working memory, where it suffers far less interference from secondary tasks.

Nevertheless, working memory is a serious limitation to human information processing capacity and it can be empirically demonstrated that working memory really limits design thinking (Anderson et al. 1984; Kavakli and Gero 2003). The limits of this system can all too easily be surpassed and this may cause severe performance risks. Therefore, it is necessary to avoid all too-demanding interaction tasks and design interfaces so that the problems can be avoided.

These examples are not the only capacity limits in the human mind, but they do give a good idea of what capacity-based explaining can mean. It is necessary to ensure that interaction with an interface does not surpass the available capacity. This is difficult because it is possible that even external conditions such as noise, interruptions or additional tasks may cause people to accidentally surpass the limits. In these cases the risk of errors naturally rises and this is why interaction should always ensure some redundancy.

Explaining by capacity is sensible, when it is possible to show that the environment is too complex for the thinking limits of the human information processing system. The key sign for capacity problems is errors caused by complexity. Naturally, the main way of reacting is to reduce the complexity. This can be done either by redesigning the interface or by improving the skills of the personnel.

5 Capacity and interaction

Forgetting a currently active navigation route or an important command in constructing command lines are typical examples of the problems which capacity may cause interaction design. Many lapses of attention and memory can be avoided if the designers understand the importance of limited capacity. It is distressing for a cognitive engineer to observe that a person wishing to purchase a ticket has to push tens of keys to get a machine to print one ticket. This can be found even in stations with only one or two main destinations. Such a system is difficult to learn to use and leads to wasted time and frustration.

The psychological notion of capacity must be transformed into a design plan. Answers to why-questions must be changed into how-questions. Psychological knowledge must be applied to understanding design problems. This is the very core idea of explanatory design. It may be useful at this point to present some illustrative examples. Image quality in screens and other displays is important, because it affects readability and communicability. Luminance, contrast, flicker, colors and character design are essentially design attributes, which are ultimately based on human perceptual capacity, discrimination threshold and attentional discrimination phenomena. This family of problems has recently received much attention, as web-page design has become an important theme (cf. Nielsen 1993; Nielsen and Tahir 2002).

Another perspective to capacity is provided by memory. Early studies on programmers illustrated that working memory capacity is an important interaction problem (Anderson et al. 1984, Broadbent 1975). Similarly it has been shown that designers have substantial problems with working memory limits (Kavakli and Gero 2003). The immediate memory capacity problems can also be seen in visual information chunking. The form of display presentation is essential for good recall and navigation. Saariluoma and Sajaniemi (1989, 1991) demonstrated that spreadsheet users utilise the visible forms of numeric information to learn and remember the systems of cell reference of the non-visible functions and calculations. Finally, it can also be shown that people use mental images in making interaction easier.

6 Emotions

Emotions provide us with a clearly different system of explanatory grounds compared to those of capacity. Emotions, for example, have contents so that it is possible to talk about positive and negative emotions, for example, while capacity is minimally emotion-based. We can fill our working memory with any imaginable emotional contents as long as the load caused by the representation does not exceed its limits. It does not really make much difference whether our working memory stores likes or dislikes, though, of course, this difference is essential from the point of view of emotions. For this reason, one cannot really effectively explain issues of emotional contents on the grounds of cognitive capacity (Saariluoma 1997, 2002).

There is very little doubt about the importance of emotions in interaction design (Norman 2004). It is an emotional issue whether one likes an interface and a specific interaction model. User acceptance and marketing dimensions such as branding are essentially very emotional issues. This is why one cannot disregard knowledge about emotions when discussing future interaction design.

It is not possible here to consider all aspects of human emotions. Less interesting and important themes such as the length of emotional states or their strength must be neglected here. Instead, attention shall be paid to the contents of emotions. Emotions are activated by a cognitive analysis of the situation (Power and Dalgleish 1997). This can be called appraisal. It is an essential process in investigating the activation of emotional states. Our emotions are reactions to prevailing situations and before we know what a situation is we have to be able to make a cognitive analysis of it. We do not know whether there is a dangerous animal around, unless we have noticed it (Lazarus 1999, Power and Dalgleish 1997). It is also possible to influence emotions by influencing cognitions (e.g., Beck 1976).

Emotional contents can be divided into two components. Firstly, there is emotional valence. Emotions normally exist in positive vs. negative pairs. Typical examples could be relief and angst, joy and sorrow or trust and mistrust. Valence is naturally very important, because we avoid unpleasant emotions and pursue pleasant ones.

A more complicated explanatory ground is provided by emotional theme. The theme is the characteristic, which separates different emotions from each other. Joy is different from grief and consequently they have different themes. It is necessary to understand the nature of important emotions in order to be able to use emotions in interaction design. Depending on the type of interaction, we might pursue very different emotional themes. In computer gaming, for example, fear and excitement might be very important but in computer programming these themes might be more harmful than useful.

Investigating emotions and using emotional explanations in interaction design is important for a number of reasons. Perhaps the most important is the close connection of emotions to motives and the role of emotions in determining the importance of issues to oneself. Emotions are important in motivation for the reason that emotions convey information about our needs (Franken 2002). If we are hungry then we feel uncomfortable. Naturally, these connections have an important role in motivating our immediate actions.

Finally, emotions are always important when we evaluate the importance of objects, issues, people or events. Emotions tell us what is important. This is why the emotional dimensions of interfaces are so important. Unless designers are able to effectively cope with emotions, the risks of design errors and failures increase.

7 Emotions and design

Many people still remember an old advert in which a Chaplin-like figure interacted with computers. This was in the early days of computers when most users were novices. Chaplin, who is a symbol of fumbling yet prevailing, was a very insightful choice of symbol for novice PC users. The advert referred to difficulties, positive humor and solving problems. In this advert emotions were notably important.

Our example is close to one of the major negative emotions in practical interaction design. This is user frustration. Interfaces which are too complex or which have slow interaction speeds easily lead to user frustration (Preece et al. 2002). The main reason to call attention to user frustration is to illustrate that emotional design is a practical necessity. Emotions have a role in interaction design whether we want them to or not.

A typical example of applying the psychology of emotions to interaction design is to analyse how the acceptability of products correlates with personality traits. This information can then be applied to the interface and usability design (Jacoby et al. 1998). A somewhat more complex example of emotion and personality-based interaction design is the so-called "brand personality" (e.g., Aaker 1997). It has been noticed that a brand may enable consumers to express their personalities (i.e., emotional patterns). Consequently, products can be designed for certain types of personalities (see, e.g., Iacocca 1984, for the design of the Ford Mustang).

In practical design, it is possible, for example, to show consumer products to people and to investigate how their emotional or personality traits explain their relations to some definable features (Bruseberg and Macdonagh-Philip 2001). This kind of activity can be called emotion or personality profiling. It can be used, for example, to find justifications for design solutions.

These examples illustrate very well the nature of emotional design. In a holistic sense it is very closely associated with personality and product communication. Marketing and design are essential in creating emotional atmosphere around a product. It is meant to provide feelings for users. The closer these feelings are to the user's emotional value system and personality, the better.

8 Apperception and mental contents

Despite their fundamental role in human action emotions have their limits as an explanatory framework. They cannot really represent important cognitive contents. We can cognitively categorise our environment in a much more detailed manner than we can emotionally categorise our environment. There is no substantial emotional difference, for example, between keyboards and screens. This is why we have to investigate mental contents in representations.

When the topic is the interface, it seems natural to assume that perceptual information is highly important. Indeed, it is important, but it is hardly the core process in constructing mental representations (Saariluoma 1990, 1995, 2001). We have numerous important non-perceivable content elements in mental representations. We talk, for example, about possible and impossible, files and storage, past and future, infinite and eternal. We also talk about laws, standards and regulations. In general, such things are non-perceivable and we cannot, even in principle, have their representations on our retina. For these reasons, it is important to draw a distinction between perception and apperception.

Apperceiving means "seeing something as something". This means the ability to give a meaning to an object instead of just perceiving the object. We can listen to an unfamiliar language without understanding a word. This means that we hear what is said but we do not understand it. Understanding is one kind of apperceptive process. Similarly, apperceptive processes are, for example, comprehending or apprehending. The key characteristic of apperception is that it constructs both conscious and subconscious parts of mental representations (Saariluoma 1990, 1992, 2001, 2003; Saariluoma and Kalakoski 1997, 1998). This is why the concept of apperception, which has been widely used over the last four hundred years is very helpful in the discussion about the construction of mental representations (Kant 1787/1985; Leibniz 1704; Stout 1890; Wundt 1913).

Working with apperception is content-based by nature. This means that apperception research works to answer problems, which can be explained by mental contents (Saariluoma 2003). Obviously, mental content is a rational ground to explain human behavior. If I ask somebody why he or she is going in that direction and he or she answers, "Because I can buy a computer there", then there is nothing strange in explaining his or her behavior on the grounds of mental content.

Of course, the above example is not very exciting, but there are much more important phenomena, in which the content-based approach is relevant. It can be shown, for example, that mental representations have a property, which can be termed functionality. This means that all elements in representations make sense or are senseful (Saariluoma 1990; Saariluoma and Maarttola 2003). Functionality means that there is always a reason why any element is incorporated into a representation. In the computer, we have a keyboard to input information and a screen to provide visual output. We use graphical interfaces, to decrease memory load. Similarly, all human constructions are knit together by networks of reason and this is why they make sense. Naturally, such schema of functions or functional reasons is a content element in mental representations.

The phenomenon of sensefulness has many consequences in interaction design. Firstly, the elements of interfaces and human actions normally make sense. We know why we use buttons or why we use a command language in constructing an interaction. We should also know why people in a shopping centre move as they do to provide themselves with effective e-computing services. A presupposition for understanding what people think and do, is the analysis and opening of the hidden functional schemata (Saariluoma 1990; Saariluoma and Maarttola 2003).

Secondly, these rules are important in investigating the phenomena of consistency and coherence (Saariluoma and Maarttola 2003). If we use blue to visualise high temperatures, we certainly are in contradiction with cultural conventions. If we print install on the screen, when the machine is actually removing programs, we violate the norms of semantic coherence. All questions of this kind implicate sensefulness and an investigation into mental contents.

Mental contents again provide a new type of explanatory framework for interaction design (Saariluoma 2003). We cannot reduce these concepts and discourses into capacity nor can we effectively express typical capacity phenomena in terms of mental contents. Naturally, the phenomenon of functional schemata is one of the many types of mental contents, which may have an explanatory value.

The example should be sufficient to illustrate that one can build around mental contents an explanatory framework. There are psychologically relevant phenomena, which can best be explained in terms of mental contents. They are determined content phenomena on which one can ground content-based explaining. This is common in clinical psychology, but it is increasingly more evident in many phenomena related to thinking, for example, presupposed content-based thinking. It is important to develop this discourse because it provides new possibilities for explanatory interaction design in future.

9 Applying apperception – experience design

Designing the interaction contents is naturally one of the most important aspects of design. It is all too easy to make concept-explainable errors. Missing one's way in the jungle of cultural differences is a typical example of such errors. Illustrations, which look nice in Finland such as those of forests and lakes may nevertheless give a very different message in the United States and signify a country's underdevelopment rather than its dynamism. As more firms increasingly operate via the WWW, these relatively common problems take on an important role.

Visual design is another practical example. At first glance, visualisation, for example, may be a pictorial and perceptual issue, but this is an oversimplification. Visualisation is important because it improves conceptual communication (Brown et al. 1995; Tufte 1983, 1990, 1997). This is evident when the issues, which are visualised, are very often non-perceivable. The temperatures in different parts of an engine or the issues of population distributions, for example, are not genuinely perceptual issues. Visualisation makes them understandable, but this does not mean that visualisation would not be perceptual; they are apperception-related problems rather than perceptual.

Interfaces for machine and architectural design may serve as an additional example of apperception and thinking-related problems. In them, thought models and other content-based explanatory concepts are important (Saariluoma 1990, 2003; Wills and Sanders 2000). In designing professional software, content-based concepts are vital, but there are numerous standard problems as well which can be resolved by applying such theoretical devices as apperception and content-based research (Saariluoma and Maarttola 2003).

10 Creativity and explanatory design

One may naturally think that an explanatory design scheme bounds creativity. It seems to be going against free innovation to think that one must base one's ideas on an explanatory schema. This is a misunderstanding in two senses. Firstly, it neglects the necessity of basing design on a scientific understanding of the world and secondly, it entails a simplified view of creativity.

Free creativity cannot neglect the laws of nature and the mind. This is why it is important to ground one's ideas in scientific knowledge. It entails the least risks and makes it possible to construct the intended solutions in real life. This is why explanatory creativity is so important.

Another misunderstanding concerning creativity is also very common. Creativity is very often seen as free-associating. Brainstorming and tests such as "uses" are typical examples of the divergent notion of creativity (Guilford 1950). However, empirical research has shown that creativity seldom works in its divergent form (Weisberg 1986, 1993). This is why Saariluoma (1997) wanted to establish a convergent form of creativity called foundational analysis.

In foundational analysis, people concentrate on analysing explicit and implicit assumptions of the existent objects and work to restructure them. The idea is to found an unfound intuitive, that is, implicit, or explicit, theoretical presupposition, which is not valid and by means of replacing the weakness with another, improved one. Creativity in this sense is analytic thinking rather than free-associating.

Of course the reconstructed ideas need not be small. In classic philosophy, for example, the very explanatory principle was always reconstructed. The principle of all explanations such as water or fire was replaced by some other principle (Zeller 1883). This means that there is no limit to the ideas, which can be reconstructed, if the reconstruction can be justified.

Naturally, explanatory design is a notion, which effectively serves convergent creativity. By means of analysing the arguments and reasons used to justify some design solution, it is possible to find problems and argumentatively resolve them. For example, the graphic interface replaced the symbolic because it provided better memory support for beginners. The true grounds were psychological and they also proved to be correct.

11 Conclusions

In this chapter, I have outlined some principles for explanatory interaction design. By this kind of design I mean that design decisions are based on various explanatory frameworks. In the ideal of explanatory design, one must look for solutions, which can be explained on the ground of scientific knowledge and from the explanatory point of view the more well argued the design decisions the better the design.

Instead of a unified psychological argumentation, we have different frameworks, which can be used to solve very different types of design questions. Three examples, capacity, emotions and mental contents have been discussed in this chapter. These frameworks are not exhaustive but they do enable the point regarding explanatory design to be made clearly. Our scientific languages are limited in their power of expression. There is no possible way to use capacity-based argumentation in solving content-originated problems. We can fill our attention or working memory with information of any contents, as long as the capacity is not limited (Saariluoma 1997, 2003). This is why it is impossible to use capacity explanations to solve problems of mental contents. Nor can capacity language help us with essentially emotional problems. Limited working memory capacity does not have much value when we work to understand why clients do not feel that an interface is emotionally intriguing.

Putting these two main lines together the chapter has outlined a meta-scientific framework for future interaction design. It should be based on natural scientific and human knowledge, design decisions should be based on explanations and explanations should be grounded on suitable explanatory frameworks.

References

Aaker JL (1997) Dimensions of brand personality. Journal of Marketing Research 34:347-357

Anderson JR, Farrell R, Sauers R (1984) Learning to program Lisp. Cognitive Science 8:87-129

Atkinson R, Shiffrin R (1968) Human memory: A proposed system. In: Spence KW, Spence JT (eds) The Psychology of Learning and Motivation, vol 2. Academic Press, New York, pp 89-195

Beck A (1976) Cognitive Therapy of Emotional Disorders. Penguin Books, Harmondsworth

Baddeley AD (1986) Working Memory. Oxford University Press, Oxford

Baddeley AD, Hitch G (1974) Working memory. In: Bower G (ed) The Psychology of Learning and Motivation, vol. 8. Academic Press, New York, pp 47-89

Broadbent D (1958) Perception and Communication. Pergamon Press, London

Broadbent D (1975) The magic number seven after twenty years. In: Kennedy R, Wilkes A (eds) Studies in Long Term Memory. Wiley, New York, pp 253-287

Brown, JR, Earnshaw, R, Jern, M, Vince, J (1995) Visualization. Wiley, New York.

Bruseberg A, Macdonagh-Philip D (2001) New product development by eliciting user experience and aspirations. International Journal of Human-Computer Studies 55:435-452

Carroll JM (1997) Human computer interaction: psychology as science of design. Annual Review of Psychology 48:61-83

Covan N (2000) The magical number four in short term memory: A reconsideration of mental storage capacity. Behavioural and Brain Sciences 24:87-185

Ericsson KA, Kintsch W (1995) Long-term working memory. Psychological Review 102:211-245

Franken RE (2002). Human Motivation. Wadsworth, Crawfordville

Goldstein B (1996) Sensation and Perception. Brooks & Cole, Belmont, CA

Guilford JP (1950) Creativity. American Psychologist 5:444-454

Hempel C (1965) Aspects of Scientific Explanation and Other Essays in the Philosophy of Science. Free Press, New York

Iacocca L (1984) Autoelämänkerta. [car autobiography, in Finnish]. WSOY, Porvoo

Jacoby J, Johar G, Morrin M (1998) Consumer behaviour. Annual Review of Psychology 49:319-344

Johnson-Laird P (1983) Mental Models: Towards a Cognitive Science of Language, Inference, and Consciousness. Harvard University Press, Cambridge, MA

Kalakoski V, Saariluoma P (2001) Taxi drivers' exceptional memory for street names. Memory & Cognition 29:634-638

Kant I (1787/1985) Kritik der Reinen Vernunft. Philip Reclam, Stuttgart

Kavakli M, Gero JS (2003) Strategic knowledge differences between an expert and a novice designer. In: Lindeman U (ed) Human Behaviour in Design: Individuals, Teams, Tools. Springer, Berlin, pp 42-52

Lazarus RS (1999) Stress and Emotion – A New Synthesis. Free Association Books, London

Leibniz G (1704) New Essays on Human Understanding, Cambridge University Press, Cambridge

Logie R (1995) Visuo-spatial Working Memory. Erlbaum, Hove

Miller GE (1956) The magical number seven plus or minus two: Some limits on our capacity for processing information. Psychological Review 63:81-97

Nickerson RS, Landauer TK (1997) Human-computer interaction: Backgrounds and issues. In: Helander M, Ladauer TK, Pradhu PV (eds) Handbook of Human-Computer Interaction. Elsevier, Amsterdam, pp 3-31

Nielsen J (1993) Usability Engineering. Academic Press, New York

Nielsen J, Tahir M (2002) Kotisivun suunnittelu [Homepage usability: 50 websites demonstrated] [In Finnish] Edita, Helsinki

Niemelä M (2003) Visual search in graphic interfaces: A user psychological approach. Jyväskylä studies in computing 34. Jyväskylä University Printing House, Jyväskylä

Norman D (1969) Memory and Attention. Wiley, Oxford

Norman D (2004) Emotional Design. Basic Books, New York

Oulasvirta A, Saariluoma P (2004) Long-term working memory and interrupting messages in human-computer interaction. Behaviour & Information Technology 23:53-64

Pahl G, Beitz W (1989) Konstruktionslehre. (in Finnish). MET, Porvoo

Pashler H (1998) The Psychology of Attention. MIT Press, Cambridge MA

Perrow C (1999) Normal Accidents: Living with High-Risk Technologies. Princeton University Press, Princeton, NJ

Power M, Dalgleish T (1997) Cognition and Emotion. From Order to Disorder. Hove, Psychology Press

Preece J, Rogers Y, Sharp H (2002) Interaction Design. Wiley, New York

Reason J (1990) Human Error. Cambridge University Press, Cambridge

Saariluoma P (1990) Apperception and restructuring in chess players' problem solving. In: Gilhooly KJ, Keane MTG, Logie RH, Erdos G (eds) Lines of Thought: Reflections on the Psychology of Thinking. Wiley, London, pp 41-57

Saariluoma P (1991) Aspects of skilled imagery in blindfold chess. Acta Psychologica 77:65-89

Saariluoma P (1992) Error in chess: Apperception restructuring view. Psychol Res 54:17-26

Saariluoma P (1995) Chess Players' Thinking. Routledge, London

Saariluoma P (1997) Foundational Analysis: Presuppositions in Experimental Psychology. Routledge, London

Saariluoma P (2001) Chess and content oriented psychology of thinking. Psihologica 22:143-164

Saariluoma P (2002) Thinking in Work Life: From Errors to Opportunities. (in Finnish). WSOY, Porvoo

Saariluoma P (2003) Apperception, content-based psychology and design. In: Lindeman U (ed) Human Behavior in Design. Springer, Berlin, pp 72-78

Saariluoma P, Kalakoski V (1997) Skilled imagery and long-term working memory. American Journal of Psychology 110:177-201

Saariluoma P, Kalakoski P (1998) Apperception and imagery in blindfold chess. Memory 6:67-90

Saariluoma P, Maarttola I (2003) Stumbling blocks in novice architectural design. Journal of Architectural and Planning Research 20:344-354

Saariluoma P, Sajaniemi J (1989) Visual information chunking in spreadsheet calculation. International Journal of Man-Machine Studies 30:475-488

Saariluoma P, Sajaniemi J (1991) Extracting implicit tree structures in spreadsheet calculation. Ergonomics: Special Issue: Cognitive Ergonomics, 34:1027-1046

Saariluoma P, Sajaniemi J (1994) Transforming verbal descriptions into mathematical formulas in spreadsheet calculations. International Journal of Human-Computer Studies 421:915-948

Shiffrin RM (1988) Attention. In: Atkinson RC, Herrnstein RJ, Lindzey G, Luce RD (eds) Stevens' Handbook of Experimental Psychology, vol 2: Learning and Cognition. Wiley, New York, pp 731-811

Simon HA (1969) The Sciences of Artificial. MIT Press, Cambridge, MA

Stout GF (1890) Analytical Psychology. MacMillan, London

Styles E (1997) The Psychology of Attention. Psychology Press, Hove

Tufte ER (1983) The Visual Display of Quantitative Information. Graphics Press, Cheshire

Tufte ER (1990) Envisioning Information. Graphics Press, Cheshire

Tufte ER (1997) Visual Explanation. Graphics Press, Cheshire
Underwood G, Everatt J (1996) Automatic and controlled information processing: The role of attention in processing novelty. In: Neuman O, Sanders AF (eds) Handbook of Perception and Action 3. Attention. Academic press, London, pp 185-227
Weisberg, R (1986) Creativity: Genius and other Myths. Freeman, San Francisco
Weisberg, R (1993) Creativity: Beyond the Myth of Genius. Freeman, New York
Wills F, Sanders D (2000) Cognitive Therapy: Transforming the Image. Sage, London
Wittgenstein L (1953) Philosophical Investigations. Basil Blackwell, Oxford
Wundt W (1913) Grundriss der Psychologie. Kröner, Stuttgart
Zeller, E (1883/1939) Outlines of the History of Greek Philosophy. Routledge and Kegan Paul, London

Toward the analysis of the interaction in the joint cognitive system

José J. Cañas[1], Ladislao Salmerón[2], Inmaculada Fajardo[3]

[1]Department of Experimental Psychology, University of Granada
Spain
delagado@ugr.es

[2]Department of Experimental Psychology, University of Granada
Spain
lalo@ugr.es

[3]Laboratory of HCI for Special Needs, ATC Department, Faculty of Computer Science, Basque Country University
Spain
acbfabri@si.ehu.es

Abstract

Traditionally, cognitive analysis of interaction has been done by applying theoretical models of human cognitive processes proposed by cognitive psychologists. However, this approach is now facing an important problem: predictions made from these models developed in laboratory settings with particular materials, tasks and people are not confirmed when we have to predict how a person interacts with a device. This failure could be explained by recognising that these theoretical models incorrectly assume that the human cognitive processes work independently of context. Furthermore, traditional analysis of interaction has also incorrectly assumed that the human being is the only cognitive agent in the interaction. We propose to replace this analysis by another one in which interaction design should be based on the idea that human cognitive processes adapt their operations to contextual changes to interact with other cognitive agents, devices, to perform jointly the task at hand. In this chapter we define some steps towards the development of this new cognitive analysis. In addition, we present the principle of "mutual dependency" that could be of much use in facing the future of interaction design.

1 Introduction

In 1969 Herbert Simon wrote a book, *The Science of the Artificial*, in which he argued that cognitive science should have its area of application in the design of devices. He proposed the foundation of a science of the artificial related with cognitive science in the sense in which we have traditionally understood the relationship between the engineering disciplines and the basic sciences. Such a science has been called cognitive ergonomics or cognitive engineering (Norman 1986).

Simon's cognitive ergonomics (1969), would be independent of cognitive science, its basic science, although both would be closely related. Cognitive science would contribute knowledge on human cognitive processes, and cognitive ergonomics would contribute concrete problems of design that should be solved in the context of the creation of devices. Norman (1986), the author that coined the term cognitive engineering, conceived it as an applied cognitive science where the knowledge of cognitive science is combined with that of engineering to solve design problems. According to Norman, its objectives would be: (1) to understand the fundamental principles of human actions important for the development of the engineering of design principles, and (2) to build systems that are pleasant in their use.

Simon's proposal of understanding cognitive engineering as an applied discipline of cognitive science has dominated the work of researchers in the last thirty years. We can find a good example of this in the first two versions of Wickens' (1992) influential book, which has marked a time in the discipline. In his introduction, Wickens declares his intention to organise the book according to human information processes. In this way, the index of chapters is the same as one found in a book on cognitive psychology: theory of signal detection, perception, attention, memory etc. In each chapter, after an explanation of each process, the author gives examples of ergonomics in which knowledge acquired in cognitive psychology can be applied.

Simon's proposal, however, is now in need of revision after recognising the evident difficulties found when applying results obtained by cognitive scientists to the explanation of the problems of design of such devices. These difficulties are causing a paradigmatic change that will have repercussions beyond cognitive ergonomics. Cognitive scientists therefore will be forced to reconsider the many fundamental questions of the paradigm that have arisen after the cognitive revolution of the fifties and sixties.

Examples of this failure in applying cognitive models to the design of artefacts can be found in several fields of cognitive ergonomics, such as HCI, educational technology, problem solving... (Cañas et al. 2003; Jonassen and Wang 1993; Huguenard et al. 1997; Lansdale et al. 1996). In addition to the published works, one can imagine a more comprehensive list of failed attempts due to the reticence of journals to publish null results. A brief revision of some of these works will help us to illustrate the difficulties faced by the classical approach and that of the alternative with its literature base. For example, Huguenard et al. (1997) applied the CAPS model of working memory (Just and Carpenter 1992) in order to predict errors that people make when interacting with a telephone-based system. The resulting data, however, did not support the hypotheses derived from the model. Another failed approach is reported by Lansdale et al. (1996). The authors attempted to apply the knowledge derived from theories of spatial cognition to the design of pictorial databases. These theories, however, were of no help to the design of the databases.

Another example can be found in a series of experiments reported by Jonassen and Wang (1993) in which they attempted to apply the semantic theories of memory organisation to hypertext design. These theories propose that information stored in memory is organised by interrelated conceptual units forming a semantic network (Anderson 1995). Jonassen and Wang (1993) reasoned that if the organisation of a hypertext mimics the memory organisation of an expert, a novice reader would achieve a higher learning level. The results of several experiments, however, showed no benefits of this approach.

Cognitive models at the time led us to contradictory predictions. For example, another source of contradictory data related to spatial cognition research comes from the study of navigation tasks. The way in which cognitive processes are involved in this task appears to be very different in each context of navigation (e.g., map vs. real environment in Garden et al. 2002). Several authors (e.g., Kim and Hirtle 1995) have suggested that the application of spatial cognition models in physical environments to the study and design of navigation in electronic environments could be useful. Research in hypertexts, however, has shown contradictory results. McDonald and Stevenson (1999), for example, found that spatial maps improve search and orientation in a hypermedia system. Spatial maps and overviews could facilitate the formation of survey knowledge, therefore enhancing the processes of searching and orientation. This finding could be interpreted as a reinforcement to the spatial nature of the hypermedia environment. Farris et al. (2002), however, found that the users' schemata of hypermedia were based more in semantic than in spatial relations, suggesting that the spatial nature of hypermedia should be re-evaluated. The question arises, therefore, is it hypertext navigation of a spatial or a semantic/verbal nature? The first authors have taken into account the new demands of interacting with hypertexts, that is, the movements of users to find information, which are similar to the process of navigation in other environments; the latter have taken into account other characteristics of hypertexts which are also present in linear text, that is, semantic processing. For this reason, each author uses a different model from cognitive psychology to explain the data, reporting only part of the reality. Therefore, it is probable that hypertext navigation tasks require an interaction of these two cognitive processes as traditional cognitive theories cannot embrace the task fully by themselves. Hypertext navigation does not solely consist of navigation and orientation processes, or semantic or verbal processing in isolation, it is an interaction of these processes. It is not just a question of how many processes there are but also the ways in which they interact. That is, we need new models, which consider both environment constraint and the interaction with cognitive processes. Examples of this approach are presented in the next paragraph.

In the research field of complex problem-solving it is also possible to find failures of applying cognitive models. This research field is particularly interested in the finding of designs that prevent dramatic human errors in real tasks such as aviation, supervision of automatic systems etc. Cañas et al. (2003) tried to predict expert behaviour during environmental changes in dynamic-complex tasks. After revising the cognitive psychology literature, they derived contradictory predictions from different cognitive models: experts' performance could drop due to their inflexible automated routines, or experts' performance could be maintained at the same level, due to the experts' multiple and flexible representations of the situation allowing them to adapt to the constraints of the new situation.

The authors noticed that predictions were derived by these models considering the cognitive processes in isolation, without any reference to environment constraints. To overcome this problem, Cañas et al. (2003) designed a research strategy which took into account both cognitive processes (expert strategies) and environment constraints (characteristics of the dynamic-complex task). The derived predictions and results following this strategy were more successful and explicative than those which could have been solely derived from the cognitive models. The results showed that only some experts dropped their performance when facing environmental changes. Experimental design allows us to throw light upon this effect. Only those environmental changes that affected the particular strategy of experts could affect their performance. Possible experimental designs derived from the cognitive models' predictions could not have explained these apparent contradictory results since these models do not consider the situational constraints (Vicente 1999; Vicente and Wang 1998).

Now, when we think about experiments such as those mentioned above, we must ask ourselves how we should interpret these data contrary to predictions derived from cognitive models. Models sufficiently tested in traditional laboratory tasks of cognitive psychology are therefore not able to make predictions in situations where they should. Therefore, if we conceive cognitive ergonomics, following Simon's proposal, as a discipline in which to apply the knowledge acquired by basic research in cognitive psychology, we should find a reasonable explanation of why the hypotheses derived from the cognitive models are not confirmed in situations in which concrete problems of design of devices have to be solved.

The key to this explanation is to recognise that it is not possible to expect a theory to be valid independent of the context, task or stimulus type that is used. The operation of the human cognitive system is not independent of the environment in which it is immersed. If the characteristics of this environment change, the operation of the cognitive system can also change. It is not, therefore, possible to think that an investigation in cognitive psychology conducted with a material type (e.g., a list of words), in a particular context (e.g., a laboratory) and where the participants perform particular tasks (e.g., priming), lead us to expect that some results have necessarily universal application. Therefore, in the current line of thinking in cognitive ergonomics, it is considered that to find a complete explanation to human behaviour it is necessary that one keeps in mind the interaction between the human being and the environment in which he or she is immersed.

Therefore, we should discard the classic conception of cognitive ergonomics, in which artefact and the human being are considered as independent units that should be modelled independently and isolated from the context where the interaction between them takes place. In this conception, the objective of ergonomists was to provide the designer of the artefact the characteristics of human information processing in order to make decisions on the design of the artefact (Wickens 1992). Accordingly, the object of the study of cognitive psychologists was the human cognitive system and the object of interest for the designers was the artefact. Therefore, when they worked together they only had to communicate what they knew about their respective objects of interest.

Contrary to this, today's cognitive ergonomists believe that Simon's proposal of a design discipline working on the creation of artefacts with the support of cognitive science, should be replaced by a new science of design that takes as its object of study a cognitive system. This is called the joint cognitive system, in which the artefact and the human being are only parts that interact to produce behaviour (Hollnagel and Woods 1983; Woods et al. 1994; Woods and Roth 1988; Rasmussen et al. 1994). This joint cognitive system is cognitive in the sense that it processes information to produce behaviour. Information processing, however, is not the sum of the operations of two independent components. On the contrary, information processing is distributed between the artefact and the human being working together to produce behaviour.

This new proposed science still needs to be developed in three essential aspects. We need to better define the object of study and the phenomena to be analysed, and to develop a research methodology appropriate for this analysis. Following in this chapter are some suggestions to develop these aspects of the new proposed science.

2 The object of the science of design: The joint cognitive system

Dowell and Long (1989, 1998) have proposed that a joint cognitive system works using knowledge to produce changes in the environment or work domains. The domains in which the system works are organised around specific objectives and include possibilities and limitations. However, we must discard the idea that this work is done by a cognitive agent, the human being, using artefacts. On the contrary, this cognitive work is done by all components of the joint cognitive system simultaneously.

To understand this idea we must begin by considering that artefacts are also cognitive agents. Technological development, mainly of computer science, has caused the devices designed today to have a level of automatism that makes them candidates to be considered as cognitive systems by themselves. These are almost at the same level as human beings, in the sense that they have their own dynamics often independent of human performance. That is, although the human being does not perform any action, the artefact continues running and producing changes in the environment. The fundamental difference between the human being and the device, considered both as cognitive systems, is that the device is designed by the human being, while the human being is not designed but modified by a process that we call learning. Cognitive devices provide us with representations of the work domain, with processes to transform these representations and with means to express these transformations (Simon 1969; Dowell and Long 1998). For example, radar in the domain of air traffic control provides representations that allow the controller to reason on the state of the domain (e.g.,, height and distances among airplanes) and to transform these representations into transmitting orders to pilots.

This idea has been developed fundamentally in one of the most active application areas of modern ergonomics, the design of systems for supervisory control. In a nuclear power station's control room, for example, there are devices and people interacting to supervise a physical process, the electric power generation starting from nuclear energy. The devices that we find in this room are designed so that they are intelligent assistants; their main role is to help the human operator in the control of the physical process. Therefore, we should think of these devices as autonomous cognitive agents with the ability to monitor the process. The analysis of accidents that happen in a control room demonstrates that erroneous actions are the result of a sequence of shortcomings in the interaction between a group of human beings and a group of devices, all conditioned by the organisational context where the interaction happens (Hollnagel and Bye 2000).

That is to say that an approach in which one does not consider the interaction between the two cognitive systems, the human being and the semiautomatic device, will be insufficient to explain the operation of a system of supervisory control. A nuclear power station's control room is an example of this. The objective of cognitive ergonomics, therefore, is to study a cognitive system integrated by human beings and artefacts.

3 The phenomenon to be explained: The interaction

When considering the device as a cognitive agent that should be modelled at the same level as the human being within the joint cognitive system, the interaction between them becomes the proper phenomenon of the study of cognitive ergonomics. According to Venda et al. (2000) the interaction is the process that includes the following components and states:

1. A group of environmental stimuli are presented to the person. These stimuli constitute the external input to the person's cognitive processes.
2. Perceptual processes transform this external input into an internal representation to be used by other cognitive processes.
3. The result of cognitive processes is an external output that acts on the environment.

4. The person's external output (behaviour) modifies the environment, which has its own internal dynamics that makes it change by itself.

In this description of interaction, the first three components would be common to any model of cognitive psychology. However, as Venda et al. (2000) pointed out, what is special in cognitive ergonomics is the insistence on the fourth component and in the recursive character of the process. In any theoretical model of cognitive psychology, interest stops at the output of the human system, which is to say in its behaviour. However, the result of this behaviour on the environment is the beginning of another cycle. Human behaviour modifies the environment, which can also change autonomously. In turn, this change in the environment is the input of the human cognitive processes. The phenomenon that interests us, therefore, is the human being interacting with other elements of the work system, and not the operation of human cognitive processes isolated from the environment.

This approach has been considered by Moray (1999) in order to clarify the study of mental models in cognitive literature. The mental model of a system is the way in which a person organises her knowledge about this system in memory (Norman 1983). This concept has been used to explain tasks as different as syllogistic problems or supervisory control in complex systems. Moray (1999) describes these tasks as opposite poles in a continuum, representing different levels of complexity and dynamism of the situations in which the tasks are performed. Other intermediate tasks considered in this continuum are those involved in HCI. The main idea proposed by the author is that as the situation of the task modelled increases in complexity and dynamism, so does the necessity to account for it as an independent agent that interacts with the person. Based on this idea it is possible to predict the level of failure when applying a classical cognitive model to the design of a task. As far as the modelled situation remains simple and static, some types of mental models should be useful for performing the task (e.g., simple HCI tasks). However, as the situation gains complexity, these models would fail to explain human behaviour in these tasks, and should, therefore, be replaced by another model that reconsiders the situation.

4 The analysis of the interaction within the joint cognitive system

To analyse the interaction that occurs between a person and a device, or between a person and other people through devices one can follow Hutchins' proposal of basically broadening cognitive analysis used by cognitive psychologists to study human information processing, to describe how the information is processed by the whole system formed by human beings and the devices within a certain sociotechnical environment (Hutchins 1996).

In cognitive psychology the unit of analysis has traditionally been the individual information processes. Cognitive psychologists have been asking questions about the processes that are responsible for the individual behaviour of a person. In their investigations they have tried to explain how information is represented inside the human cognitive system, and the way in which these representations are transformed, combined and processed inside the system (Simon 1969). However, it is possible to broaden this analysis to encompass the study of units of more than one person where several people with several devices have to interact within a sociotechnical context. To illustrate this point, Hutchins (1996) uses the aeroplane cockpit as one example where one can see how cognitive analysis can be applied to describe the way in which crew members of a commercial aeroplane perform their tasks with the help of a group of devices. Taking as a unit of analysis the cockpit, with all the devices together with the two pilots, Hutchins analyses how the speed of the aeroplane is memorised before landing.

When the aeroplane is taking off or landing, the speed is slow and so the shape of the wings is inappropriate. To correct this situation aeroplanes have devices called "flats" and "slats" that modify the shape and the area of the wings. These flats and slats have to be extended and configured every time the aeroplane lands. Configuration depends on the speed at which the aeroplane will land, and this in turn will depend on a series of factors such as the longitude of the landing area, the speed of wind etc. Therefore, a task that the pilots have to perform every time that they approach an airport to land is to calculate the appropriate configuration. To perform this task the pilots have to maintain in memory the speed at which the aeroplane goes and the speed at which it should land.

Under these conditions, Hutchins wonders if this task of remembering only concerns the pilots, or whether it is the responsibility of the whole cockpit, the pilots and all the instruments. Would it be possible to make a cognitive analysis of a cognitive system that we would call the cockpit? To answer this question, Hutchins suggests that we should think of what defines a cognitive system. According to the tradition of cognitive science, a cognitive system is a system in which information is represented and processed. From this point of view, Hutchins proposes that it is the whole cockpit that represents and processes information and that, therefore, the whole cockpit takes responsibility in the task of memorising.

What are the cognitive activities of pilots? The first task that they have to perform is to calculate the speeds that correspond to the aeroplane's weight. To do this they have at their disposal a set of cards, the correspondence between speed and weight. Using the cards, they don't have to remember these data; they only have to select the appropriate card. Once the appropriate card has been selected, the values are marked in the speed indicators. Evidently, the individual working memory of the pilot is involved in this task as has been demonstrated in the frequency of conversion errors (Norman 1988; Wickens and Flach 1988). However, we could consider that the task is also performed based on the book with the cards with the correspondence amongst weight, speed and the atmospheric conditions that constitute the long-term memory of the cockpit.

The appropriate card for the weight of the aeroplane is placed in the cockpit in a visible way so that the pilot and co-pilot can use it, just as we could hope they would recover and put the information on the person's individual working memory according to the analysis of traditional cognitive psychology. The position of the card in the cockpit is such that both the pilot and the co-pilot can see it and check that it is the correct one. It is also placed near the fuel indicator, so that the pilot can check that the co-pilot has selected the correct card. Therefore, we can think of a working memory shared between two crew members and the cards.

The marks in the speed indicator are made by the pilot with the values that are given to him by the co-pilot. These marks have the function of storing information. Without them, the pilot needs to remember the approach speed during landing, read the air speed, and make all the calculations to know what the speed of an appropriate approach is. With the marks, he will no longer have to read the air speed indicator, calculate the approach speeds and remember them. Therefore, what would be a task requiring memory, reading and reasoning becomes a task of space judgements because the pilot only has to judge if the needle has surpassed a mark or not.

When they begin to use marks of speeds, we can observe the following: the marks show spaces in the indicator that correspond to the speeds at which the flats and slats should be configured. The pilot, therefore, not only has to perceive the marks, he also has to interpret them and to give them meaning in terms of configurations of the flats and slats. That is to say, although with the marks it is not necessary that the pilot remember the speeds, he should remember the configurations that correspond to each speed.

Therefore, we can distinguish two types of representation in the cockpit. In the first place, we have observable representation such as the indicator of the weight of the aeroplane, the card with the correspondence amongst weight, atmospheric conditions and speeds, the marks in the speed indicator and the verbal communications between the pilot and co-pilot. In the second place, we have the non-observable representation that is in the pilot's and co-pilot's minds. These human mental representations can be considered as storage at the same level as the representations the other flight instruments store.

However, we could also recognise that the marks in the speed indicator have really modified the cognitive task of crew members. We could say that it is not a memory task anymore but a judgement task. By using artefacts the cognitive processes that used to be implied in the task have been replaced by others. This fact would not be observed from an analysis done from the point of view of the pilot's cognitive processes. Hutchins points out how these marks form what Luria (1979) called a "functional system". A functional system is a constellation of structures, some internal but others external to the human being, implied in some tasks that are frequently performed. Although these marks are also called by some "memory aids" (Norman 1991), Hutchins points out that they are not really so because their function is not to improve the pilot's memory. The function of these marks is one of improving the cockpit's memory. In a cockpit without the marks, the function of remembering speeds corresponds to the pilot's memory. In a cockpit with the marks, the function of memorising speeds no longer corresponds to the pilot's memory. The pilot, however, who has to perform another cognitive task without the marks, would have to read them and to interpret them in terms of the configuration of the flats and slats. Therefore, when introducing the marks in the design of the cockpit they redistribute the cognitive functions amongst people and the device. Since the working memory of people is subject to errors, the marks that can be considered as long-term memory because they are permanent improve the cockpit memory, not the pilot's memory, since the marks eliminate the necessity to memorise speeds. The pilot without marks should memorise the speeds and read the scales in the speed indicator. With the marks, he doesn't even need to read the speeds in the indicator. With the marks, the task becomes a task of space judgement.

This point is essential in understanding why Hutchins proposes that we should consider the cockpit as a unit of analysis, and not the human cognitive system in cognitive ergonomics. The memory in cognitive psychology is considered the individual's internal function. However, tasks performed in the cockpit of an aeroplane have to be considered from the point of view of a functional system. In cognitive ergonomics this is called a joint cognitive system that transcends to the individual. These tasks are performed as much for the individual as for the devices that compose the system. Speeds are only partially remembered by individuals that are in the cockpit. They are also represented and remembered by the devices. When the pilot and co-pilot have to decide if the speed at which the aeroplane goes in a certain moment is quick or slow, the task is carried out by comparing the speed with the data in the pilot's memory, or with the marks in the indicator. Therefore, we cannot consider that the pilot's task of memorising is only the recovery of information from her long-term memory. A correct cognitive analysis of this task of memorising should be made considering that the information is stored not so much in the pilot's memory, as in that of the co-pilot and, mainly, in the devices that are in the cockpit. For this reason, in cognitive ergonomics it is considered that a cognitive task such as this is performed by the whole system where we can observe a continuous interaction amongst people and devices. However, the interaction thus considered as a cognitive unit of analysis would be a complex activity. Therefore, it would be very helpful to have a way of describing it to facilitate its analysis.

With this goal in mind Cañas and Waern (2001) have proposed a framework of reference that allows us to describe the interaction at several levels making the stress in the relationship between particular cognitive processes and types of artefacts that when introduced would affect the human cognitive agent. An adaptation of this framework can be seen in Table 1. In the left column of the table there are examples of cognitive artefacts. Each cognitive level represents a level of analysis. In the right column of the table we have the aspects of human cognition and behaviour affected by the introduction of one artefact.

Table 1. Reference framework to explain interaction phenomena (Cañas and Waern 2001).

Cognitive artefacts	Cognitive levels	Aspects of human cognition and behaviour affected
CMC, e-mail, e-conferences, MUD	Sociocultural	Organisation, history, culture, virtual communities
CSCW, workflow	Cooperation	Communication and coordination
Knowledge-based systems, support systems for decision making	Complex information processing	Knowledge representation, decision making, problem solving
Data display systems (visual, auditory, tactile etc.), direct manipulation systems.	Simple information processing	Perception, attention, memory, comprehension etc.
Output and input systems, virtual reality	Sensory motor	Afferent and efferent human system

Starting from the bottom of the table, the first cognitive level that we find is the sensory motor. In this level interaction is described from the point of view of the characteristics of the human sensorial and motor systems. Interaction occurs when the output of the device, be this visual, auditory or of any other physical type, is captured by human sensorial receivers. In the same way, human behaviour would be given through the motor system; it is necessary that the device have the necessary input systems to receive it in the appropriate way. For example, we can be interested here in how people learn to adapt and to use neuronal implants cognitively. When a person receives an implant of an artificial motor organ, a hand, for example, his actions are not the same as they were before, fundamentally because he doesn't have direct sensorial feedback. Since many motor functions are dependent on sensitive feedback, any device that compensates for the loss of a motor organ would have to be designed with this in mind. Therefore, it is a challenge for cognitive ergonomics to consider how a compensatory type of feedback could be designed, how a person could learn to manage the device as well as his compensatory feedback and the possible secondary effects of such feedback. The process of feedback described could be reflecting the last level of interaction proposed by Venda et al. (2000). Another possible example that is of enormous interest today in this level is "virtual reality", where people are provided with a three-dimensional experience of the world and where at least some motor actions are allowed to change this experience. Topics of interest for cognitive ergonomics are, for example, the real sensations in the virtual world, and the interactions between virtual reality and natural reality.

Going up a step in the table we find the individual information processing level. In this level we can begin to speak about symbolic information processing. The aspects of devices that are important in this level are related to their performance.

The cognitive aspects refer to how the objects are presented by the device (on the screen, for example) and how they are perceived by the user. It is important to know, for example, if the objects indicate the pertinent action in a unique way, and the interpretations that the objects confront. The "affordance" concept taken from Gibson (1979) is useful to analyse the difficulty that the user has in understanding what will happen when certain actions act on certain objects (also see Norman 1986).

An important part of the work done in cognitive ergonomics has been developed in this level. For example, when we are studying how people understand items on a menu, whether verbal, or represented as icons, or when we are answering questions with regard to how much information can be put on the screen, we are in this level. The necessary attention to carry out a task as well as information overload, are also aspects that are considered in this level.

The use of hypertext systems for instructional purposes is an example of the changes caused by the introduction of a new cognitive artefact for accomplishing an automated task such as reading. When reading and learning from a hypertext readers use different cognitive processes than those required in a linear text (Wenger and Payne 1996). The main reason for this change is the fact that in hypertext readers can choose freely the order in which they read the content, whereas in linear text the order is established by the author (Salmerón et al. 2003).

The new cognitive demands of hypertext could improve the performance of users with special characteristics. For example, deaf users seem to take advantage of the more complex visuospatial configuration of hypertext structures due to a working memory process adapted to maintain and remember this kind of information during the use of sign language (Fajardo et al. 2003). Data such as these could not be explained by models of working memory, which do not consider the flexibility of the cognitive system to adapt to environmental changes. In this example, both the human cognitive system and artefact cognitive representation of information have changed. To explain the results, it is necessary to analyse the interaction between them.

In the following level we find the topics that concern complex individual information processing. The devices that are important in this level are, for example, knowledge management systems and those that support decision making and complex problem solving.

New topics that are of interest in this level refer to knowledge awareness, mental models and situational awareness. For example, it is important to know how the conceptual model of a computer system should be presented so that the user can form a corresponding mental model that allows him to work correctly with it (Cañas et al. 1994). To make decisions and to solve problems people develop heuristics, that is to say, strategies of information processing that allow them to solve problems efficiently (Newell and Simon 1972).

Cognitive ergonomics studies how people can understand the concepts and principles used in support systems, to solve a problem or to elaborate a decision. For example, the search heuristic used by the computer can be different from that used by the human user. It is possible to wonder then, if it will be necessary that the device be transparent, that is to say that the human user will be able to understand the search heuristic that she uses, or that it is enough that it carries out some algorithms correctly without revealing them (Waern and Hägglund 1997).

Next, we meet with higher topics, when people cooperate to perform a task. Many tasks require cooperation for reasons of effectiveness. For example, on some occasions, it would take a person too much time to make all the decisions for the design of a mechanical device. Many tasks require cooperation because the knowledge of several people is needed. For example, medical work in a hospital uses the abilities of laboratory personel, medicine, surgery and psychiatry, sometimes applied to one patient alone.

In this level, individual information processing covered in inferior levels should be considered from the point of view of the communication and the coordination that takes place amongst the participants of a task. Of course, individual information processing is still important, but the result of team information processing will be different and will depend on interactions within the team.

Devices that are good for communication and coordination belong to the category called, with its English initials, "CSCW" (Computer-Supported Cooperative Work). They can vary from the simple support of communication, such as e-mail, to complex systems of support in coordination, such as systems of work flow.

In this level, topics of interest for cognitive ergonomics are, for example, studying how CSCW systems affect the habits, strategies or styles of people's communication, how to adapt such systems to the ways of working that have developed in a work place, and how to allow them to organise tasks flexibly and to distribute the tasks efficiently.

Finally, the level with a wider reach is the one that covers the sociocultural aspects of knowledge. In this level it is recognised that actions of people, as well as their expectations are built on historical tradition, where the mutual social influences as well as the devices that are used jointly, play an important role. The devices in this level can help to build a community and keep the historical memory of it. For example, we could discuss at this level how people who use the Internet extensively form a virtual community, with similar effects to a community in real life, from the point of view of traditions and expectations, but where the rules for interaction and action can be different from theirs.

This level is so high that it is debatable if it can really affect the design. A community is not designed, but develops over a long period of time. Its members can experience problems and make errors, and they can try to find for themselves the different ways to overcome them. Solutions are given based on mutual agreements without external advice, and built on general cognitive or social principles in general.

Topics of interest for cognitive ergonomics in this level are then, more to do with analysis than with design. Methods and concepts of cognitive ergonomics could help participants to mediate its practices, and allow them to choose solutions that favour its goals and own values. For example, some problems can be solved with purely social action, while other problems can be solved technically (O'Day et al. 1996).

This reference framework, therefore, offers us three or four levels where cognitive ergonomics can offer very pertinent explanations. Although levels overlap, interaction problems can be considered in any single level. An analysis in a higher level does not exclude problems in a different one. It is obvious that solutions at the organisational level are not sufficient to solve perceptual problems and vice versa. In this way, a wider level will also be required to consider other levels.

However, we should stress an important point that could help us to understand what happens when we introduce a change in the joint cognitive system. A change in one of the components of the joint cognitive system always means a change in the distribution of cognitive functions that artefacts and people play in their interaction. Artefacts could be introduced or redesigned. People could learn, or suffer changes, due to, for example, age or disability. When some or all of these changes occur we can observe changes within, or between, levels of explanations. All these changes involve modifications in the distribution of functions amongst people and artefacts. This is particularly true when a change in a level corresponds to a change in another level modifying the tasks and mainly the distribution of functions between devices and human beings. We will illustrate this point with one example taken from a study from Lanzi and Marti (2002) about artefacts used in the air traffic control room.

Over the decades the activity of controllers has been based on a very consolidated and sure work environment, where the relationship amongst workers is mediated by several paper ribbons where they write data about the aeroplanes that they are controlling. The ribbons are inserted in some supports and these in turn are placed horizontally on a board.

We could conceive these paper ribbons as the centre of the whole joint cognitive system because the controllers are moving them continually up and down on the board to represent visually the status of aeroplanes and their relationships. The form, as these paper ribbons are manipulated, defines the different roles of controllers and the distribution of the tasks amongst them. The roles are defined by the type of paper ribbon used, the action that it is made with and what is written on it. For example, the assisting controller is the one who makes the marks on the ribbons and passes them to the controller who orders them.

From some years to date, authorities have looked for alternative artefacts to substitute this system based on paper ribbons due to the problems associated with the necessity of coordinating activities through the telephone or manually. This type of coordination makes the time factor very important when air traffic increases. It takes time to stuff the ribbons and to manage them on the board. Also, the information that is on the ribbons has to be combined with what the controllers see on the radar. To combine information, for example, to project the future trajectory of an aeroplane, the controller has to continually switch attention from the ribbons to the radar and vice versa.

For this reason, an intense investigation is now taking place, as much in Europe as in the United States, to find a system for substituting paper ribbons. At the moment, both advantages and inconveniences of the following alternative systems are being compared: (1) systems with electronic ribbons that contain the same information as the paper ribbons but have the advantage of being able to communicate directly with the radar; (2) systems without ribbons where the controllers have computers that receive information directly and with which they interact through the standard input systems (keyboard and mouse); and (3) systems with semielectronic ribbons. However, after years of investigation in Europe and in America, a universally accepted alternative does not exist. We are in a situation in Europe where almost every airport has a different system. Results of these investigations have not been able to show which is the better system.

According to Lanzi and Marti (2002) the reason for this situation is the impossibility of comparing systems without bearing in mind the activity of the controllers is different in each system. The question is not which of the proposed systems is better in terms of efficiency of the software. The question is to know how each alternative proposal needs to be accompanied by a change in the form as the controllers carry out its work.

Field studies (Fields et al. 1998) have demonstrated that controllers perceive the static two-dimensional representation of ribbons on a board as a dynamic three-dimensional representation of the progression of aeroplanes towards a defined area of air space. Therefore they have a mental map of air traffic. This representation is dynamic and three-dimensional; it is built with the combined information of ribbons and radar, respectively. It contains the whole of air traffic as much in the present as in the future, and it is shared by all controllers. For example, the controller who drifts and the controller who executes actions have the same representations because both use the same devices, ribbons and radar. They are also mutually helped to structure this mental representation correctly. For example, when the controller who is planning retires a ribbon from the board, he puts it before the controller executioner's eyes to let him know just what he is doing, sometimes saying aloud something like, "I am retiring the ribbon of this aeroplane."

In the systems without ribbons each controller has his own screen which decreases collaboration and the possibility of creating a common mental representation. Each controller has his own mental map that cannot coincide with that of the other ones. The authors mention an example of a critical situation in which two aeroplanes run the risk of colliding. This shows how the activity of the controllers changes when a new device is introduced, changing the joint cognitive system in its entirety. With the system of ribbons the two aeroplanes are in the same region of the controllers' mental map, while in the system without ribbons, the aeroplanes are in different regions of the mental map of each of the controllers.

The same idea can be exemplified with a situation that is common to many investigators that at the present time use statistical programs with graphics to analyse their data. In this situation it is normal that the data are subject to many analysis types until finding an interpretation that is in consonance with the research hypotheses. After each analysis, the investigator usually represents the data in a graph using one of many formats that the program offers. Each graph is stored in the investigator's memory while she evaluates the validity of its interpretation. In this way, we can say that the cognitive representation of data is simultaneously in the investigator's mind and in the interface of the computer. If the investigator changes the format of the graph she will simultaneously change the representation in her memory and, more importantly, the interpretation that she makes of that same data. Therefore, we cannot analyse mental representation from the point of view of the human cognitive system without considering mental representation from the point of view of the device, because both are part of a joint cognitive system. In this sense, we have to say that interpretation of the data that is the object of the cognitive processing that is performed, is carried out by the whole joint cognitive system, and not only by the human cognitive system.

In the case of failed experiments mentioned in the introduction, it can simply mean that models that have been proven fundamentally with a particular material in the laboratory, and to explain behaviour in particular types of tasks, cannot be applied to explain the operation of cognitive processes in interaction with other types of material.

5 Consequences for the future of interaction design: The principle of "mutual dependency"

According to the arguments mentioned above, we can foresee cognitive ergonomists generating knowledge during the design process that would lead to the development of formal theories of interaction. To do this they would have to:

1. Identify which is the cognitive task that has to be performed by the joint cognitive system.
2. Identify the cognitive aspects of information processing carried out by the joint cognitive system to perform that particular task.
3. Identify the particular distribution of cognitive functions and tasks between devices and human beings.
4. Model the information processing of the whole system.

In this analysis there is an important aspect that could have clear consequences for the future of interaction design: when the system changes (e.g., the artefact is redesigned or the human being learns to perform the task better), so does information processing, possibly changing the roles of the cognitive functions that each component of the system carries out. The practical consequence of this proposal could be expressed as a design principle that we call "mutual dependency". This principle states that the human cognitive functions implied in the task will depend on the functions that are present in the interface. Furthermore, the functions of the interface that help to perform a task will be those that are more appropriate to the human cognitive functions that are implied in the task. For example, the appropriate interface functions will be those that correspond to the structure and function of the human working memory.

Therefore, according to this principle of mutual dependency, designers should consider that any modification, substitution or introduction of a new function in the interface will imply a change in the human cognitive functions that intervene in the task. In addition, anything that is particular or constraining in the characteristics of the human cognitive functions that are present in some or in all users will imply a limitation in the possible functions that are included in the interface. For example, users that have some limitations on their working memory functions would require interface functions that overlook these limitations.

Let us consider one example of an application of this principle. One of the most important developments in today's interface design is the introduction of virtual reality environments. The design of these environments will require us to consider two important questions. One of these questions will be related to the functioning of the human cognitive system. When a person is immersed in a three-dimensional virtual reality environment, the perceptual processes will be forced to process information in ways that have not been possible before. For example, human perceptual processes are not used to dealing with perceptual information when flying as birds. Since virtual reality environments will allow human beings to have the experience of flying, it is possible to think that perceiving in virtual reality environments will be different from that of perceiving in our own three-dimensional real world. Therefore, a design strategy consisting of simply applying our lab-generated knowledge on human perception will not be informative enough here.

The second question to be considered concerns the design of the system linked to the particular user's cognitive functioning. Consider, for example, a change in an existing virtual reality environment consisting of allowing the user to jump outside the gravity laws. The designer must not only consider new perceptual rules associated with this new environment, but also the possible consequences of this change in the overall user cognitive system (e.g., feeling of nausea associated with an unnatural jump).

We don't want to finish this chapter without mentioning that this proposal does not only have its repercussions in the work of designers. It also has repercussions in the work of cognitive psychologists, because this proposal is related to an intense debate happening at the moment within cognitive psychology. Some authors have being proposing for some years that we should consider the environment as part of the cognitive system (Beer 1995, 2000). Although the idea is not shared by all authors, it is undeniable that it is receiving important attention. In the words of one of their opponents, Wilson (2002), the proposal fails to consider that two types of systems exist, the "facultative" and the "obligate". A facultative system would be one that changes when conditions change, while an obligate system would be more or less independent of changes in the environment that surrounds it. Although no cognitive psychologist would defend a strong version of the obligate system to describe the human cognitive system, some are defending something that would be on-line with the proposal of the joint cognitive system. This is the position Wilson (2002) calls the "mind-more-the situation". That is to say, it would be considered that the human cognitive system has some characteristics more or less permanent, but to explain its behaviour completely it is necessary to keep the environment in mind. Mainly, if we want to make predictions on how the system will behave in a certain situation, it is completely necessary to consider the characteristics of that situation. Taking an example used by Wilson (2002) himself we can think of hydrogen. Evidently, the scientific knowledge about hydrogen is based on what we have discovered of its atomic structure, but to know how it behaves with other chemical elements, this knowledge is not enough.

References

Anderson JR (1995) Cognitive Psychology and Its Implications. Freeman, New York

Beer RD (1995) A dynamical systems perspective on agent-environment interaction. Artificial Intelligence 72:173-215

Beer RD (2000) Dynamical approaches to cognitive science. Trends in Cognitive Science 4:91-99

Cañas JJ, Bajo MT, Gonzalvo P (1994) Mental models and computer programming. International Journal of Human-Computer Studies 40:795-811

Cañas JJ, Quesada JF, Antolí A, Fajardo I (2003) Cognitive flexibility and adaptability to environmental changes in dynamic complex problem solving tasks. Ergonomics 46:482-501

Cañas JJ, Waern Y (2001) Ergonomía Cognitiva. Editorial Médica Panamericana, Madrid

Dowell J, Long JB (1989) Towards a conception for an engineering discipline of human factors. Ergonomics 32:1513-1535

Dowell J, Long JB (1998) Conception of the cognitive engineering design problem. Ergonomics 41:126-139

Fajardo I, Cañas J, Salmerón L, Abascal J (2003) Towards a cognitive accessibility guideline based on empirical evidences of deaf users Web interaction. In: Stephanidis C (ed) Universal Access in HCI. Inclusive Design in the Information Society, vol 4, pp 950-954. LEA, London

Farris JS, Jones KS, Elgin PD (2002) Users' schemata of hypermedia: What is so "spatial" about a Website? Interacting with Computers 14:487-502

Fields R, Wright P, Marti P, Palmonari M (1998) Air traffic control as a distributed cognitive system: A case study of external representations. In: Green TRG, Bannon L, Warren CP, Buckley J (eds) ECCE9 Proceedings of the ninth European Conference on Cognitive Ergonomics. EACE, Limerick, Ireland

Garden S, Cornoldi C, Logie R (2002) Visuo-spatial working memory in navigation. Applied Cognitive Psychology 16(1):35-50

Gibson JJ (1979) The Ecological Approach to Visual Perception. Houghton Mifflin, Boston, MA

Hollnagel E, Bye A (2000) Principles for modelling function allocation. International Journal of Man-Machine Studies 52:253-265

Hollnagel E, Woods DD (1983) Cognitive systems engineering: New wine in new bottles. International Journal of Man-Machine Studies 18:583-600

Huguenard BR, Lerch FJ, Junker BW, Patz RJ, Kass RE (1997) Working-memory failure in phone-based interaction. ACM Transactions on Computer-Human Interaction 4:67-102

Hutchins E (1996) How a cockpit remember its speeds. Cognitive Science 19:265-288

Jonassen DH, Wang S (1993) Acquiring structural knowledge from semantically structured hypertext. Journal of Computer-Based Instruction 20:1-8

Just MA, Carpenter PA (1992) A capacity theory of comprehension: Individual differences in working memory. Psychological Review 99:122-149

Kim H, Hirtle SC (1995) Spatial metaphors and disorientation in hypertext browsing. Behaviour and Information Technology 14:239–250

Lansdale MW, Scrivener SAR, Woodcock A (1996) Developing practice with theory in HCI: Applying models of spatial cognition for the design of pictorial databases. International Journal of Human-Computer Studies 44:777-799

Lanzi P, Marti P (2002) Innovate or preserve: When technology questions co-operative processes. In: Bagnara S, Pozzi S, Rizzo A, Wright P (eds) ECCE11 Proceedings of the eleventh European Conference on Cognitive Ergonomics. CNR, Catania, Italy

Luria AR (1979) The Making of Mind: A Personal Account of Soviet Psychology. MIT Press, Cambridge, MA

McDonald S, Stevenson RJ (1999) Spatial versus conceptual maps as learning tools in hypertext. Journal of Education Multimedia and Hypermedia 8(1):43-64

Moray N (1999) Mental models in theory and practice. In: Gopher D, Koriat A (eds) Attention and Performance XVII: Cognitive Regulation of Performance: Interaction of Theory and Application. The MIT Press, Cambridge, MA, pp 223-258

Newell A, Simon HA (1972) Human Problem Solving. Prentice-Hall, Englewood Cliffs, NJ

Norman DA (1983) Some observations on mental models. In: Gentner D, Stevens AL (eds) Mental Models. Lawrence Erlbaum, Hillsdale, NJ, pp 7-14

Norman DA (1986) Cognitive engineering. In: Norman DA, Draper SW (eds) User Centred System Design. Lawrence Erlbaum, Hillsdale, NJ, pp 32-65

Norman DA (1988) The Psychology of Everyday Things. Basic Books, New York

Norman DA (1991) Cognitive artefacts. In: Carroll JM (ed) Designing Interactions: Psychology at the Human-Computer Interactions. Cambridge University Press, New York, pp 17-38

O'Day VL, Bobrow DG, Shirley M (1996) The socio-technical design cycle. In: Proceedings from CSCW 1996, pp 160-169

Rasmussen WB, Pejtersen A, Goodstein L (1994) Cognitive Systems Engineering. Wiley, New York

Salmerón L, Fajardo I, Cañas JJ (2003) An online method for assessing text comprehension in hypertext systems. Paper presented at the thirteenth Meeting of the Society for Text and Discourse, Madrid, Spain

Simon H (1969) The Science of the Artificial. MIT Press, Cambridge, MA

Venda VF, Tribus RJ, Venda NI (2000) Cognitive ergonomics: Theory, laws, and graphic. International Journal of Cognitive Ergonomics 4:331-349

Vicente KJ (1999) Cognitive Work Analysis: Toward Safe, Productive and Healthy Computer Based Work. Erlbaum, Mahwah, NJ

Vicente KJ, Wang JH (1998) An ecological theory of expertise effects in memory recall. Psychological Review 105:33-57

Waern Y, Hägglund S (1997) User aspects of knowledge systems. In: Helander I, Landauer MG, Prabhu TK (eds) Handbook of Human-Computer Interaction, 2nd edn. Elsevier Science, Amsterdam, The Netherlands

Wenger MJ, Payne DG (1996) Comprehension and retention of nonlinear text: Considerations of working memory and material-appropriate processing. American Journal of Psychology 109:94-130

Wickens CD (1992) Engineering Psychology and Human Performance. Harper Collins, New York

Wickens CD, Flach J (1988) Information processing. In: Wiener E, Angel D (eds) Human Factor in Aviation. Academia Press, New York

Wilson M (2002) Six views of embodied cognition. Psychonomics Bulletin and Review 9:625-636

Woods DD, Johannesen LJ, Cook RI, Sater NB (1994) Behind human error: Cognitive systems, computers and hindsight. CSERIAC, Columbus, Ohio

Woods DD, Roth EM (1988) Cognitive systems engineering. In: Helander M (ed) Handbook of Human Computer Interaction. Elsevier, Amsterdam

To simulate or to stimulate? In search of the power of metaphor in design

Antti Pirhonen

Department of Computer Science and Information Systems
University of Jyväskylä
Finland
pianta@cc.jyu.fi

Abstract

Metaphors are a key part of human conceptualisation processes. Conceptualising contemporary information and communication technology is no exception. The way we communicate with and with the help of modern technology can be understood and conceptualised as a matter of metaphor. Within the context of interaction design, however, the term metaphor has been used in a way that is not coherent with its use in metaphor theories, which arise from linguistics. The conceptual vagueness in the context of interaction design has resulted in mistrust toward metaphor as a design principle. In this chapter metaphor is redefined for the needs of design. It is argued that the questioning of the power of metaphor in design is a consequence of using the concept in a loose manner. Contemporary metaphor theories provide an extremely interesting perspective to design. In this chapter, a sample design is analysed in terms of the proposed theoretical framework.

1 Metaphor lifecycle: From dawn to dusk

1.1 The nature of metaphor

The concept and related term metaphor may mean very different things in different contexts. Firstly, the term metaphor is used in everyday language and corresponds to common dictionary definitions. Secondly, metaphor has been an object of broad academic discussion since Aristotle, resulting in theories of metaphor. Thirdly, the use of the concept in the context of user interfaces has to be handled separately, since it differs markedly from both everyday and theoretical usage.

Everyday use of the term, relying on typical dictionary definitions, accords clearly with the Aristotelian view of metaphor. Central to this view is the strong connection with the verbal modality. The most common definition, as found, for example, in the *Oxford English Dictionary* (*OED*) is a "figure of speech". As in everyday usage there is seldom the need to perform a detailed analysis of the meaning of verbal expressions, it is quite natural that the domain of the concept is not too strictly defined. Therefore, the term metaphor is often used as a general term referring to all figurative language. Related concepts such as metonymy are rare and usually the term metaphor is used instead.

The most traditional view of the concept of metaphor was probably first articulated by Aristotle. In his books he handled metaphor in poetics and rhetoric. For Aristotle, metaphor was a means of communicating meanings effectively. The keyword in this view is similarity: a new and unfamiliar entity is expressed with the help of familiar concepts by pointing out the similarities between the two. The rationale for the usage of metaphors is to help the learning process. In addition, Aristotle saw metaphors as an effective way of enlivening presentation, illustrating and clarifying, directing emotions, as well as expressing things with no name (Aristotle 1984).

The concept and term metaphor, in the way it is used in everyday language and as Aristotle formulated it, satisfies the needs of everyday communication. Philologists and cognitive scientists, however, seem far too intrigued with the phenomenon of the metaphor to content themselves with the rather simple and easily adoptable Aristotelian view. The first major change in the Aristotelian view were the interaction theories (e.g., Black 1962), which shifted the focus from similarities onto the interaction between semantic contents (Searle 1993). Still, these are merely further developments of the Aristotelian view in a sense that they, like the Aristotelian view,

1. concern verbal expressions, and
2. are based on juxtaposition between literal and metaphorical meaning.

The contemporary theory of metaphor (Lakoff 1993; Lakoff and Johnson 1980, 1999) goes far beyond the traditional view. The brief version of the definition of metaphor as *cross-domain mapping* tells us clearly that this view is much broader than the traditional one. In contemporary theory, metaphor is seen as a basis for all abstract conceptualisation. This theory makes the distinction between metaphor and metaphorical expression. Seen from inside the paradigm of contemporary theory, it can be argued that it was *metaphorical expression* that was called a metaphor in the traditional view. In this chapter, to be consistent in the usage of terminology, we should always make a clear distinction between the terms metaphor and metaphorical expression. However, in the name of readability, the distinction is not always made if the context clearly reveals to which one (metaphor or metaphorical expression) is being referred. Sometimes it is not even possible to separate metaphor (in the conceptual sense) and its concrete expression.

The shift of focus from metaphorical expressions (the traditional view) to conceptual cross-domain mappings (contemporary theory) provides an opportunity to understand metaphorical expressions that are non-verbal in nature. In principle, the adaptation of contemporary theory thus justifies the use of the concept of metaphor in the context of the design of multimodal environments. This opportunity is widely used, but unfortunately the usage of the term in UI-design has not respected its roots. At the time of the introduction of the GUI, metaphor was a buzzword which was rapidly being used by anyone and everyone. The spread of the use of the term probably led to the everyday comprehension of the concept. Thus, the usage of the term in the context of UI-design seems to integrate the mundane usage with the justification of modern metaphor theory to use the concept in non-verbal environments.

One might argue that language changes continuously anyway and that the current usage of the word metaphor in multimodal environments has only enriched the meaning of the word. However, this combination of mundane meaning and conceptual nature that arises from the contemporary theory is very problematic from the perspective of the content of the concept. It is problematic from the theoretical viewpoint, but also in practical UI-design. The main problem is the inflation of the concept. Throughout human history, metaphor has shown its power in human communication. Recently, its appropriateness has been questioned in UI-design. What then has changed? I argue that it is not the human communication needs nor anything else that is firmly grounded in human nature. Nor is it the change in technical environment. What has changed is the usage of the concept of metaphor. Before we totally discard metaphor as a design principle, we should take a look at the nature of metaphor and discover the secret of its well-known power in communication.

The rationale of this work is to find relevant theoretical and practical points that sharpen the usage of the concept of metaphor in UI-design. The work is conceptually based on core properties of metaphor theories in linguistics. These theoretical aspects are applied in the context of UI-design. Furthermore, the work contributes to the development of metaphor theory as a whole by analysing the dynamics of metaphor.

1.2 The core properties of metaphor in the context of UI-design

Whether referring to the traditional or modern metaphor theories or even the mundane usage of the term, there is a lot in common. First, in all of these conceptions metaphor contains two domains, which are paralleled in one way or another. Second, the major rationale of using metaphor is to support the conceptualisation process. This is usually expressed as learning support. Even if there is this wide mutual understanding, it is not enough. These two properties alone do not justify calling a parallel a metaphor. Linguists separate several tropes, of which metaphor is just one example. Most of these (metonyms, irony, hyperbole and understatement, oxymoron, idioms) are often referred to as metaphors in everyday language. In UI-design, all kinds of parallels that contain similarity are called metaphors. My point is that if we tried to broaden our vocabulary, even in UI-context, we would have the whole power of metaphor available to use. Once we had separated the concept of metaphor from related concepts, we would understand its unique power and could utilise it, too.

In the following Sections 2.1 and 2.2 I will illustrate the strange understanding of the concept of metaphor in the context of the GUI by analysing two common objections to the use of metaphors in design. From the later analysis I then derive a discussion about the metaphor lifecycle in Sections 2.2.1 and 2.2.2.

2 Concept of metaphor in the context of GUI vs. in rhetoric

2.1 Objection 1: "Metaphor can never cover the whole domain of Its referent"

The most familiar argument against the use of metaphor as a design principle is that in a metaphorical setting, the virtual entity and its real-world counterpart differ from each other. It is argued that this difference misleads the interpreter of the metaphor (user). It is further argued that when trying to imitate a real world entity with a virtual artefact, the functionality of the virtual entity is restricted (Harrison et al. 1998; Johnson 1987; Nardi and Zarmer 1993).

Creating a metaphor means finding analogies between the known and the new. Certainly, a metaphor can never have all of the properties of the entity it refers to – and vice versa. However, it has to be noticed that the endeavour toward similarity between a metaphor and its referent is unique in the UI-context. Elsewhere, it is actually the differences that are seen as the strength of a metaphor. Hamilton (2000) argues that the mismatch is the core of a metaphor. She writes how the mismatch makes one pay attention to "parallels not immediately apparent from the direct comparison". Referring to the same thing, Carroll and Mack (1985) write about the open-endedness of metaphors and find this a strength, essential for the stimulating effect of a metaphor: "It is this property of metaphor that affords cognitively constructive processes which can lead to new knowledge. From the perspective of active learning, the open-endedness of these kernel comparisons is intrinsic to the mechanism that allows them to work" (p. 395).

The idea that a metaphor and its referent should resemble each other as much as possible collides with all central definitions of metaphor. A good example of the strange usage of the concept of metaphor in GUIs is a push-button. No doubt, most people who have followed the development of GUIs would call a virtual push-button a metaphor. In the contemporary GUI, a virtual push-button looks (even when pushed) and possibly sounds like its physical counterpart. With the development of computer graphics, a push-button has been developed to resemble more and more a physical one. This tendency would lead to a situation where the difference between a virtual and real push-button cannot be perceived. Aristotle (1984) declared the ability to create good metaphors as "a sign of genius", an innate talent to see "similarity in dissimilars" (p. 2335). He would hardly have found a virtual push-button with its obvious similarities to be a metaphor at all.

If we are trying to imitate a real-world entity as accurately as possible, we have a good concept already in use. The *Oxford English Dictionary* (*OED*) defines the verb simulate as follows: "To imitate… by means of a model…". The OED's description of the corresponding noun simulation is in accordance with this. We conclude that when striving towards the highest possible similarity between a virtual and a real object, we are talking about simulations, not metaphors.

Simulations and metaphors should be distinguished conceptually from each other in design. This is simply because they have different strengths and should be used accordingly. However, making the distinction between these two in practical design is not that simple. These problems are discussed later with reference to our sample design.

We conclude that two important features of metaphors are neglected when flattening the use of the concept of metaphor to the imitation of real-world entities.

1. The first argument concerns the designer. We argue that a working metaphor demands from the designer creativity, inventiveness and a deep view of human mental processes. Creating a metaphor that is simultaneously appropriate (makes essential qualities salient) and unexpected (stimulating) demands much more than simple imitation of the most obvious point of comparison in the real world.
2. The second argument deals with the user. The key question is: do we see the user as a passive receiver of the ideas of the designer or do we count on the active mental processes of the user? Again, we refer to Carroll and Mack (1985), who describe metaphors as a way to make users pose problems for themselves. In other words, rather than using metaphors as a means to transfer knowledge or understanding from one person to another, this view underlines their role as inspiring a user's own imagination and creativity.

Giving a role to something like the user's imagination and creativity might sound frightening in its uncertainty and indefiniteness. It sounds safer to search for strategies that provide methods to control the meaning construction process, rather than inspire it. Still, whether we acknowledge it or not, constructing meanings and mental representations is always subjective in nature. The process is tied to previous experiences and to other subjective qualities.

The difference outlined between the traditional meaning of metaphor and its somewhat loose use (when imitating real-world entities) has important implications. When creating a simulator (e.g., a flight simulator), we have a clear target: our model is perfect when the user of the simulator cannot sense the difference between it and its real-world counterpart. Therefore, a simulator is in practice always a more or less imperfect substitute for something else. It is used, for example, because of safety or economy. But the simulation itself can hardly ever equal what it simulates. Metaphor, in the sense in which it is traditionally used, does not even have this kind of concrete counterpart with which it could be compared. Since the aim of a metaphor is to make something essentially salient by drawing a parallel between contextually unrelated entities, the success of a metaphor cannot be evaluated in as simple a manner as the success of a simulation. Whether a metaphor works or not is dependent on both the metaphor and its interpreter. So there is no theoretical end-point called "the perfect metaphor". For one person it might work just as its creator wished; for another person the same metaphor might fail totally. To express it in another way: To develop a simulation is a highly mechanical reproduction process. In turn, to develop a metaphor is a creative communication process.

2.2 Objection 2: "Once learned, the metaphor becomes useless"

The strength and rationale of metaphors in GUIs, according to the usual argument, is their power in facilitating learning how to use the computer (Carroll and Mack 1985; Hamilton 2000; Nardi and Zarmer 1993). However, we may ask (see Gentner and Nielson 1996; Johnson 1987): why use the metaphor after having learned to use the application?

Cooper (1986) analyses the concept of the dead metaphor. Even a brilliant metaphor may gradually become an idiom, thus losing its literal meaning. This idea could be applied to UI design when creating either verbal or non-verbal metaphors. Why couldn't we let a metaphor die in peace? A durable metaphor could then have a different function for a novice user and an expert. For a novice user it could be a metaphor (in the traditional meaning), providing insights into the nature of a function or application. Gradually, it turns into an idiom for the experienced user, still having some communicative value.

A dead metaphor, or a metaphor which has turned into an idiom, is something that has been born as a metaphor. The connection to the source of the metaphor has supported it for a period of time, but gradually the need to maintain the associations with its source has reduced. Finally, it becomes totally independent of its "parent" and lives its own life. The only thing (if any) that reminds us of its roots is perhaps its name or other symbolic presentation. Later, this new independent concept may be a source for – or give birth to – a new metaphor. The dynamics of the metaphor lifecycle are discussed further in Sections 2.2.1 and 2.2.2.

Again, we ended up with the subjective nature of metaphors. Being coherent in our concepts, we shouldn't actually even talk about the creation of metaphor as the task of the designer. Rather, the challenge of the designer is to support the user's metaphor creation process. This way we also turn from the classical or Aristotelian metaphor conception to what is usually referred to as the modern theory of metaphor (Lakoff 1993; Lakoff and Johnson 1980, 1999). In it, metaphor is seen as a key means for a human being to construct knowledge. The underlying idea of the metaphorical expression is the designer's own metaphor, which he is trying to communicate to the user with the help of an appropriate expression.

From now on, we shall still refer to metaphors and simulations as if they were something that could be designed. The term metaphor should therefore be interpreted merely as "a support for metaphor creation". The same applies to simulation in our conceptual analysis, even if simulations can also be understood much more mechanically.

2.2.1 The transformation of metaphor

The lifecycle of the metaphor is handled in the literature in the form of analysis of the concept of the dead metaphor (e.g., Cooper 1986; Fraser 1993; Searle 1993). Usually, the concept of the dead metaphor (or idiom, see Gibbs 1993) is taken as the other stage of an expression that once was a metaphor. In other words, the lifecycle of a metaphor is seen to contain two stages: life, with metaphorical meaning, and death, with no metaphorical meaning. However, Fraser (1993) brings up the obvious fact that the dying process of the metaphor is hardly sudden. Fraser (p. 330) speaks about a continuum from live to dead metaphor. The continuum must mean that live and dead metaphors are the ends and that there are several intermediate forms between these. This continuum is referred to here as the lifecycle of the metaphor.

Figure 1 illustrates the lifecycle of one metaphor. When the metaphorical expression is interpreted for the first time and given metaphorical meaning, the metaphor is born. It activates the interpreter (for instance, the user of an information system) and causes strong insight into the key properties of the target domain. After this interpretation process the metaphorical power is at its strongest. Gradually, the strong first impression caused by insight experience fades out. Finally, there is no more need for this kind of experience, and the whole expression moves to the lexicon of everyday expressions. The metaphorical power is worn out and the expression has become an idiom.

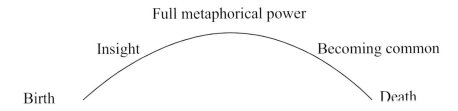

Full metaphorical power

Insight   Becoming common

Birth   Death

Fig. 1. A rough illustration of a lifecycle of a metaphor: The metaphorical power as a function of time

This description and related illustration (Figure 1) is, in most cases, certainly over-simplified. First, as the drawing illustrates the change of the metaphorical power as a function of time, the curve in the drawing means that the time required for the insight is about the same as the length of time of the gradual transformation to idiom. These are phenomena that are probably impossible to measure, but with common sense we can infer that the insight may be (and usually is) very rapid, and that the death probably takes rather a long time. Therefore, the shape of the curve in Figure 2 illustrates, probably better than the one in Figure 1, an average metaphor lifecycle. *At this point, when starting to elaborate upon the curves in more detail, it is important to stress that the purpose of these curves is not to support any empirical findings but to illustrate the relationships among the analysed concepts.*

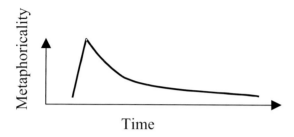

Fig. 2. A credible lifecycle curve

However, even the curve in Figure 2 shouldn't be seen as a general or average lifecycle of a metaphor. A curve of this kind presupposes first of all a skilfully prepared, even ingenious design of a metaphor (metaphorical expression). So it has to support insights, and become an integral part of the interpreter's knowledge structures so that it can be gradually disconnected from its source. Second, this kind of curve makes sense only if the metaphor is in rather regular use. If not, it is possible that the meaning of metaphorical expression is more or less forgotten and there is once again a use for its metaphorical nature. Figure 3 illustrates this kind of situation. In this fictitious case, the marked points in the time axis refer to the points of time when the metaphor is processed. In practice, the points could refer to the exposure to the metaphorical expression. The curve illustrates how the metaphor becomes mundane during the periods of regular use, but after periods of no use the metaphorical nature is of use once again. In this case, three periods of regular use have been adequate to turn the metaphor into an idiom.

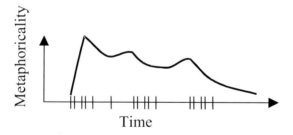

Fig. 3. Discontinuous decrease of metaphorical power

It is essential to understand that in the previous illustrations the value indicates metaphorical power or, to be more exact in the use of chosen concepts, the degree of metaphorical value of the expression. So it does not indicate the overall communicative value. The descending shapes of the curves might be misleading in this sense. We should keep in mind that the degree of idiomaticalness increases along with the decrease of metaphoricalness. As the degree of metaphoricalness is in inverse relation to the degree of idiomaticalness, the combined communicative value of metaphorical and idiomatical nature remains relatively stable ("Sum value" in Figure 4). In the interpretation of Figure 4 it has to be noted that the Idiomaticalness-curve only starts from the point of insight (peak in the Metaphoricalness-curve). That is because there is no sense making assessments about the idiomatic nature of a concept before an initial concept exists.

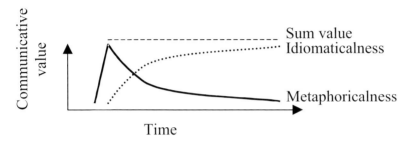

Fig. 4. The dynamics of overall communicative value

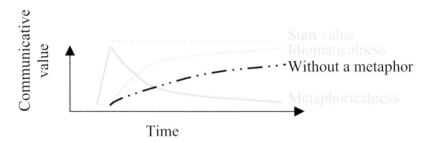

Fig. 5. Communicative value without a metaphorical expression

Figure 4 may raise a new question: why use metaphors, if the overall communicative value remains at a high level regardless of whether the value is mainly caused by the metaphorical or idiomatic nature of the concept at a certain point of time? The answer is illustrated in Figure 5. As can be seen, the overall communicative value ("Sum value" in Figure 4 and Figure 5) does not stay at a high level just like that. The message of the illustration is that this high level of communicative value results from a skilful support of metaphor construction. In Figure 5 we can see a curve that illustrates the conceptualisation process without the support. Most probably, after a prolonged use, this concept has been adopted (or, more precisely expressed, "fully constructed") and the communicative value is at a high level. The construction of the concept might still be highly metaphorical. However, if there is no explicit support for metaphor construction, the first attempts may lead to irrelevant direction. In other words, the metaphor might be chosen on an irrelevant basis; or using Richards' (1950) terminology, the *ground* of the metaphor is irrelevant. Testing the relevancy of the metaphor candidate might take a lot of time and resources, resulting in a delay in the effective use of the concept. Gradually, when using the concept in appropriate context, a more or less relevant metaphor might be found and it then turns into an idiom in time. On the contrary, if support is provided for the metaphor creation, high communicative value is reached rapidly. This value is first constituted mainly by metaphor, but later is more the result of its idiomatic quality.

The very basic idea of creating a metaphor is to parallel the unknown with the known. Thus it could be argued that it would be better to let the user freely create the metaphor, without trying to evoke certain kinds of associations, as the designer can hardly ever be aware of the user's life in any real depth. In other words, the designer does not know what kind of metaphor would speak most to the user. However, it is the designer if anyone who understands the nature of the concept she has created. Therefore, detailed knowledge about the nature of the concept to be introduced is probably a more fruitful basis for assessing the need for metaphoric support than detailed information about the life of each potential user. Knowledge about the users could be handled at a cultural level instead and then only experiences that are assumed to be shared within a certain culture should be taken into account.

It is important to discuss the communicative value of an expression as a whole. Otherwise, focusing solely on the metaphorical nature, the lifecycle with its end in "death", might evoke irrelevant connotations. Actually, even the (highly metaphorical) word choice "death" is not necessarily ideal. I would prefer to talk about a *maturation* of a metaphor. The death of a metaphor could best be compared to the growth of human being from childhood to adulthood. Becoming grown up could be characterised as the death of childhood. Childhood is a unique, valuable and essential part of the human lifecycle but all parents are waiting for their children to grow and they carefully follow all the little steps in that process. Finally, it might be even plaintive to notice that the baby is an independent adult, but still the parents understand that this is what was to happen anyway and what they wished. Likewise, it is very natural that the delight for gaining an insight of a metaphor is fading out and the "tenor" (Richards 1950) of a metaphor mature to a basic element of the user's conceptual system.

2.2.2 Metaphors of culture and individual

The cases of the metaphor lifecycle described earlier concern setting, in which a person faces a new entity and is actively seeking a way of connecting it with the existing mental structures. In this process, the person creates a metaphor that helps to understand some key properties of the new entity. However, there are cases in which this kind of process cannot be possible. One example of a metaphor that cannot be explained this way is an ordinary light switch. It is a technical device that is very much a part of our everyday life. There can hardly be in the industrialised world someone who doesn't take a light switch beside a door as given or "natural" design. But when discussing the logic of switch functions, we find that the standard UI has no basis in the "natural" behaviour of human beings. Presumably when oil and gas lamps were changed to light bulbs with switches, there was a metaphor (or metaphors) on which the UI of the switch as we know it today was based. Still, nobody remembers the first time using this simple but ingenius tiny gadget. This is because we all learned to know about light switches at an age from which we do not have clear memories. Even if we had memories from this time, the process of learning to use the switch would hardly have been similar to the one of our ancestors when they changed from their familiar oil lamps to its electrical successor: little baby does not have the same kind of conceptual system as we grownups have. In other words, for us, a light switch has been an integral part of our everyday life for as long as we can remember. We were born in the middle of a culture that contains light switches. In the same way that we do not wonder why we sit on chairs in front of a table and not on the floor when eating, we do not wonder why the light switch is just beside the door and why that switch has to be pushed.

A light switch is thus based on metaphor, but for us all it is an idiom. This kind of entity, which has been introduced for the whole society and has gradually become a mundane concept for everyone, I call a cultural metaphor. Its lifecycle has to be contemplated from a broader perspective and across a longer time span than the lifecycle of a metaphor in the mental structures of an individual.

3 Metaphors in a sample design: Utilising the theoretical framework when analysing the design process of a portable music player

In this chapter, we describe the design process of an application, in which it is possible to evaluate the applicability of metaphor theories in design. We implemented two prototypes of portable music players, on an iPaq hand-held computer. The original idea was to find interaction techniques that would be useful in mobile environments. We ended up by using simple gestures across the touch screen of the iPaq as the input method and providing feedback in the form of non-speech stereophonic sounds, earcons, following systematic guidelines (Brewster et al. 1995). This was because these could be used on the move, without looking at the device. Gaze was thus released for other use. The reasons for choosing a portable music player as the application were that

1. It could be used with a small number of commands. The number of simple gestures on the touch-screen that could be reliably distinguished from each other is rather small, and
2. A concept of a portable music player and its standard functions could be assumed to be familiar to most of the potential users. Thus, the mental representations could be assumed to be based on previous experience of similar devices. These assumed representations could be used as one of the determinants of the design.

Our ideas and implementations of the interaction techniques first took a form of TouchPlayer. On the basis of evaluations a new design, GestureJukeBox, was implemented. These two prototypes and their different versions illustrate how the concept of metaphor can be used when analysing design and user behaviour.

3.1 Basic functions

3.1.1 Controlling gestures

The basic functions of both TouchPlayer and GestureJukeBox were: play/stop, next/previous track and volume up/down. In addition, GestureJukeBox had separate functions for going to the first and the last track. Gestures were made by the user moving a finger across the screen (instead of the stylus). We could then recognise our gestures in the same way as normal stylus interactions on the screen. After initial design discussions we decided upon the gestures that can be seen in Table 1.

Table 1. Basic functions and related gestures.

Function	TouchPlayer	GestureJukeBox
Next track	Sweep across screen left -> right	Sweep across screen left -> right
Previous track	Sweep across screen right -> left	Sweep across screen right -> left
Play / Stop	Single tap	Double tap
Volume up	Sweep from bottom -> top of screen	Circular gesture clockwise
Volume down	Sweep from top -> bottom of screen	Circular gesture anti-clockwise
Last track	-	Sweep left -> right + tap
First track	-	Sweep right -> left + tap

Some of the gestures of TouchPlayer are illustrated in Figure 6. As can be seen, the key metaphors used in our application were related to the parallel between physical directions and logical order.

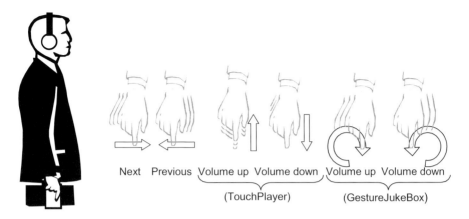

Next   Previous   Volume up Volume down   Volume up Volume down

(TouchPlayer)   (GestureJukeBox)

Fig. 6. Directions of some control gestures

3.1.2 Feedback sounds

We used feedback sounds to confirm the recognition of a gesture. The sounds used were earcons (Blattner et al. 1989; Brewster et al. 1993) as these have been shown to be effective in improving the usability of mobile devices (Brewster and Cryer 1999). It was important to provide feedback on the gestures as users would not see anything but would still need to know the state of the device.

The design of the feedback sounds was supposed to illustrate each function. Since the device was intended to be used with headphones and it supported stereo sounds, there were several ways of providing information in an audio format at our disposal. In this chapter we concentrate upon pitch and location, since the usage of these properties in our sample designs has clear connections to metaphors.

The play and stop sounds were both very short and simple in accordance with the related gesture – single or double tap – thus illustrating a very basic idea.

The logical directions of the playlist were linked in the feedback sounds to conform to the Western left-to-right writing system: Functions that shifted the pointer of the playlist backwards (to "previous track" and in GestureJukeBox, also to "first track") had feedback sounds from the left channel, and the functions relating to forward direction had sounds from the right. Apart from conforming to writing directions, this design was seen to accord with the standard control panel of almost any music player. The play/stop-feedback sound was in the middle.

The pitch – or more precisely the change in the pitch – of the feedback sound was logically linked to the directions in the playlist: forward direction corresponded to an increasing pitch and backward direction to a decreasing pitch in both sample designs.

We did not give any explicit audio feedback for volume changes, as the change in the volume of the music playing would indicate this change implicitly. However, in GestureJukeBox, there was a separate feedback sound to illustrate the change of the volume adjustment when the music was not playing.

3.2 Analysis of the metaphors

Next/previous. The idea of this design was to parallel logical directions in the playlist with physical directions of the user on the move: going forward in the playlist was performed by a sweep forward. Respectively, a sweep backwards shifted the pointer one step backwards in the playlist. This parallel was assumed to be intuitive. Also, from the point of view of metaphor theories, this control can be argued to be a real, strong metaphor when paralleling the new (browsing the playlist with sweeps) with the familiar. The familiar thing in this case was the universal convention of understanding the front and back of human being: what is in front of your sight when your head is not turned, is *in front of* you. The space in the opposite direction is *behind* you. Also, the natural direction of walking or running is to go in the direction of your sight, thus the understanding of going forward and backwards have an extremely sound basis in our natural behaviour.

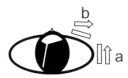

Fig. 7. The change of directional "forward" metaphor in the change of fixing point

Even if our assumptions concerning the directions felt obvious, a couple of things are worth noticing. First, we found out that the location of the fixing point of the device was critical in terms of the directional metaphor. In order to parallel physical and logical forward-backward directions, the sweep has to happen in a back-front direction. Thus the device has to be fixed on the side of the user (case "a" in Figure 7). In practice, a side fixing point depends very much on the clothing of the user. Concerning the height, the best point is a typical trousers pocket. In ordinary jeans the edge of the pocket meets the side seam of the jeans in a relatively horizontal position, offering a natural point to hang up the device (Figure 8) so that it is clearly on the side of the user ("a" in Figure 7). However, if the device is fixed merely in front (case "b", Figure 7), which is possible on a jeans pocket, the directional metaphor loses its ground. In this case, the most likely association of directions is related to writing directions, in which forward means from left to right. As can be seen in Figure 7, case "b", this conflicts with the directions in case "a".

Fig. 8. Fixing in jeans

Another remark about directions popped up from the evaluation data. In the video-based evaluations of both TouchPlayer and GestureJukeBox we could observe that one participant (out of ten) in both evaluations obstinately tried to go forward in the playlist with sweeps backward. Neither of them could explain their exceptional behaviour. Whatever the reason, the metaphor created by these two participants must have been something different from the assumed one. It might have something to do with some human ways of moving forward. A swimmer, for

Fig. 9. Mixing desk

example, pushes the water backwards in order to get forward. Also, a skier pushes backwards with sticks when striving forwards.

Volume up/down. As illustrated in Figure 6, the volume control gestures were vertical sweeps. The initial idea was to parallel an increase in volume to a sweep upward (and a decrease in volume to a sweep downwards, respectively). In our theoretical framework, this kind of design meant associating physical vertical directions with intensity. Since these two, physical directions and intensity, do not have any obvious connection, the connection can be described as metaphorical. However, we found another possible interpretation of the connection between the directions and intensity: In a mixing desk (Figure 9), volume is increased by pushing the fader away, decreased by pulling it back. If a user would associate vertical sweeps with this kind of fader, the directions should be reversed to the directions of the up/down metaphor: when pushing the imaginary fader away from you (providing that the device is hanging on your side), you actually sweep downwards when increasing volume. Whether the users' first idea would be the up/down metaphor or a fader, could only be found out with a user test. We carried out an initial think aloud trial with seven users to investigate all the gestures developed. We gave the users sets of gestures to perform and recorded the correctness of the gestures made. We then interviewed them to see what they felt about the gestures and if they were appropriate. Users performed the gestures well with very few instances of mistakes. The users rated the gestures as very natural and none felt that the "push" gesture was appropriate for volume increase. Thus, at least in this case, a clearly metaphorical design was much stronger than a simulation of a fader. This case and the differences between a metaphor and simulation, reveals one of the central problems of simulations: a virtual fader can never compete with a real one. It is really only a substitute. An imaginary fader lacks almost all the essential physical properties of a real fader. In particular, the lack of tactile contact with the knob, the position of which indicates the current intensity, makes the virtual fader a poor substitute for a real controller.

The initial idea was to enable the user to adjust with a one single vertical sweep the volume in any level between full and zero. However, because of the small size of the touch-screen, it proved very difficult to fine adjust the volume in this way. Therefore in the final design, each vertical sweep only caused a small adjustment in the volume level. Larger adjustments required several sweeps. This was possible since we had already decided to count on the up/down metaphor; if we had gone for a fader simulation, the idea of several sweeps would have been inappropriate.

Play/Stop. In the design of TouchPlayer, play and stop functions were performed with the same gesture, a single tap on the touch-screen. This accords with the convention of most music players, since they usually have one single button for these two functions. So when music is playing, the function is stop and when the music is stopped the function is play. This control does not provide that clear basis for analysing the underpinning metaphors. Single tap might be associated with pushing a button as well as a mouse click, for instance. Both of these alternatives could only be seen as simulations. However, since there surely is metaphorical meaning behind a mouse click and pushing a button, discussion of these would lead us away from the current design. Furthermore, these gestures and the possible underlying metaphors do not have their basis in directions such as playlist browsing and volume controls. Therefore, we leave a more detailed analysis of these functions for future discussion elsewhere.

4. What did we learn?

In his keynote speech in APCHI'98 conference Alan C. Kay (1998) demonstrated just what an immature feature of our culture computer applications are. He wondered how is it possible that after 50 years of commercial computing, we are still imitating paper culture. He also showed a number of videos from the late sixties; the films were about the computer applications of that time. Kay argued that nothing really new has happened in the basic use of a computer since then. The basic ideas and concepts of human-computer interaction in, for example, word processing, vector graphics and video conferencing have remained the same.

Certainly, something has happened since the sixties. But the change mainly concerns quantity; the number of computers is obviously something that has increased compared to 40 years ago, so has the number of users and application areas. These changes have had a well-documented effect on the whole of Western culture. But the ways we interact with computers have not changed in relation to the growth of the computational power of processors. In other words, we have not been able to utilise the increase of computational power in interaction design.

It is typical human behaviour to cling to the familiar and the safe. However, the continuous search for stability often prevents us from finding innovative creative solutions. In the worst case, unimaginative imitation of the safe and familiar leads to regression. For example, when the command line interface forced a rethink of the structure and nature of many applications, there was an opportunity to start to design many practices from the very beginning, having only the task, user and computational power. But what happened: in windows-style GUIs many UI-elements proved to be clumsy imitations of the technology that we had before microprocessors. Instead of utilising the new situation and designing interaction in terms of the actual task, we accepted simulations that inevitably brought along the limitations of ancient technology.

I'll give two familiar examples of an approach in which contemporary technology has been harnessed to imitate old practices. These old practices originally got their form mainly due to technical limitations. Now those constraints are transferred to the new technological environment, sometimes in the name of metaphor.

The first, obvious, example concerns word processing. It is clear that a mechanical typewriter is the primary predecessor of word processing. If there hadn't been a mechanical typewriter as a model for the keyboard and GUI of a typical word processor, we would hardly have, for example, this "QWERTY"-order of keys.

The other cautionary example is the typical educational usage of video-conferencing systems. The old technology for presenting information to a large number of students at the same time was a lecture hall. The strength of that technology was that a skilful lecturer had a rich variety of presentation modalities in use (voice, body language, blackboard etc.), which made it possible to create an impressive presentation. The central limitation of that technology was, especially when the number of students was large, that the opportunities for true interaction between a teacher and a student were limited. Now we have transferred the same educational setting to the Internet and implemented it with a video conferencing application. The result was that we failed to bring anything essentially new to the teaching act – above all, the communication remained relatively unidirectional. The quality of presentation worsened compared to a real lecture, due to the technical limitations of video and audio. The rationale was either that the new technology did not require the lecturer and students to be in the same physical location, thus enabling distance education, or that the number of students was not restricted by the size of a lecture hall. In other words, from the point of view of supporting the learning process of an individual student, the quality was worsened but the quantity was raised – a typical phenomenon from industrial automatization: skilful handicraftsman is replaced with a machine with a cost to the quality, in the name of profitability.

I argue that the main reason for continuing to use past practices and forms instead of creating new forms is not due to the use of metaphors in GUIs. On the contrary, the reason could be said to be that metaphors are hardly used at all! I strongly disagree with Nelson (1994) in that metaphors are one cause of poor design. He even defines metaphor (p. 236) in a way that shows that his conception has nothing to do with metaphors. In the same volume Kay (1994) also attacks the use of metaphors in design. He proposes something he calls "user illusion" (p. 199) as a substitute for metaphors. On closer inspection, however, his ideas about this "user illusion" prove to be in accordance with the traditional view of the metaphor. In other words, he actually attacked "GUI metaphors" and proposed real metaphors instead. So the problem – at least in Kay's and Nelson's case – is not that metaphors were out of date but that metaphors have been misunderstood in the context of GUI. If only we were able to articulate the nature of metaphor in terms of design, and then communicate it within the HCI community, we would have a powerful tool to use – much more powerful than the one that resulted in the virtual desktop.

Acknowledgements

Dedicated to the memory of Stuart Tasker, a talented computer science student, who was responsible for the implementation of GestureJukeBox. Thanks to Prof. Stephen Brewster for cooperation in all stages of the work and Chris Holguin for the implementation of TouchPlayer. I'm also grateful for the whole staff of the Department of Computing in Glasgow University for providing a friendly and inspiring research environment.

References

Aristotle (1984) The Complete Works of Aristotle: The Revised Oxford Translation / ed by Jonathan Barnes, 1 ed, vol 2. Princeton University Press, Princeton, NJ

Black M (1962) Models and Metaphors. Cornell University Press, New York

Blattner M, Sumikawa D, Greenberg R (1989) Earcons and icons: Their structure and common design principles. Human Computer Interaction 4(1):11-44

Brewster SA, Cryer PG (1999) Maximising screen-space on mobile computing devices. Summary Proceedings of ACM CHI'99 (Pittsburgh, PA). ACM Press, pp 224-225

Brewster SA, Wright P, Edwards ADN (1993) An evaluation of earcons for use in auditory human-computer interfaces. Proceedings of ACM/IFIP INTERCHI'93 (Amsterdam, Holland). Addison-Wesley, Reading, MA, pp 222-227

Brewster SA, Wright P, Edwards ADN (1995) Experimentally derived guidelines for the creation of earcons. Adjunct Proceedings of HCI'95, Huddersfield, UK, pp 155-159

Carroll JM, Mack RL (1985) Metaphor, computing systems, and active learning. International Journal of Man-Machine Studies 22(1):39-57

Cooper DE (1986) Metaphor. Billing & Sons, Worcester

Fraser B (1993) Interpretation of novel metaphors. In: Ortony A (ed) Metaphor and Thought, 2nd ed. Cambridge University Press, Cambridge, pp 329-341

Gentner D, Nielsen J (1996) The anti-mac interface. Communications of the ACM 39(8):70-82

Gibbs RWJ (1993) Making sense of tropes. In: Ortony A (ed) Metaphor and Thought, 2nd ed. Cambridge University Press, Cambridge, pp 252-276

Hamilton A (2000) Metaphor in theory and practice: the influence of metaphors on expectations. ACM Journal of Computer Documentation 24(4):237-253

Harrison BL, Fishkin KP, Gujar A, Mochon C, Want R (1998) Squeeze me, hold me, tilt me! An exploration of manipulative user interfaces. CHI'98, Conference Proceedings on Human Factors in Computing Systems. ACM Press Addison-Wesley, Los Angeles, CA, pp 17-24

Johnson J (1987) How faithfully should the electronic office simulate the real one? SIGCHI Bulletin 19(2):21-25

Kay AC (1994) User interface: a personal view. In: Laurel B (ed) The Art of Human-Computer Interface Design. Addison Wesley, Reading, MA, pp 191-207

Kay AC (1998) The computer revolution hasn't happened yet. In: Werner B (ed) APCHI 98. IEEE, Los Alamitos, CA, p xviii

Lakoff G (1993) The contemporary theory of metaphor. In: Ortony A (ed) Metaphor and Thought, 2nd ed. Cambridge University Press, Cambridge, pp 202-251

Lakoff G, Johnson M (1980) Metaphors We Live by. The University of Chicago Press, Chicago

Lakoff G, Johnson M (1999) Philosophy in the Flesh: The Embodied Mind and Its Challenge to Western Thought. Basic Books, New York

Nardi BA, Zarmer CL (1993) Beyond models and metaphors: Visual formalisms in user interface design. Journal of Visual Languages and Computing 4:5-33

Nelson TH (1994) The right way to think about software design. In: Laurel B (ed) The Art of Human-Computer Interface Design. Addison Wesley, Reading, MA, pp 235-243

Richards IA (1950) The Philosophy of Rhetoric, 2nd ed. Oxford University Press, New York

Searle JR (1993) Metaphor. In: Ortony A (ed) Metaphor and Thought, 2nd ed. Cambridge University Press, Cambridge, pp 83-111

Designing ubiquitous computer-human interaction: The case of the connected family

Panos Markopoulos

Technische Universiteit Eindhoven
The Netherlands
p.markopoulos@tue.nl

Abstract

The forecast advent of ubiquitous computing promises to bring about a radical shift in our way of interacting with computing systems. It is expected that people will interact continuously with computation, in an ever-increasing range of forms, situations and locations. Current user-centred design methodology is severely stretched when applied to this new context. This chapter discusses the nature of ubiquitous computer-human interaction and proposes a set of five design principles that can inform some of the choices interaction designers need to make when shaping the human experience of a ubiquitous computing environment. We discuss these principles in the context of designing for the connected family: how to support communication within families and across generations. We describe some lessons from our research in designing for enhanced social communication between family members and some of the research challenges ahead.

1 The nature of interaction with ubiquitous computing environments

The research vision of ubiquitous computing (*ubicomp*) is expected to materialise in the form of products and services in the marketplace gradually, perhaps between four to six years from now (Lyytinen and Yoo 2002). Major technology manufacturers and research institutes have put forward their own relevant research visions and roadmaps. Such visions are *Ambient Intelligence* (Philips), *Pervasive Computing* (IBM) and *Cooltown* (Hewlett Packard) to name a few. Important nuances distinguish these visions that should be influential in shaping the interactive experiences of their users. On the other hand, they all share an impetus towards embedding computation in our social and physical interactions making it an inseparable part of our daily life.

For the field of human-computer interaction it is a serious challenge to foresee problems and solutions for a situation that does not yet exist. Currently only modest scale demonstrators of ubiquitous computing technologies exist. This limitation of scale hampers our ability to predict and understand the nature of interaction with ubicomp systems, because the scaling up of human-computer interaction is a quintessential characteristic of ubicomp (Abowd and Mynatt 2000). This scaling up may concern the number of devices deployed and used, the duration of interaction and the range of places where ubicomp is used. Some of the reasons for which ubiquitous computer-human interaction (*ubichi*) differs from traditional computer-human interaction are discussed briefly in the paragraphs that follow.

1.1 Ubichi is immersive, potentially continuous and prolonged

By its nature, ubicomp technology will alter the places where it is deployed. Rather than facing an interface through a screen, people will be expected to populate ubicomp environments, reside in them, work within their physical and functional boundaries or simply pass through these boundaries. As a consequence, ubichi departs from traditional patterns of interaction in what one could call their respective "rules of engagement". In current user interfaces, interaction is intermittent, it starts, suspends or resumes, as and when the user decides; that is, if the user provides input and consumes output, then interaction is taking place. Even in the case of process control where computational processes do not stop, users interact with the system intermittently. In contrast, ubichi may be continuous and implicit. Simply entering an ubicomp environment may mean interacting with it without necessarily having or expressing such intent. Suspension and resumption of interaction with the environment can be, potentially, outside the control of the user. An important dimension of designing ubichi is designing these rules of engagement: Compared to conventional interaction more options are available and deciding how much control to provide to the users becomes even more critical for the acceptance of a system. Too much control, and the user can be occupied all too often by negotiations with an intrusive system. Too little control and the user may be threatened by a system that takes too much initiative and threatens his privacy. An important concept relating to achieving the "right" balance between control and automation has been encapsulated by the notion of calmness (Weiser and Brown 1996). Calmness requires that users should be empowered without being overwhelmed with information and control tasks. It amounts to enhancing people's peripheral reach by enabling information, which is outside one's current focus of attention, to be perceived and interpreted by preattentive processes and to be summoned to the foreground of attention with great ease.

1.2 Ubichi bridges the real and the virtual world

A critical component of ubicomp is that computation should embed itself in our physical world (Weiser 1991). As a result physical objects acquire digital manifestations when electronics and computation are added to them. An example is the "media cup" prototype (Beigl et al. 2001). This cup can sense when it is used (through temperature) and can communicate this to a system, which can thus speculate the sort of activity that is taking place (e.g., a coffee break). Conversely, virtual objects (e.g., information artefacts) acquire physical manifestations, as is the case with tangible user interfaces (Ullmer and Ishii 2000). The design of ubichi goes beyond the consideration of input and output tasks and their dependencies as it entails determining and communicating to people the physical boundaries of places, where different social, organisational and technical contexts are relevant (Kindberg and Fox 2002).

New interactive technologies need to be developed to bridge the two worlds. Such technologies may concern the means for supporting users to interact with a ubicomp environment, as, for example, the World cursor project from Microsoft (Wilson and Pham 2003).

Bridging physical and virtual worlds brings about hard pragmatic concerns from engineering and interaction design perspectives. The fact that ubicomp needs to blend in with physical spaces may entail new, open and extensible ways of configuring systems. For example, while a current desktop computer may have a lifetime of three to five years in a modern office environment, technology that becomes embedded in buildings should have a considerably longer lifespan, should be extensible to allow new functionality or new system components to be added and should allow easy integration with existing systems, some of which will be adapted to the environment or even personalised to the current users. As the ubicomp vision will gradually materialise, the onus of configuring systems and combining different ubicomp system components is passed on to the end-user. Further, bridging the real and virtual worlds means that interaction design practice will increasingly overlap with product design and architectural design.

1.3 Ubichi is social

As many people use, inhabit or pass through the same physical space, they need to coordinate their activities and share resources. Ubicomp environments may facilitate, mediate or even interfere with social interactions that occur within their boundaries.

Access to a common communication and computational infrastructure enables interaction across physical boundaries as users share services. Traditional implications for connecting people to a network (e.g., Metcalf's law) will arise also in the context of ubicomp. The value of a ubicomp system may depend on the reachability of one's social network through this system. Conversely, if a person lets the system monitor her activities and her whereabouts, or share her opinions about content consumed, the system itself acquires more value for this person's social network. The perceived usefulness of a ubicomp system may eventually depend on the content users are willing to provide and the degree to which they embed it into their current social interactions. Looking at ubicomp in this way means that it is a scaled-up development of groupware. Most challenges for groupware design (Grudin 1994) apply also to the design of the ubiquitous computing environment: disparity of work and benefits, reaching a critical mass of users, possible disruption of extant social processes etc. Where traditional groupware supports work activities, ubicomp may be deployed to serve needs, practices and rituals of social life and leisure activities. In this domain it is even more critical and challenging to balance effort with benefits and to reach a critical mass of users.

1.4 Ubichi is disparate

Research demonstrators for ubicomp give an indication of the variety of forms of interactive devices that might be involved: floors, cups, speech, gestures and door handles have been shown to be viable means of interacting with computing systems. The ubichi designer cannot assume interaction through a standard and predetermined set of devices as is the case with graphical user interface design. The complete set of input/output devices that might be used to access a system is likely to be unknown to the designer of any individual application or service. This set of devices and services is likely to be numerous, diverse and expanding over time. Any environment may have its own legacy devices and applications. New devices and applications may need to be added to the system after its initial installation. Contrary to traditional interaction design, ubichi needs to become "open" in the sense that it should be designed to be extended and to be combined with other, initially unknown, forms of interaction.

The eventual form of the interactive experience will depend as much on any particular interactive product as upon the technological, social and the physical contexts in which this product will be experienced. This implies an even more important role of context in designing and engineering interactive systems but also a need to ensure extendibility and adaptability to such contexts. This openness necessitates the ability for the users to extend and adapt system behaviour, combining different products and services (Newman et al. 2002). The high context dependency of the ubichi experience affects the way that such experiences should be tested. Usability of individual products and services will remain an important factor for their eventual acceptance and adoption. However, user testing should go beyond uncovering usability problems specific to the interaction between one user and a product under test. Such testing should examine the use of a single device or an application or a service as a constituent part of large arrays of devices and services, examining also the longer term impact upon the life of a person, his thoughts and emotions and upon his pattern of living (Abowd and Mynatt 2000).

2 Current thoughts for addressing the challenges of ubichi design

So far, we have examined ways in which ubichi is expected to differ from current human-computer interaction. This discussion is a continuing endeavour for ubicomp researchers, who have proposed several ways to address the challenges discussed so far. In this section we review some of these proposals and discuss their relations.

Although in some cases researchers seem to subscribe to a shared common vision, there appear to be two dimensions along which most approaches will differ:

- The universal information appliance versus the disappearing computer, and
- The intelligent and proactive system versus a collection of tools.

These concepts are discussed briefly in the following sections and are the basis for proposing some design principles that concern the form of the interaction and the methodology for understanding the user requirements for ubichi.

2.1 Information appliances: Universal or task specific?

Since the earliest writings on interaction with ubiquitous computing environments we can distinguish two apparently contrasting visions regarding the nature of the devices that will sit in the boundary between a user and a ubicomp system. These visions have co-existed, have competed but also have developed in tandem. The first vision has been most eloquently articulated by Mark Weiser in his seminal article in the *Scientific American* magazine (Weiser 1991), where he described the notion of "disappearance" for the computer and its embedding in humble objects of daily use. Donald Norman (1998) explored this vision of ubicomp further in his book *The Invisible Computer* where he elaborated on Weiser's concept of an information appliance. Norman defines an information appliance as a machine or tool adapted for a special purpose, that provides specialised access to information (as opposed to an embedded control device). Further, a distinguishing feature of information appliances is their ability to share information amongst themselves.

Purpose specificity and connectivity are essential to Norman's conception of information appliances. Purpose-specific appliances are gradually entering the marketplace, for example, electronic organisers, translating devices, GPS-based navigation aids, electronic books etc. This specificity of an information appliance is in stark contrast to the most generic of tools, the personal computer. Apart from the personal computer itself, the consumer electronics market is already populated by generic devices such as hand-held personal computers, smart phones etc., that can host a rich collection of applications. It appears that general-purpose devices have not yet had their day. Quite the opposite! MIT's influential Oxygen project (Dertouzos 1999) promotes the idea of the "Handy21", a hand-held, configurable, general-purpose device that can be transparently personalised to the user who will pick it up and provide access to a dynamic and extensible combination of applications and services.

The term "information appliance" has been used to refer to both these concepts; however, it seems that researchers are pursuing two radically different conceptions for the relationship between human and computer. The purpose-specific version aims for invisibility of the computer as they become so easy to use that people are no longer aware that they use them. The concept of a universal information appliance emphasises the notions of adaptivity and of access "anywhere, anytime".

Following the approach of the universal information appliance, hardware platforms will still exist in various forms, sizes and capabilities to fit the user and context of use but will also host applications that will mould themselves to the platform capabilities and adapt to person and context of use. The latter requirement for interactive software has been best encapsulated as the notion of plasticity of the user interface: the capacity of a multitarget user interface to preserve usability across targets and contexts of use (Calvary et al. 2001). Currently, the objective of a plastic user interface has not yet been attained. The state of the art concerns mostly retargeting user interfaces and migrating interaction dynamically from one platform to another.

The two concepts of a universal or a purpose-specific appliance have opposing philosophies but are not mutually exclusive. There are good reasons for users to carry general-purpose tools with them and to own general-purpose tools for the home such as the PC. It is also true that the expansion in the number of devices that are used will necessitate cognitive disappearance through the development of purpose-specific information appliances. In both cases the ultimate criterion for success shall be the extent to which a particular device, service or application becomes a useful element in the collection of devices used by people at any particular time and place.

2.2 Ubicomp environments: Butlers or tools?

Another dimension for characterising work in the domain of ubicomp is the intended social relationship between human and computational system. While Norman's view of the information appliance was that of a tool, elsewhere as for example, in the Ambient Intelligence vision or in the context of perceptual user interfaces (Pentland 2000), an important role is advocated for anticipating user needs through adaptivity and intelligence.

A traditional scenario for adaptivity has been that the system has the role of an old-fashioned butler: discreetly staying in the background anticipating user needs and taking initiative when appropriate. Alternatively when wearable devices are concerned the system turns into a personal assistant: "...like a person who travels with you, seeing and hearing everything you do, and trying to anticipate your needs and generally smooth your way" (Pentland 2000). These concepts of a butler or a personal assistant attempt to appease fears of an Orwellian Big Brother watching every move one makes.

However, the butler and the personal assistant are elusive targets because of their genericity. It is very hard for systems to provide meaningful and useful adaptivity for the range and complexity of contexts, social and physical, characterising our daily lives. The anticipation and the proactivity illustrated by the butler and the personal assistant may not be appropriate in all situations. Interpersonal relationships are characterised by a much richer variety of relationships: e.g., caregiver-patient, teacher-student, master-apprentice, etc. Such relationships are context specific and can inform the designer in choosing the extent of pro-activity and intelligence required by the system. Further, these relationships could be dynamic, evolving and negotiated as is done in human social interactions. It may be that ubicomp designers and developers need to seek a richer variety of metaphors for the relationship between human and computational environment that will encourage people to accept the role of intelligence and to shape their expectations from adaptive technologies.

The difference between viewing a computer as a tool or a butler pertains more to the desired role of computational intelligence and less to its technological feasibility. In his writings on calm computing Weiser (Weiser and Brown 1996) positioned himself on the tool-side, suggesting that ubiquitous computing can be achieved without intelligence but, rather, with the appropriate binding of computing to context and objects. Intelligence often involves a trade-off in reducing the complexity of a system at the cost of reduced control by the user. In most cases such loss of control is problematic and the deployment of intelligence has to be justified by the reduction in the complexity of people's tasks and by the perceived value that this intelligence offers to people. For example, tracking people's movements at their home only to save them the effort of flicking a light switch as they enter or exit a room, is not likely to be an acceptable use of machine perception.

2.3 Designing the ubiquitous computer-human interaction

Compared to the volume of writings on the technological developments relevant to ubicomp, there has been relatively little published to guide the design of the resulting user experiences. Perhaps this sparseness is because only concept demonstrators and experimental systems have been built of truly ubiquitous computing applications and services (with just a few possible exceptions). There is, as yet, no current user base and no significant body of design experience to which to refer.

Calmness and disappearance present a useful conceptual framework for the user-experience designer. These concepts have been well espoused by the research community, but the cases where researchers or designers could claim to achieve disappearance or calmness are few and far between.

Don Norman in his treatise on information appliances (Norman 1998) proposed three "axioms" for the design of information appliances, which are repeated in their short form below:

- Simplicity. The complexity of the appliance is that of the tool. The technology is invisible.
- Versatility. Information appliances are designed to allow and encourage novel creative interaction.
- Pleasurability. Products should be pleasurable, fun and enjoyable – a joy to use, a joy to own.

These axioms seem sound and relevant but do not yet address how designing ubiquitous interaction differs from standard interaction design. Simplicity has been considered a critical trait of good interface design since the earliest days of the field of human-computer interaction. For example, one of Nielsen's popular heuristics (Nielsen 1994) for user interface design promotes aesthetic and minimalist design and encourages designers to be parsimonious in the inclusion of information or features in the user interface. Simplicity and more recently the concept of *pleasurability* apply equally well to existing computing and consumer electronic devices (cf. Jordan 2000). Versatility as introduced by Norman is a property inherent in our personal computers, exactly the one that has enabled them to become so popular. A personal computer is a platform that lends itself to unexpected uses, a host for many applications and an access point for services not foreseen by its designers.

3 Designing for the connected family

The challenges for ubichi design have so far been discussed in the abstract outside the context of a particular application or human activity that ubicomp may support. In this section we discuss how these challenges manifested themselves in a series of design cases, that explored how ubicomp could be applied in a domestic and leisure context to support social communication within families. This choice of application domain reflects our intention to provide significant benefits to the user that will justify the adoption of the required innovations and the potential changes of lifestyle.

Social communication can be a major driver for technology adoption. E-mail, instant messaging, mobile telephony and short messaging services are examples of how the adoption of technology for social communication often surpasses the expectations of their inventors. Emigration and the high mobility of professionals are increasingly common in modern society, leading to people living far away from loved ones or being apart quite regularly and for prolonged periods of time. Such individuals may experience benefits from technologies designed to enhance social communication with their families. The elderly are a particularly relevant target group as they tend to live away from their children and social circles, at their own homes or in communities for the elderly.

prototypes, simple simulations or functional vertical prototypes) are created and field-tested in the intended context of use over a long period of time (much longer than a typical usability test in the laboratory). This way the critical question of how the technology under design could affect the daily life of its intended users can be more reliably addressed.

In this approach, diaries are an indispensable data collection method. Diaries traditionally allow the collection of information about the human activity studied at the place where this activity takes place and close in time to its occurrence. Data can be less vulnerable to recollection errors and can be rich in contextual details compared to an interview or a questionnaire-based survey. However, diary keeping can be irregular or erratic, or may encourage a dry and factual rather than reflective type of information to be solicited by the informants. For these reasons diaries are typically combined with interviews for collecting information outside the time-span of the diary keeping and for uncovering more covert feelings, thoughts and deeper explanations by informants. Van Vugt and Markopoulos (2003) report a combination of situated prototyping with diaries, which were triangulated with interviews (briefing and debriefing interviews) and logs of the prototype use. This triangulation is a necessary precaution for not missing important information about people's thoughts, emotions and attitudes that they might refrain to mention, and to check for potentially flawed diary keeping. In that study, a picture-based communication was completely simulated using a slide show, which would simulate the reception of "electronic postcards". Informants could get an impression of the nature of the communication and how they would themselves monitor the intended appliance for the reception of new items. In several cases, even though they realised the communication was "canned" rather than real (i.e., a prefabricated collection of items was shown), informants reported feelings of satisfaction and of closeness to the sender.

Another study combining diaries with photo projects and situated prototyping is reported by Markopoulos et al. (2003). In order to explore how the elderly might be supported in communicating with their grandchildren more often, a hypothetical system to support this communication was first simulated with a cardboard pin-board. Participants, both elderly and children, were given lightweight digital cameras with which they could capture images from the day they wanted to share with the other. As often as they could, they would post handwritten messages on the paper pin-board. In each of these situations they would update a diary where they were requested to describe their feelings, their motivation for this communication. Researchers uploaded the pictures captured during the day and effected the exchange of messages and pictures by e-mail. A critical component of the design concept was that the facial expression of someone receiving a message should be automatically recorded and provided as feedback to the sender of the message. This technically challenging functionality was easy to simulate in this setting, with the experimenters taking a picture of the receiver's reaction and sending it back to the sender of the original picture. This study lasted two weeks, giving a good account of the sort of communication that might take place, the motivation for both parties to communicate and the value associated with both. An important element of such prototype testing is the "staging" of the intended experience that the experimenters must create.

The diaries were designed to set the tone of the reporting needed. Rather than having a list of questions that informants should answer, prompts were inserted in the margins to set a direction and a tone for the type of information that was sought. This contrasts cultural probes where the intentions and interest of the researcher are not so clearly communicated to the informant.

Diaries were given to both elderly and children. They were designed carefully and crafted to fit the desired tone of the dialogue between the researchers and each age group; for example, the diary designed for the children had a humourous picture of an adult on the cover and required less information to be recorded. This attention to the visual design of the diary itself is a lesson learnt from the cultural probes technique. Elderly informants turned out to be very thorough diary keepers and sometimes very reflective authors, a pattern that we found in subsequent studies as well. They were able to answer very direct questions about their emotional needs and their experiences from visits and communication.

It is useful here to contrast Cultural Probes and diaries as methods for understanding user needs. The former is a useful tool for inspiration, a means for embodying interaction between designer and informant. This communication succeeds if the values, the taste and the preferences of the informant are conveyed to the designer and if the latter manages to acquire empathy for the end-user and inspiration for design solutions. The diary is a data collection technique: it succeeds if it gives accurate, dense and context-sensitive data that has high face validity. Nevertheless the description above shows that the borders between the two are blurred: diaries may require the informant or the researcher to become creative and they also may focus on an in-depth understanding of smaller numbers of informants rather than gathering data amenable to statistical analysis.

So far, numerous diary studies of communication needs between family members have been conducted. We have explored the elderly living alone, grandparents and grandchildren, three-generation families, parents and adult children living in different countries and close friends living apart. These studies confirm the salience of the need to stay in touch with close friends and family and that this need is not sufficiently served by current technologies. Ultra-low effort asynchronous communication with images and short messages seems to emerge as a plausible complement to actual visits and telephone communication. This emerging class of systems and services helps satisfy the emotional need to be aware of the activities and daily lives of dear individuals, while circumventing some of the difficulties of timing the communication in a way to fit the differing daily routines of the people connected. Relevant communication appliances are required to fit practically, socially and aesthetically in a particular "place" reserved for communication in a home (see Markopoulos et al. 2003).

Fig. 1. The diary covers (above) for the children and for the elderly, aimed to set a relaxed and playful tone in the communication with the informants. Below, a page filled by a twelve-year-old subject, showing the prompts in the margins. In her text she describes a soccer game with her friends and the picture she took to send to her grandparents.

3.2 Designing an information appliance for intrafamily messaging

From studies such as those mentioned above, we have seen that intrafamily communication differs from other communication activities in several ways. It has a very high emotional value. In a recent study of intrafamily communication of three-generation families spread across two households in the Netherlands (cf. Romero et al. 2003), such communications represented roughly half of our informants' communication activities. Communications can be very frequent and very regular, with lots of short communication acts being used for coordination on a daily basis and longer telephone calls, helping people stay in touch and be reassured of the well being of their loved ones.

The FRIDGE prototype (Vroubel et al. 2001) was designed as an exploration into the concept of information appliances for the home environment. FRIDGE was intended as an information appliance for intrafamily messaging. FRIDGE is an augmented reality prototype supporting interaction with a projected display in the genre of systems that followed Xerox's Digital Desk (Wellner 1993). The mail facility is a very limited electronic mail application. The intention has been to make electronic mailing and message posting easily accessible in situations where, normally, it would not be: for example, replying to a message that arrives while cooking, or a enabling a child, too young to read and write, to send a drawing to grandparents.

The experience of designing FRIDGE illustrated two issues for designing ubicomp: one is the limitations of evaluation in a laboratory setting and the second is how taking the "tool" approach to designing information appliances necessitates the definition of purpose-specific interaction styles. The term interaction style is used here as a combination of:

Input devices (e.g., tangible input devices, mouse, keyboard, etc.),

Output devices (e.g., projected image, audio, etc.),

Interaction structure (e.g., choice, selection, etc.), and

Context: user(s), physical and social environment, platform constraints.

For example, consider the task of selecting a date for an appointment. In current graphical user interfaces, this task can be supported by drop-down menus (interaction structure) that are operated with a mouse or a stylus (input devices), on a desktop screen or on a hand-held display (output devices). The context may be the physical and social environment where we expect this device to be used; for example, the hand-held computer may be used on the bus or a touch-screen may be mounted on the fridgedoor and used in the kitchen.

Fig. 2. Interacting with the FRIDGE prototype in a laboratory: manipulating electronic notes with a tangible user interface and using an electronic stylus strictly as a pen

To address the challenges of ubichi, purpose-specific interaction styles need to be developed, where hardware and software and the product form of the appliance need to be designed in tandem. While the functional requirements from an intra-family messaging system may be much simpler than those of a generic electronic agenda or mail client (e.g., less need for address books, shared agenda, etc.), the interaction requirements tend to be very idiosyncratic for this context of use: traditional keyboard and mouse solutions would not work, the display is likely not to be put horizontally on a kitchen surface etc.

FRIDGE was designed to support freehand pen-input with no handwriting recognition, which is combined with a tangible user interface (Ullmer and Ishii 2000). Having two input techniques helps avoid overloading a single device, so it is easier to guess and to remember how to use the system: the pen is not seen as a general-purpose pointing device, but is used only for writing or drawing.

Pen-input for writing and drawing is arguably a very natural form of interaction. Excluding handwriting recognition is essential to preserve the naturalness of pen-input: first, with physical pens there is no recognition going on, and second, with handwriting recognition technology the user is required to monitor and correct the recognition process. Notes in FRIDGE behave like paper-slips in several ways. They are not resizable and scrollable, they cannot be "minimised" but they can be moved, rotated and stacked. Unlike files on a desktop, notes are not grouped in folders, backed up or recycled. Thus, it was hoped, a simple conceptual model of the interaction should result.

3.3 Evaluating ubichi

The second lesson drawn from the FRIDGE design case concerned the limitations of user testing in the laboratory. Field testing was difficult with FRIDGE. Performance limitations that are usually accepted in the laboratory are unacceptable in a realistic context. For example, the FRIDGE prototype was very sensitive to variations in lighting and was very noisy. A major limitation for the purpose of assessing the intended user experience was that evaluation participants who were asked to assess the usefulness of this concept and how they would use it, had to project from a usage experience in the laboratory to their daily habits. Very likely, the subjects would have different reactions had the testing been done at their homes, or in a situation closely resembling their everyday lives. To test the fit of this information appliance to their daily lives, its use should be embedded with current communication patterns of people, integrating it with existing communication systems and other messaging facilities. For example, our test participants expected to access messages sent to their FRIDGE through other mail and messaging applications.

In summary, context appropriateness does not only pertain to resolving technical constraints. It is very difficult to anticipate the user experience based on what can be enacted in a laboratory-based evaluation or from interviews. As suggested by Davies and Gellersen (2002), understanding how new artefacts can be used requires realistic and serious deployment. Fitness for context therefore, needs to be resolved from the stage of user needs analysis. Even more important, it must be reflected in the set-up of the evaluation procedure that needs to be sensitive to the intended context of use.

Usability testing in the traditional way, as was done for the FRIDGE prototype, is a necessary but insufficient criterion for assessing the quality of a design. In a more recent project called ASTRA (Romero et al. 2003), an awareness system to support intrafamily communication was designed. The prototype featured communication through pictures with handwritten notes, and it enabled communication of a household with mobile members of the broader family; for example, the grandparents would receive pictures and messages on a home device, which were generated by the mobile grandchild with a mobile device. In this study a laboratory usability test was conducted as a precursor to a more extensive field test where the prototype was deployed.

An artificial situation was created for the purposes of the laboratory test. Some family members were taken for a morning out in a neighbouring open-air museum and were set the task of sending a few pictures back to the laboratory-based participants throughout the morning. As in the evaluation of FRIDGE described above, it turned out that in this artificial situation the test subjects could not imagine what role this appliance could occupy within their current communication habits and needs (Romero et al. 2003; van Baren and Romero 2003). However, the laboratory study was followed by an extensive two-week field study, where our informants used the prototype system at their homes. This time, it was possible for users to experience the intended affective benefits first hand and for the research team to observe emerging communication patterns. For example, test participants experienced strong affective benefits, like feeling closer to the other person, feeling in touch, and reported feeling higher levels of group attraction when compared to not using the designed appliance. In this case, the realism of the experience lends much more credibility to these results in relation to the results of the laboratory test. Nevertheless, to gain more confidence in our findings we continue the efforts to scale up the system including larger components of one's family and social network and to test over longer periods of time.

3.4 Implicit interaction and automated capture in domestic environments

Two essential parts of ubichi are implicit input and automated capture (Abowd and Mynatt 2000). Interaction becomes implicit when the users do not have to perform any purpose-specific interactions to communicate their intents to the system explicitly. Rather, implicit human-computer interaction relies on the system perceiving the users' behaviour and its context and then using this information as input.

In the context of social communication, the potential usefulness of implicit input seems to be much less salient. Implicit input can be used for automatic adaptation and personalisation of a system or a service. From the user perspective these features involve a trade-off in the amount of information captured about the user and the benefits they bring. This trade-off must be experienced before the initial inhibition for any user modeling by the system is overcome. For example, if one were asked if he would mind using and carrying a device that tracks his position through the day, the answer is almost certainly that this is unacceptable. However, given a mobile phone that allows being connected through the day most people are willing to accept it, especially after a long socialisation to mobile telephony, through which people have learnt to accept this trade-off and not to consider the ownership of such devices strange. Currently, mobile phone service providers are able to locate mobile phone users fairly accurately and transmit that information to other users. It remains to be seen how such functionality may be adopted by users and whether they will be socialised to accept this apparent threat to their privacy. Corresponding experiences with using person-tracking indoors within an office environment have been positive although it had raised fears with the wider public when first announced (Davies and Gellersen 2002).

Hypothetical ubicomp scenarios, (e.g., describing the automated and regular capture of pictures at home) can easily provoke negative gut reactions. Automatic capture of information can help family members stay connected in several ways. A home can, for example, be aware whether its inhabitants are in or out. Information regarding the use of power and water at home can be projected to a remote home, to give an imprecise but reassuring impression about the happenings at a connected household (Eggen et al. 2003). More precise information capture (e.g., whether someone is alone at home, what program is currently playing on the TV, etc.), is easy both to register and to disseminate through the Internet. The spectre of the Big Brother haunts such technologically motivated proposals and emerges as a major obstacle for the end-user acceptance of ubiquitous computing technologies for the home.

In the context of interpersonal communication, the reticence to let the system capture and disseminate information on the resident's behalf is pretty much justifiable. In several ethnographic studies on intrafamily social communication, people's reluctance to accept automatic capture of audio/visual data in their homes was noted. People are pretty good at deciding when to communicate what to whom and they are very likely to resent a system taking initiative. These choices are a crucial component of our daily interactions and one that is critical in how we project ourselves socially. Semiautomated capture is of course much more promising, that is, the user staying involved in the decision of what information to give to whom and managing a system that is able to support the collection and aggregation of such data. In practical terms, automatic capture can be as simple as capturing someone's facial expression in reaction to reading a message or seeing a picture. It has been found (Markopoulos et al. 2003) that automatic capture of the facial expression of the receiver of photographs and messages was perceived to add value to communication.

4 Hypothesising principles for the design of ubichi

In the next paragraphs we put forward some design principles that try to address the departures of ubichi with respect to standard user-centred design techniques. The principles are described epigrammatically and are followed by an explanation of their rationale.

4.1 Design for the person and not the user

The difference in the "rules of engagement" for ubichi and standard computer-human interaction discussed earlier, suggests that ubichi can have a further reaching impact on a person's life when compared to current computing.

Considering an individual as a user of a system currently concerns only a small "slice" of their activities, interests and concerns. Ubichi can be expected to increase this slice in more ways than just the time-span of interaction and the activities concerned. The ubichi designer is invited to design for the user as a person, to address her needs and consider a potentially constant interaction with computers that has no explicit beginning or end. Designing for the person requires a more holistic view of people than traditionally has been the case with user-centred design. Traditional task analytical techniques that use abstractions such as roles and tasks are perhaps less suitable than holistic views of users as goal-driven personas (Cooper 1999). Using such richer representations of users that aim to create some empathy in the design and development team is an emerging trend already apparent in the domain of industrial design of consumer electronics. Creating and utilising such rich views of users within structured design processes is still an active research topic, leading to several proposals by researchers on variations of the techniques of personas and cultural probes. Such adaptations, suitable for the emerging domain of ubichi still need to be developed and validated in practice.

The designer is challenged to be parsimonious in extending the reach of the computing environment and to do so only while addressing true and significant user needs. This challenge pertains also to how people want to live and how they want to be perceived by others.

An individual may perceive a system as intrusive when it does not match his or her habits, lifestyle and values. Consider, for example, early scenarios of ubiquitous computing, envisioning that dietary advice should be offered on the fridge door or rewards should be given to people for doing their workout at the gym. For many people, a system that would provide such a commentary on their activities would be perceived as annoying and obtrusive. Similarly, introducing a system that advises one to exercise, move or take medication will be likely to antagonise many. This mismatch between the values designed into a system and the individual's personal values is avoidable. Coming back to the lifestyle example, it is better to let the users set their targets for improving their lifestyle and what type of feedback they want to receive. In this case the difficulty of making a system that is not socially "inept" is overcome by handing back control to people.

In conclusion, designing for the person means:

- Needs analyses should strive for holistic and dense representations of persons rather than narrow views describing them only by means of their relation to a system.
- Let people be who they want to be. Ubicomp systems should serve a person's own needs, ideals and values. Values designed into the ubicomp system should be possible for the user to inspect or even modify.

4.2 Empower people

To enable pleasurable interaction, it is essential that users can be and can feel in control of the resulting ubichi experience. To some extent adaptation to user and to context of use can remain transparent to users, perhaps supported by advanced middleware or adaptive algorithms. In this case, user comfort comes at the expense of situation awareness and control. Another possibility is to let the users construct their own experiences, by assembling desired devices, applications and services and setting personalised preferences. People can become in this way the architects or constructors of their environments and ubichi experiences. This approach is perhaps counterintuitive when one thinks of making interfaces easy to use and to learn. It appears like regressing to the days where the computer user needed to be a scientist or a specialised technician. Indeed the extent to which we can deliver the benefits of personalised computational environment or personalised access to ubiquitous computing services without requiring that the users be programmers seems to be a critical challenge for future research. Tasks currently reserved for programmers will need to be reallocated to the person who will interact with the components of the ubiquitous computing environment. The untrained user will need support for this job. A minimal (necessary but not sufficient) requirement then is that the end-user/programmer should be treated at least as well as the programmer: the user should be able to inspect the computing system, to modify it, debug it etc. This must be possible in at least those parts that affect him or her as a person, for example, sharing personal information, adaptivity to context and habits etc. (Mavromatti et al. 2003).

Clearly "opening up the box" comes at a cost for the end-user and it is not easy to decide how much of system adaptivity should be automated or handed over to the end-user. Focusing on the impact of ubicomp on daily life, we would like that reactive behaviour should be observable and reconfigurable by users, for example, parents should be able to determine the behaviour of the environment watching over their child, or doctors should be able to reconfigure a patient-monitoring system.

Apart from the behaviour of ubicomp systems, the very fact that they can be perceptive and that they are networked brings about critical privacy threats. People's presence in the digital world becomes ubiquitous and leaves a permanent trace (Grudin 2002), and perhaps is more threatening in terms of privacy than most individuals can foresee. Informing people about the information capturing behaviour of a ubicomp system is one important step. Solutions need to be found to enable users to master and control this complexity; see, for example, Langheinrich (2001).

In conclusion empowerment implies the need to:

- Help individuals to shape their ubichi experience, for example, by personalisation and end-user programming.
- Help people stay aware and in control of how information about them is assembled and shared by a ubicomp environment.

4.3 Design purpose specific interaction styles

Returning to the concept of information appliances, we note that the general principles of Norman for simplicity and pleasurability entail two major design challenges. One concerns minimalism and simplicity and concerns scoping the functionality to only that which provides value to people. The second, which becomes essential in designing ubichi is to design purpose-specific interaction styles.

Interaction styles concern just as much the design of hardware as the software. Ubichi bridges the virtual and physical worlds, so interaction design extends to designing how computing is embedded in physical artefacts as well as physical spaces. Consider, for example, location-aware services. What is becoming a canonical problem for researchers in this field is the design of navigation aids that will provide guidance or location-sensitive information to users as a result of being able to track their position through positioning services. A plethora of proposals have been made for accessing such information from mobile devices, most often using the interaction techniques provided as a standard to the hardware platform (e.g., interaction with a stylus on a hand-held screen). While appropriate for some situations, clearly the image of people walking through cities "head down" monitoring their PDA screens is not convincing. Attention to context may suggest other forms of interaction, tailor made for the intended task and context of use. For example, Bossman et al. (2003) discuss how navigation information can be provided with haptic output devices strapped on the wrists of the user. Crucially, the GentleGuide prototype they designed does not solve a general navigation problem, but is a "pick up and use" system for first-time visitors in large indoor spaces. During iterative design and testing of this device it turned out that haptic guidance need only be very minimal and coarse. Test users showed impressive effectiveness and efficiency in interpreting haptic signals, in conjunction with their perception of their surroundings and using them to find their way. As a case study, GentleGuide demonstrates clearly the potential of developing novel interaction styles, narrowly targeting the intended task and context of use.

4.4 Design the "101st device"

It was mentioned earlier how multiple computers need to be coordinated to provide the ubichi experience. Consider the current problems users face with their personal computers and how often they need to consult help desks to resolve technical problems. With this in mind, the promised scaling up of computer use seems very problematic. Scalability here concerns at least two aspects of ubichi: one is learning to use a system and the second is staying in control of it.

From the perspective of usability, it is not sufficient to consider the learnability of a single device or application. While a single technical or usability problem may not be insurmountable, the emerging complexity of an environment where each of the devices populating it will have its own tricks to learn would result in an unacceptable experience. Learnability and, more generally, usability in the ubicomp era concern how to use valued functionality from a latest addition to an array of devices already deployed, adopted and serving the needs of some individual. To put it epigrammatically, usability does not concern the use of one device or application but, rather, using the 101st device inserted to a ubicomp environment along with those used already. Testing for usability should take place in the intended context of use, not only for reasons of general ecological validity but, crucially, so that the actual interaction of a particular person and his own, personal and dynamically forming emergent ubiquitous computing environment will be evaluated. For practical purposes some basic level of usability has to be first established through laboratory testing but, clearly, field tests should be part of the agenda for interaction designers.

Persons interacting with a ubicomp environment may be unable to comprehend the complexity of their workings, for example, which service or which persons can access their information, or what could be the side effects of interacting with a particular device. This pertains to what Thomas Green (Green and Petre 1996) has described as "hidden dependencies", a critical cognitive dimension for characterising how people perceive information artefacts. The ubichi designer has to make technical complexity transparent so that the user can stay in control of the system, whether this concerns automating tasks or information capture and sharing. Contrary to Green who studied visual notations, graphical user interfaces and other information artefacts, the ubichi designer cannot consider only the difficulties of one person interacting with a system on her own. Given the social nature of ubichi discussed earlier, the way multiple users interact with the system and the way private information is dealt with, are more important than in standard computer-human interaction. The multiplication of information stored and processed by a ubicomp system means that abstraction is not a sufficient answer for hiding detail as, for example, a notational viewpoint might suggest. The notion of calmness discussed above is a critical yardstick for empowering users without overloading them with information.

Assuming the user is already equipped, familiarised and busy with the use of some devices, the designer can no longer afford to consider the experience of a designed product in isolation. The user, by the nature of ubicomp, will already have a life saturated with technology. Striving for calmness in the terms described by Weiser should aim to eliminate this saturation or at least eliminate its side effects such as information overload and disruptiveness. Solutions for reducing the disruptiveness of technology may involve ambient displays, (cf. Wisneski et al. 1998), minimalism as advocated by Norman or the use of agents for mediating with the environment.

In conclusion, designing for the 101st device amounts to the following.

- Design for calmness.
- Strive for realism in implementation and testing.

4.5 Apply implicit interaction and automated capture parsimoniously

It was discussed earlier how implicit interaction is a critical departure of ubichi when compared to traditional human-computer interaction; it does not need though to be omnipresent. Implicit interaction brings about two "costs" for the end-user: First it requires monitoring user activity, which needs to be justified to the user by commensurate benefits. Second it brings about a loss of control to the users, who are no longer explicitly instigating interaction.

These negative aspects of implicit interaction do not necessarily discredit it, but require careful attention of the designer. Individuals will not readily accept being monitored or to relinquish control to a ubicomp environment if the benefits are not compelling. Focus of ubichi demonstrators on switching on lights may be necessary for creating feasibility demonstrators, but more value has to be provided to the individual before they forfeit control, money and privacy for getting the functionality in return.

We argue that implicit interaction can bring benefits when:

- It cannot be replaced by explicit interaction, for example, round-the-clock health monitoring.
- The value of the service or function delivered through this interaction compensates for the loss of predictability and control.

5 Discussion

This chapter has proposed a set of design principles for the design of interaction with ubiquitous computing environments. Their relevance to design has been motivated by a few design studies regarding intrafamily social communication. The design principles are listed in a summative form.

1. Design for the person and not the user.
2. Empower people.
3. Design purpose-specific interaction styles.
4. Design the 101st device.
5. Apply implicit interaction and automated capture parsimoniously.

The first two principles are consistent with current trends in designing interactive systems. The espoused goals of designing for the person, of providing value to the user in an affective sense and for providing fun, are becoming increasingly accepted also for the design of consumer products (e.g., see Jordan 2000). The third principle, about the design of purpose-specific interaction styles, extends the scope of interaction design to address hardware design. This is already the case with current industrial design, for example, in the domain of consumer electronics or automobiles. In the case of ubichi, however, further than the repackaging and re-tailoring of known interaction styles, radical innovations in input and display technologies are called for, as was shown with the GentleGuide and the FRIDGE prototypes. The final two principles are specific to the ubicomp era. The "design of the 101st device" pertains to the challenge of scaling up computer-human interaction and attaining fit to a dynamic social and technological context. The latest studies reported show some first steps at including more realism both at the stage of understanding users and at assessing the success of ubichi designs. The last principle is the most specific to ubicomp and the least explored to date. It remains a goal for future research to examine the viability of automated capture and implicit interaction from a human-centric perspective.

The comparison to current practices and trends shows that we do not anticipate that ubichi design will be radically different in terms of the techniques used and the design process. There does though appear to be a qualitative shift. The typical activities of collecting requirements and of testing will become very complex and brittle, because of the richness of the factors involved. Ubichi design needs to be much more informed from scientific methods applied for collecting and interpreting requirements or to gauge the success of a prototype. Current methodological research still needs to bridge the distance between the more research-oriented techniques such as ethnography, task analysis and the more intuitive, evocative and impressionistic techniques such as personas and probes. The combination of field testing and diaries advocated, addresses several methodological challenges for the ubichi designer: anticipating a situation that does not yet exist, designing for a complex social and technological context which is very much variable for different individuals and households and understanding and designing for the values and needs of a person.

In operational terms two important refinements to standard ethnographically inspired, user-centred design practices have been discussed.

- A critical component of a requirements analysis is to simulate as much as possible the intended user experience in the field, by use of situated prototypes, preliminary versions of a system and "staging" the intended user experience.
- Diaries emerge as an excellent tool for embedding data collection within the daily lives of people. However, diaries should be triangulated with methods such as interviewing, logging, focus groups or even design-oriented techniques such as Cultural Probes and personas.

Dunne in his essay "InHuman Factors" (1999) pointed out that "every product has an enormous impact upon the way we think; the relationship between artefacts and people is dynamic, especially when beliefs, values and aesthetics are involved". This, we believe, will be even more pronounced with ubiquitous computing systems that, as was argued above, can affect people very profoundly and can easily embed values and lifestyle choices foreign to the intended user population.

In a similar vein to Dunne, Gaver (2002) has suggested the need to introduce ambiguity in the design of products, letting the interpretation of designs emerge through the interaction with their users. Dunne and Gaver have gone a long way into counterbalancing the almost mechanistic methodologies proposed by the human-computer interaction community that aim to optimise user-system interaction as a work-system, thereby assuming a constant drive to increase efficiency and productivity. Their works suggest the need to question the values embedded in our designs and to address a broader range of needs of a person, including play or even appreciation of art. On the other hand, there is a significant distance that needs to be covered between products created for design research and those intended to be inserted into people's daily lives. Much of the inspiring designs proposed by researchers in interaction design are primarily embodiments of theses and arguments relevant to an audience of researchers and designers. Research is still needed to create a track record of designing ubichi experiences that move beyond the technological demonstrator or the evocative concept. Such designs will need to demonstrate that they help people obtain promised benefits, whether these concern pleasure and fun, self-actualisation, social interactions or even the more mundane cognitive benefits of easy access.

6 Acknowledgements

Many thanks to Wijnand IJsselsteijn, Boris De Ruyter, Natalia Romero, Joy van Baren, Claire Huijnen, Onno Romijn, Alexandros Philopoulos, Henriette van Vugt and Irene Mavromatti, whose collaboration has been instrumental in developing the ideas presented. Thanks also to Ilse Bakx and Lisa Cherian for their constructive critique while proofreading this chapter.

References

Abowd GD, Mynatt ED (2000) Charting past, present, and future research in ubiquitous computing. ACM ToCHI 7(2):29-58

Beigl M, Gellersen HW, Schmidt A (2001) Media cups: Experience with design and use of computer-augmented everyday objects. Computer Networks 35(4):401-409

Bossman S, Groenendal B, Findlater JW, Visser T, de Graaf M, Markopoulos P (2003) GentleGuide: An exploration of haptic output for indoors-pedestrian guidance. In: Paternó F (ed) Human Computer Interaction with Mobile Devices. Udine, Italy, LNCS 2411, Springer, Berlin-Heidelberg

Calvary G, Coutaz J, Thevenin D (2001) Supporting context changes for plastic user interfaces: Process and mechanism. In: Blanford A, Van-derdonckt J, Gray P (eds) People and Computers, vol. XV. Springer, pp 349-364

Cooper A (1999) The inmates are running the asylum. SAMS

Davies N, Gellersen HW (2002) Beyond prototypes: Challenges in deploying ubiquitous computing systems. Pervasive Computing 1(1):26-35

Dertouzos M (1999) The Oxygen project: The future of computing. Scientific American 52-55

Dray S, Mrazek D (1996) A day in the life of a family: An international ethnographic study. In: Wixon D, Ramey J (eds) Field Methods Case-book for Software Design. Wiley & Sons, New York, pp 145-156

Dunne T (1999) Hertzian Tales. UK: RCA CRD Research Publications

Eggen B, Hollemans G, van de Sluis R (2003) Exploring and enhancing the home experience. Cognition Technology and Work 5:44-54

Gaver B (2002) Designing for Homo Ludens. i3 Magazine 2-6

Gaver B, Dunne T, Pacenti E (1999) Cultural probes. Interactions 6(1):21-29

Green TRG, Petre M (1996) Usability analysis of visual programming environments: A cognitive dimensions framework. Journal of Visual Languages and Computing 131-174

Grudin J (1994) Groupware and social dynamics: Eight challenges for developers. Communications of the ACM 37(1):92-105

Grudin J (2002) Group dynamics in ubiquitous computing. Communications of the ACM 45(12):74-78

Hutchinson H, Mackay W, Westerlund B, Bederson BB, Druin A, Plaisant C, Beaudoin-Lafon M, Conversy S, Evans H, Hansen H, Roussel N, Eiderbäck B, Lindquist S, Sundblad Y (2003) Technology probes: Inspiring design for and with families. CHI Conference, ACM Press, pp 17-24

Jordan P (2000) Designing Pleasurable Products. Taylor & Francis, London

Kindberg T, Fox A (2002) System software for ubiquitous computing. Pervasive Computing 1(1):70-81

Langheinrich M (2001) Privacy by Design – Principles of Privacy-Aware Ubiquitous Systems. Ubicomp 2001, LNCS 2201. Springer, pp 273-291

Lyytinen K, Yoo Y (2002) Issues and challenges in ubiquitous computing. Communications of the ACM 45(12):63-65

Markopoulos P, IJsselsteijn W, Huijnen C, Romijn OPA (2003) Supporting relationships through awareness systems. In: Riva G, Davide F, IJsselsteijn WA (eds) Being There: Concepts, Effects and Measurements of User Presence in Synthetic Environments. IOS Press, Amsterdam, The Netherlands, pp 262-279

Mavromatti I, Kameas A, Markopoulos P (2003) Visibility and accessibility of a component based approach for ubiquitous computing applications: The e-gadgets case. In: Stephanidis C, Jacko J (eds) HCI International. Lawrence Erlbaum, New York, pp 178-182

Newman M, Sedivy JZ, Edwards K, Smith TF, Marcelo K, Neuwirth CM, Hong JI, Izadi S (2002) Designing for Serendipity: Supporting End-User Configurations of Ubiquitous Computing Environments. Designing Interactive Systems, DIS 2002. ACM Press. London, pp 25-28

Nielsen J (1994) Heuristic evaluation. In: Nielsen J, Mack RL (eds) Usability Inspection Methods. Wiley & Sons, New York

Norman DA (1998) The Invisible Computer. MIT Press, Cambridge, MA

O'Brien J, Rodden T, Rouncefield M, Hughes J (2000) At home with technology: An ethnographic study of a set-top box trial. ACM ToCHI 6(3):282-308

Pentland A (2000) Perceptual intelligence. Communications of the ACM 43(3):35-44

Romero N, v.Baren J, Markopoulos P, de Ruyter B, IJsselsteijn W (2003) Addressing interpersonal communication needs through ubiquitous connectivity: Home and away. In: Aarts E, Collier R, v.Loenen E, de Ruyter B (eds) Ambient Intelligence, LNCS 2875. Springer, pp 419-430

Ullmer B, Ishii H (2000) Emerging frameworks for tangible user interfaces. IBM Systems Journal 39(3&4):915-931

van Baren J, Romero N (2003) Design of an awareness service and assessment of its affective benefits. Master Thesis, User System Interaction Programme, Technical University of Eindhoven, The Netherlands

van Vugt H, Markopoulos P (2003) Evaluating technologies in domestic contexts: Extending diary techniques with field-testing of prototypes. Proceedings HCI International, vol. III. Lawrence Erlbaum, Hillsdale, NJ, pp 1039-1044

Vroubel M, Markopoulos P, Bekker MM (2001) FRIDGE: exploring intuitive interaction styles for home information appliances. In: Jacko J, Sears A (eds) CHI 2001, Extended Abstracts. ACM Press, pp 207-209

Weiser M (1991) The computer for the 21st century. Scientific American 265:94-104

Weiser M, Brown JS (1996) Designing calm technology. Power Grid Journal 1(1)

Wellner P (1993) Interacting with paper on the DigitalDesk. Communications of the ACM 36(3):87-96

Wilson A, Pham H (2003) Pointing in Intelligent Environments with the World Cursor. Interact 2003. IOS Press, pp 495-502

Wisneski C, Ishii H, Dahley A, Gorbet M, Brave S, Ullmer B, Yarin P (1998) Ambient displays: Turning architectual space into an interface between people and digital information. CoBuild '98. Springer, Darmstadt,Germany, pp 22-32

Older adults: Key factors in design

Mary Zajicek

Department of Computing, School of Technology, Oxford Brookes University
UK
mzajicek@brookes.ac.uk
http://www.brookes.ac.uk/speech

Abstract

The western world is experiencing a rapid increase in the use of computers and other interactive electronic products by people of all ages and all walks of life. Computer interaction is no longer restricted to the workplace and for use by those "at work" and is now found everywhere including over the phone and in many useful electronic products.

The envelope of the user group for computer interaction is stretching to incorporate a wide range of people and abilities. Designers can no longer rely on their target user coping with the intricacies of multitasking, multifunction systems of the workplace machine, and must look to the needs of the wider population.

The focus of this contribution is special design which will enable a particularly large group of new users, older adults, to participate fully in the use of information technology, and which will also help them to stay happy, healthy and independent for longer.

1 Introduction

The chapter addresses the demographic, legislative and economic forces which dictate the need for a re-evaluation of the provision of technology for older adults, together with the reasons why satisfactory inclusive design has not yet been achieved. It then documents the unique attributes of older adults as contributors to the system design process and as users of technology, which dictate that a radically different and more inclusive approach to system design is required. Several interface design methodologies are reviewed as offering potential solutions to the challenge of building systems for older adults.

Two exemplar software systems that have proved successful for older adults are outlined together with reports of evaluation studies carried out to learn more about older adults' interaction. In this context firstly BrookesTalk, a voice Web browser used as a platform to explore information retention from speech output, is described, with reflections on how dynamic diversity can be supported at the interface. Second, a speech system built in Voice XML which uses familiar telephone technology, enabling older adults to talk and listen to a Web-based database, acts as an exemplar for new systems which use old and familiar technology thus avoiding the interaction problems found with more technologically advanced interactive systems.

The final part of this chapter pulls together the evidence to identify key factors which contribute to usable interfaces for older adults, optimum interface design for older adults and discusses the possibility of future systems which will enhance the lives of older adults and help them to stay more independent for longer.

2 Why a change in approach?

In order to discuss design for older adults we need to define what we mean by older adults. It is inappropriate to define the group by age alone because as we will see later in this chapter there exists an amazing diversity within older adults in the rate at which they experience the effects of ageing. Dulude (2002) found that individuals in the group of older adults that she worked with either experienced considerable effects of ageing or experienced none at all, with bi-polar results. Conversely Hawthorn (2000) found that the effects of ageing start to become noticeable from the mid-forties. The people who tested the software developed at Oxford Brookes University described in Sections 5 and 6 attended a centre at Age Concern Oxfordshire and tended to be over seventy years old and lived independently. This group therefore is difficult to pin down save to say that they are a group of people that experience the effects of ageing in terms of memory loss and reduced ability to build strategies at the computer interface more than younger people.

Older adults form a significant proportion of the population, which is set to rise in the coming years. The trend of an increasing ageing population has important social and economic implications, which have been recognised by the UK and other governments (Sutherland 1999; Foresight Ageing Population Panel 2000). There are therefore considerable social and economic reasons why interface designers should rise to the challenge of designing interfaces, which are usable by older adults. The number of the "oldest old" (those over eighty) is growing more quickly than that of all the other segments of the population. This will have an impact on the cost of social care unless technological solutions can be found to enable people to stay in their own homes for longer.

Designers of interactive electronic products must take into account the special needs of such a significant population who often find current products difficult and complicated to use. Failure to do so will result in this large and growing group of citizens becoming marginalised through lack of access to information and services and also excluded from the use of interactive electronic products such as stair lifts and alarm systems which could enable them to remain living independently for longer.

There is also legislative pressure for the development of systems which are accessible to older and disabled people. The 1990 Americans with Disabilities Act (ADA) asserts the individual's right to use products and services on an equal access basis. In 1995, the United Kingdom implemented the Disability Discrimination Act (DDA). European governments have also recognised that enabling legislation for combating discrimination is necessary for the promotion of independent living, extending quality life and promoting the concept of participation in the "information society" (Buhler 2002). While we have seen significant changes in physical access to buildings etc. the barriers to access to software are harder to detect and more difficult to overcome.

A recent study commissioned by Help the Aged (2002a) showed that local authorities across the UK are concerned about the level of resources required to provide for increasing numbers of older adults. To alleviate pressure on housing and care services it is anticipated that there will be a greater emphasis on assisting those eligible for services within their own homes (Dewsbury and Edge 2000). This has advantages for both service providers and clients, as over eighty percent of older adults' consider their independence and living in their own home as "very important" (Help the Aged 2002b). The development of usable technologies to assist older adults with living independently in their own homes creates opportunities for new design approaches and has considerable potential to improve the lives of older adults.

Unfortunately, industry has not yet recognised the significant benefits of more accessible design (Keates et al. 2000). Most providers continue to produce products that are primarily aimed at younger people. Keates et al. (2000) argue that the typical researchers or developers find it easier to design for someone like themselves and that young developers may find it difficult to fully understand the day-to-day impact of age-related impairments, and the needs of older people which are significantly different from their own.

3 Older adults' requirements and their impact on interface design

3.1 The effects of ageing

It is inevitable that ageing affects our ability to carry out certain tasks: 88 percent of those aged 20 to 29 years are perfectly fit compared with 69 percent of those aged 50 to 59 years (Office for National Statistics). Increases in the number of older people in the United Kingdom will affect the number of people who experience a sensory loss (blind or partially sighted, deaf or hearing impaired). Most people in the United Kingdom experience poorer sight in later life as part of the general ageing process and more than one person in six over the age of 75 is blind or partially sighted. (Bruce et al. 1991)

Other effects of ageing can include:

- Reduced strength, reduced stamina and reduced dexterity which can affect a person's ability to successfully operate a computer and machines such as video recorders and other devices,
- Sensory loss such as hearing or sight impairment which affect the amount of information absorbed. A person with poorer sight may not be able to utilise visual information on an interactive device, or pick up on orientation and navigation clues. People with poorer hearing may also miss audio cues and may find difficulty in asking for and receiving spoken information,
- Reduced cognitive ability such as poorer memory or less ability to process information makes it more difficult for a person to remember and process information at the interface.

Although the degree of any particular effect of ageing may be small, the combined effect can be greater than the sum of the parts; it is also very difficult to predict the amount and type of information that a person with multiple minor effects of ageing is receiving and is able to use.

3.2 Dynamic diversity and design methodology

Each of the effects of ageing detailed in Section 3.1 will be manifest at different rates relative to each other for each individual. This pattern of capabilities varies widely between individuals, and as people grow older, the variability increases (Myatt et al. 2000). In addition, any given individual's capabilities vary in the short term due to a variety of causes including illness, blood sugar levels and just plain tiredness.

This collection of phenomena presents a fundamental problem for the designers of interfaces to computing systems, whether they be generic systems for use by all ages, or specific systems to compensate for loss of function. The "typical user" of standard systems is assumed to have abilities which are broadly similar for everybody, and crucially these abilities are perceived to remain static over time. Not only is this view wrong in that it does not take account of the wide diversity of abilities among traditional users, but it also ignores the fact that for all users, abilities are dynamic over time. Both the abilities and the rate at which they change also vary between individuals and between cultures, and these variations can be very much more pronounced for older users.

Current software design typically produces an artefact which is static and which has no, or very limited, means of adapting to the changing needs of users as their abilities change. The user-centred paradigm outlined by Nielsen (1993) and adopted as the most useful approach for human-computer interface design, tends to rely upon homogeneous groups for user testing in order to focus on design decisions.

The interface development tools and methods we currently use are not effective in meeting the needs of diverse user groups or addressing the dynamic nature of diversity. There is an urgent need to address the issues implicit in design for this dynamic diversity. New processes and practices are required which address these design issues.

3.3 Aspects of requirements capture

Although there is a raised awareness of the need for universal access many questions concerning suitable methodologies for design for this group remain hotly debated. Designing for this group of users is not easy, and the cultural and experiential gap between designers and older people already outlined can be especially large when developing new technology (Eisma et al. 2003). Younger people through familiarity with the technology can more easily participate as users in user-focused activities. Older adults are commonly unaware of the possibilities of new technologies, and this can severely limit their ability to contribute actively to a discussion about their requirements.

Initial requirements for a system are commonly elicited by way of a focus group, which has proved to be a challenging area when working with older adults. There are instances of successful use of focus groups with older adults, Kirakawski (1997), for example, reports instances where standard focus group procedures were used successfully for requirements elicitation with older adults, and that no adjustments for this user group were required. However, more recent work has demonstrated that focus groups must be adapted for older adults and that their organisation requires considerable interpersonal skills. For example, when gathering requirements for an interactive memory aid researchers at Dundee University (Inglis et al. 2002) reported difficulties in managing focus groups comprising more than three older adults. They reported that auditory impairment was affecting older adults' attention and the ability to follow a discussion, and that where depth and volume of information are important smaller groups or individual interviews were required.

Lines and Hone (2002) also found that older adults are inclined to "wander" from the topic under discussion, providing unrelated anecdotes and chatting amongst themselves. They reported that it was difficult to keep the participants' attention focused on the task and felt that smaller numbers in sessions were preferable, allowing everybody time to contribute and those who appeared nervous to be drawn into the discussion more easily by the moderators. These comments highlight the challenges involved in defining systems requirements from older adults' experience and perspectives. The issue is addressed below in Section 3.4 where User Sensitive Inclusive Design is proposed.

3.4 User sensitive inclusive design

As older people are likely to have very different characteristics from the people designing for them, extensive user involvement should be employed in the development of appropriate technology for this user group (Gregor and Newell 1999). Standard methodologies involving users, however, have been developed for user groups with relatively homogeneous characteristics. As we have seen "older people" encompass a considerably diverse group of users, and even small subsets of this group tend to have a greater diversity of functionality than is found in groups of younger people. They increase the range of abilities and combinations of abilities of which the designer should be aware.

An additional complication is that there can be serious ethical issues related to the use of such people as "subjects". Some of these are medically related, but also include, for example, the ability to obtain informed consent. It is suggested therefore that the standard methodology of User-Centred Design (UCD) is not appropriate for designing for this user group. It is proposed (Gregor et al. 2002) that the techniques of UCD should be modified to be appropriate for older people.

A new methodology, User Sensitive Inclusive Design (USID), is required, which addresses the following issues:

- Much greater variety of user characteristics and functionality,
- Finding and recruiting "representative users" (McGregor 1995),
- Conflicts of interest between user groups (including "temporarily able-bodied"),
- The need to specify exactly the characteristics and functionality of the user group,
- Tailored, personalisable and adaptive interfaces, and
- Provision for accessibility using additional components (hardware and software).

The word "sensitive", rather than "centred" reflects:

- The lack of a truly representative user group,
- Difficulties of communication with users,
- Ethical issues (Alm 1994; Balandin and Raghavendra 1999),
- That different paradigms are needed to standard UCD paradigms,
- That there must be a different attitude of mind of the designer.

3.5 Configurable interfaces

Adaptable interfaces, where the user can adapt a generic interface for his or her disability, are frequently put forward as a solution for the dynamic diversity exhibited in older users discussed in this chapter. Some people might say that those with different needs are supported by systems that allow the users to configure the interface to their own requirements. Microsoft Windows, for example, offers several adaptations, which can be invoked by the users to help them use the interface.

The problem here is that the adaptation itself requires considerable skill to set up, and some configuration options actually require a change in the way that the user interacts with the system, and those who would benefit from them do not always use the configuration facilities. Shari Trewin (2000) identified the following reasons for this.

1. Lack of confidence in performing the configuration.
2. Lack of knowledge of how to change the configuration.
3. Lack of awareness of the available options. Trewin and Pain (1999) found that in a study of keyboard configuration, only 35 percent of the participants with disabilities had a computer teacher available. Others relied on themselves, friends, colleagues and family members for support.
4. Difficulty in identifying the appropriate solution to a problem. For example, it can be difficult for a user, or indeed an observer, to tell if two copies of a character appeared because they pressed the key for too long or accidentally pressed it twice. In current systems users often choose configuration settings by a process of trial and error.
5. Lack of control over the unconfigured interface. For example, a user who is unfamiliar with a default system language may be unable to find out how to change the language themselves. A novice user with a disability affecting her use of the mouse may have difficulty in controlling the mouse well enough to find out about keyboard shortcuts, or to access the control panel in which she can adjust the mouse sensitivity.

Microsoft Windows 98 and later versions provide the "Accessibility Wizard", which helps users by asking them about their requirements and implements their choice of accessibility options. Wizards address the first two points above and provide a partial solution to the third; however, they provide little help in understanding the options offered or in choosing appropriate settings. Configuration can be useful therefore in accommodating diversity but not if it is complicated to set up.

4 Proposed design methodologies for older adults

Ageing can result in a combination of accessibility issues. The decline in sensory, perceptual, motor and cognitive abilities that occurs with the normal ageing process have considerable implications for interface design. Many of these are catalogued by Morrow and Leirer (1997), whereas Morris (1994), Czaja (1996) and Hawthorn (2000) have described the different declines in abilities that occur with age and the implications of these for human-computer interface design. While there is considerable awareness of the difficulties involved, very little research has been carried out into what makes an interface easy to use by older adults and what features are found to be most useful. There have also been calls for personalisation of user interfaces for different ability ranges (Myatt et al. 2000) and adaptive interfaces for older users with cognitive disabilities (Myatt et al. 2000). This section aims to review the progress made in the field.

The design methodologies proposed in this section each address the dynamic diversity outlined in Section 3 and follow the User Sensitive Inclusive Design approach in that they aim to include a wide range of representative user groups and balance the sometimes conflicting requirements of a diverse user group.

4.1 The inclusive design approach

Keates and Clarkson (2003) are active in addressing issues of inclusive design and present what they have named the 7-Level approach, based on the stages of interaction set out by Nielsen (1993) together with usability heuristic evaluations. To address the issue of dynamic diversity their approach aims to focus on interface design from multiple perspectives, essentially addressing social and practical acceptability goals identified by Nielsen (1993). Here practical acceptability is considered to consist of three components: utility (functionality), usability and accessibility. Social acceptability includes attributes such as desirability.

The 7-Level approach developed by Keates and Clarkson comprises the following components (levels here refer to the stages in the procedure of interface design).

Level 1 defines the user needs (i.e. social motivation for designing the product).
Level 2 focuses on specifying the required utility of the product.
Levels 3 to 5 focus on the stages of interaction.
Level 3 addresses how the user perceives information from the system.
Level 4 assesses the matching of the system contents and behaviour to the user mental model.
Level 5 focuses on the user input to the system.
Level 6 involves the evaluation of the complete system to ensure satisfactory utility, usability and accessibility.
Level 7 assesses the resultant system against the user needs.

Thus Level 2 forces more consideration of how the product fits the user's need. The Keates and Clarkson approach can potentially encapsulate the special requirements of older adults, because it explicitly addresses the problem from the accessibility perspective. However the approach necessarily assumes a clearly defined user group in Level 1, although this could be extended to define a set of user needs for each range of users, which they suggest could be defined by government statistics, and does not explicitly address the conflicting requirements issues or dynamic diversity.

4.2 The role of task artefact theory and claims

Task artefact theory together with interface design patterns covered in Section 4.3 aim to encapsulate user experience, as uncovered by experimentation, in specific instances of design. Task artefact theory takes a more proactive approach towards using HCI and psychological theory to inform HCI design and asserts that well-founded HCI designs should relate to theoretically grounded knowledge using an iterative approach (Sutcliffe and Carroll 1999). Original designs are arrived at through task analysis and application of existing theory and are then evaluated and improved. Design principles are then isolated as psychologically motivated design rationales or claims. Claims present design knowledge based on the following

3.1 The need for social communication with the extended family

To understand the people involved and their needs beyond soliciting ergonomics and usability requirements, ubichi design necessitates an in-depth understanding of their needs and social and physical environment. Such an understanding is not simply about obtaining information that will be translated into a requirements document. It extends to understanding persons, their needs and aspirations. The cultural probes method by Gaver et al. (1999) helps designers understand intended users, empathise with them and understand their values and aesthetic preferences. It supports a two-way communication between designers and intended users, by giving participants small design assignments and letting them become creative and express their needs constructively.

Recent methodological research by the InterLiving project (Hutchinson et al. 2003) has extended traditional participatory design. Participants act as partners in the design team, in creative workshops. An innovation by the InterLiving project is the Technology Probes technique, inspired from Cultural Probes. With this method a system prototype is placed at the home of participants to provoke their reactions and to study the perhaps unexpected usage and interaction of people with these technological artefacts.

In our research we have opted for the ethnographic rather than the participatory design approach for studying intrafamily communication. Our studies have had a threefold aim: to create knowledge and understanding of people's activities and needs, to create an empathy with the people whose needs we are trying to address and to feed ideas into the design of purpose-specific information appliances. These aims are very similar to the purposes of cultural probes; compared to the work in the *Presence* project described by Gaver et al. (1999) we have been more concerned with the veracity of the information collected and its ecological validity. Ethnographic methods, which have become established for understanding work, are severely stretched when we consider technologies for the home and for personal use. Becoming either a participant or an observer of a family or generally (in one household or many) is very hard for practical reasons; for example, it is difficult to stay a sufficiently long time with a family and live with them. Also, the researcher can at most observe but will not be an equal participant in the communication between family members. Adaptations of ethnography for the study of home life attempt to compromise the need for collection of data in the intended context of use, in the domestic social and physical setting by shortening the duration of the field study to a few visits (O'Brien et al. 2000; Dray and Mrazek 1996).

In our studies, this "rapid" ethnography has been enhanced with the idea of *situated prototyping*, a technique similar in its conception to the Technology Probes technique developed independently by the InterLiving project. Like traditional prototyping approaches for the rapid development of graphical user interfaces, this approach requires the simulation of the intended user experience as part of the requirements gathering process and it assumes that several iterations should take place before achieving a design fitting the needs of the intended users. To simulate the intended user experience prototypes (ranging from paper parameters: scenario of use, design rationale to express the trade-offs of applying the claim within the scenario of use, and the design artefact to help interpretation. Thus a thoroughly tested set of claims is put forward which provides a resource upon which designers can call. Using this method one could envisage the development of a range of sample artefacts that are tried and tested for older adults together with claims concerning their efficacy.

The range of individual differences presented by older adults, however, suggests that the one-design-fits-all strategy might be rather limited. Designers would need to develop individual profiles of users so that systems could be adjusted to their particular needs. However, carrying out usability analyses for every design is expensive and depends on the availability of a reliable sample of target users. In order to provide a useful resource for would-be designers for older adults the knowledge gained from the task artefact cycle should be generalised to make reusable profiles of users with a particular disability.

Once again this approach does not provide explicitly for dynamic diversity in individuals and as we see from the statistics provided in Section 2 it is unrealistic to design for older adults with only one disability. Section 3.1 also demonstrates that age related impairments seldom appear in isolation necessitating the provision of many different claims for all combinations of disability.

4.3 Interface design patterns

The idea for patterns and pattern language originated in the domain of architecture with the publication more than twenty years ago of Christopher Alexander's book *The Timeless Way of Building* (1979). He proposed that one could achieve excellence in architecture by learning and using a carefully defined set of design rules, or patterns, and although the essence of a beautifully designed building is hard to define, the application of patterns for room design etc. can contribute to the good design of the whole building or groups of buildings.

A pattern describes an element of design possibly together with how and why you would achieve it. For example, Alexander has created patterns that describe ways of placing windows in a room and designing a porch, which achieves a successful transition between inside and outside a building. These include textual descriptions and diagrams or photos (Alexander et al. 1977).

Patterns for human-computer interface design were first discussed in the late nineties, and there is a range of different pattern forms. Some pattern builders choose a purely narrative approach whereas others are more structured. Martin van Welie, for example, sets out patterns under the headings *Problem and Solution* (2002). A comprehensive list of pattern forms can be found at Sally Fincher's *Pattern Form Gallery* (2003a). The pattern form used in this chapter to describe patterns for speech interface design for older adults, is based on Jennifer Tidwell's *UI Patterns and Techniques* (2002), where the pattern has four sections, *Use When, Why, How*, and *Examples*. A fifth section entitled *Tradeoffs* has been included from the claims approach, as there are always trade-offs when designing speech dialogues and these should be made explicit.

Interface designers are rarely older adults themselves and therefore have no concept of how it would feel to access a computer when you are experiencing the combined effects of memory, sight and mobility loss coupled with reduced confidence that comes with slower processing of visual, spatial and verbal information. Furthermore, as we see in Section 3 the dynamic diversity of ability in older adults poses particular challenges for interface designers.

A robust set of design patterns with a linking language is therefore a particularly important requirement for those designing systems for use by older adults. A set of clear and informative patterns together with information on how the patterns may be used together in a system (i.e., the pattern language) would enable interface designers to access best practice and help them to create sympathetic and successful designs for older adults. Importantly the patterns will reflect the experience of older adults through experimentation and observation, which the designers themselves are lacking. This in itself will nurture good design and provide a framework within which some of the main pitfalls in interface design for older adults can be avoided.

The author has developed many patterns for speech systems for older adults, which can be found in Zajicek (2003). Patterns for speech systems possess different properties compared with the more visually oriented graphical user interface patterns of Tidwell (2002) and van Welie (2002), and indeed the architectural patterns of Alexander (1977). Speech dialogues use two forms of input, speech and keypad, and output in the form of a speech message. The usability of the dialogue hinges on its structure and the quality of the output messages. An example pattern, the "Error Recovery Loop", is provided here.

Errors and error recovery represent the main usability problem for speech systems. Standard menu-driven systems often start with a long set of instructions in a bid to avoid errors happening. Older users are not able to remember these messages, which also slow down the dialogue, rendering them useless. The pattern described here directs designers to embed instructions in an error recovery loop: in effect to wait for the error to happen and then try to recover from it.

This approach is most useful in dialogues which are used mostly by experienced users who are unlikely to require any instruction and will if they use the dialogue successfully never have to listen to an error recovery message.

Pattern name: Error Recovery Loop
  Use when: When errors in data input are likely to occur.
  Why: Because older adults cannot remember lengthy preliminary spoken instructions about data input. It is best to let them try to input data and if it goes wrong invoke an error recovery message.
  How: Count how many times a data input occurs and on each count invoke an increasingly detailed error recovery message. In the examples below, Example 1 simply gives instructions for efficient input, but the more detailed Example 2 provides information about which might help the user work better with the system.

Example: 1. Your name has not been recognised. Please speak slowly and clearly into the telephone.
2. The system is trying to match your name against the names it holds in the database. Please try to speak your name in the same way that you did when you registered for the Voice-activated Booking System.

Trade-offs: This form of error recovery does not prepare the user in advance for possible errors, as they have to create the error before it is invoked. The trade-off is against providing long instructions before the user embarks on a task.

The very existence of a set of patterns for design for older adults can have the effect of sensitising interface designers to the design considerations expressed in the patterns, and enable them to consult a body of good practice. The small selection of patterns in the domain of speech interaction for older adults which can be found in van Welie (2002), should encourage designers to think in terms of the functionality of output messages, and should clarify their perception of the components of the dialogue and the part they play in its overall construction. Patterns also have an important role to play as a stimulus to useful debate around usability and best practice, where they can be challenged, improved or discarded at any time.

The pattern "Error Recovery Loop" above also supports Design for Dynamic Diversity as it provides a means of supporting older adults who might make more errors on data entry while not slowing up others with long warning messages, if they enter data successfully; that is, the diversity of need for error support is provided for.

5 Design solutions in voice web browsing

Voice Web browsing for older adults has been explored by researchers at Oxford Brookes University with particular focus on memory impairment and how it affects the user's ability to construct conceptual models (Zajicek and Morrissey 2001a). This section shows how dynamic diversity, memory loss and confidence can be supported in a voice Web browser called BrookesTalk (Zajicek et al. 1998a). It also explains how standard user-centred design methodology was used in the development of BrookesTalk, and what follows serves to illustrate the weaknesses of this approach, and demonstrate how a User Sensitive Inclusive Design methodology could have been more effective.

5.1 Accommodating visual diversity

BrookesTalk, a voice Web browser for visually impaired people, supports visual diversity in its user group by providing different modalities.

1. A set of function keys as input with speech output, enabling its use by totally blind people.
2. A text banner, which provides a large text version of the spoken output, which enables people with some residual vision to read what is being spoken as they hear it. Users can adjust the size of text, and the number of lines of text shown and the colour and contrast of text, which is particularly important for older adults (Hawthorn 2000), thus enabling use by people with a wide range of visual disabilities.
3. A standard graphical rendering of the page, enabling visually impaired people to work alongside sighted colleagues, pooling resources through access to several forms of output.

Figure 1 shows the configuration of the interface. Users can adjust the proportion of screen used for the text banner or standard graphical interface depending on their level of visual impairment and working conditions (i.e., if a sighted person is present).

Dynamic diversity in vision can be accommodated therefore by adjusting the settings for the screen layout using function key F7, and stepping through a relatively long list of different settings to change the font size and the number of lines displayed in the text banner. Although the interface supports dynamic diversity the complexity involved in setting these options illustrates the difficulties inherent in configurable interfaces covered in Section 4.4.

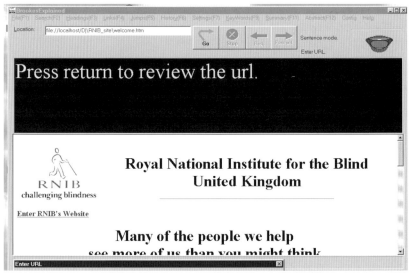

Fig. 1. The configuration of the interface for BrookesTalk showing the configurable text banner and standard graphical Web interface

5.2 Supporting memory loss with voice help

BrookesTalk was evaluated by 200 people in a large-scale exercise among visually impaired users, where one of the most important and unanticipated outcomes of the evaluation was that 82 percent of older adults were unable to even get started with BrookesTalk. During observation of their interaction, it was noted that older adults appeared to lack confidence in building conceptual models of the interface and the application. At the interaction level difficulties can be attributed to two main factors, which interfere with conceptual model development, age-associated memory impairment and visual impairment, both of which reduce the user's ability to benefit from visual clues and contexts.

To help users with memory loss and visual impairment Voice Help, a speaking front end, was built into BrookesTalk to support the users in their construction of conceptual models by "talking" them through their interaction. For each possible state of BrookesTalk an optional spoken output is provided, where the user is informed as to where he was in the interaction and which actions were possible at that point. Optional further details were also available to describe the consequences of each action. After listening to the message the user chooses an option, presses the appropriate function key and receives another message describing the new state of the system and the options available. The spoken output for those who have just started up BrookesTalk would be:

Welcome to BrookesTalk, your speaking Web browser
There is currently no page loaded. Would you like to:
Enter the URL of a page, press F1
Start an Internet search, press F2
Change the settings of the browser, press F7
Hear more details about options available to you, press F3
Repeat the options, press return

With such messages reinforcing users' knowledge of the state of the system and explaining to them what they can do next, the development of conceptual models can be accelerated, and the user no longer needs to rely on memory to know which set of actions is required at each point. With Voice Help, the user can function at the beginning of the interaction, with limited and underdeveloped conceptual models by using the system like a telephone answering system, simply responding to questions, and then in time begin to "see" what to do next without waiting for the message. Dynamic Diversity is supported here in that users can switch off Voice Help at the point at which they no longer need it.

In trials to establish whether the design innovation of Voice Help was useful in supporting memory loss (Zajicek and Hall 2000), we found that several older adults who used BrookesTalk with Voice Help were able use the Web successfully where they had been unable to with the standard BrookesTalk. Thus the "talking the user through" approach, provided by Voice Help, enabled users to achieve interaction where it had previously been impossible.

Diversity among users was noted in the amount of time they needed with Voice Help before moving on to standard BrookesTalk. Thus diversity is supported within the design since users could decide for themselves when they no longer needed Voice Help, and could be confident that they were ready to use standard BrookesTalk.

5.3 Supporting confidence with confirmation

In addition to vision and memory problems, many older people lack confidence in using IT systems, and it is important that we take this into account in the design process. An experiment was carried out using BrookesTalk with Voice Help, whereby older adults were provided with extra confidence in the form of a personal helper, who provided support by answering yes or no to users' questions as they interacted with the software. Users could confirm decisions they were making at the interface, and talk through strategies as they developed. It was assumed that this would increase the users' confidence in the conceptual models they were developing. Simple yes or no answers were given by the personal helper as any further support would be too difficult to monitor for consistency.

Those users who were provided with personal support were more able to get up and running with BrookesTalk with Voice Help than those who worked without support (Zajicek and Hall 2000). The confidence created by the reinforcement that they were doing the right thing built the users' confidence in their creation of conceptual models. Even within this user group there was considerable diversity in the levels of confidence they displayed, and this could change very rapidly apparently solely due to the users' experience with the system. Each user's personal confidence increased markedly following a particularly successful interaction, and decreased following a disaster.

These results are in line with other research (Zajicek and Arnold 1999; Zajicek et al. 1998b) where Bed and Breakfast operators of all ages, who were unable to use computers unaided, found off-line support to be essential when getting started. We see how users' confidence in their actions at the interface is important for users of all ages. Designers of interfaces for older adults therefore should seek to build confidence boosting and confirming messages into their systems. The use of confirmation in speech dialogues is discussed in Section 6. We can also infer from this work that in many cases it is just not reasonable to expect older adults to interact with walk-up-and-use software completely on their own.

5.4 Spoken information retention is different for older adults

The work described in this section was prompted by observation of older adults experiencing problems as they struggled to recall the long synthetic speech messages in the BrookesTalk Voice Help. Many people appeared to require simpler and shorter instruction messages, as they could not absorb or remember large amounts of information.

An experiment was carried out (Zajicek and Morrissey 2001a) to determine whether long speech output messages were actually causing older adults to remember less. The subjects, at Age Concern Day Centres in Oxfordshire, formed a relatively homogeneous group, average age 84 years, who showed normal age-related sensory impairment. They were able to look after themselves, but benefited from attendance at the centre for meals, companionship and organised activities. None of them had used a computer before and they had rather sketchy ideas of what the World Wide Web might be about.

The experimental results confirmed that information retention at the interface works differently for older adults compared to younger ones (Zajicek and Morrissey 2001b, 2003). While younger adults are able to accommodate differences of length of output message and retain the same amount of information from the messages, older adults were confused by the extra information in long messages and actually remembered less. These results indicate that there are important memory-related factors playing their part in interface design for older adults, which do not affect younger people. Design advice therefore would be to make output messages as short as possible at all times.

The results above indicate that the message length in Voice Help should be reduced for older adults. Shorter messages, however, mean that fewer options can be presented, and this implies that functionality should be reduced. In addition it is known that low functionality systems are easier to learn and understand. Other research also points to the need for low functionality systems, with the possibility of adding in extra facilities when a few simple actions have been mastered. For example Czaja (1996) found that older adults were happy to add extra facilities once they had mastered a low functionality e-mail system. Diversity in functional requirement is achieved by offering low functionality as older adults are learning how a system works and developing their conceptual models, and adding in more functionality later.

5.5 User sensitive inclusive design: a useful framework

Although the developers of BrookesTalk were aware of the potential diversity in their user group, they followed a traditional user-centred design methodology. For example, in the experiments described in Section 5.4 every effort was made to ensure that the experimental user group was homogeneous, that is, had the same memory levels, so that other factors would not confound the changes being monitored in the amount remembered in shorter and longer messages. The researchers even performed a memory test to ensure similar memory levels in the two subject groups, which would be standard practice in user-centred design.

Despite these precautions, they were particularly struck by the marked difference in ways of memorising, and indeed what was remembered in this supposedly homogeneous group of older people. It is particularly significant that the standard user-centred design approach used with the first version of BrookesTalk was based on the mistaken assumption that the group of two hundred users across the world, using a variety of machines and indeed languages, was homogeneous and would all use BrookesTalk in more or less the same way.

At the time researchers were genuinely surprised that older users were not able to use BrookesTalk, although five minutes spent observing a visually impaired older adult trying to get going with the software would have made this clear. As the researchers were not looking for diversity, they did not see it. In contrast User Sensitive Inclusive Design encourages designers to seek out diversity, and had it been employed in the development of BrookesTalk the problems experienced by older adults would have been factored into the design at an earlier point in its development.

It could be argued that User Sensitive Inclusive Design is simply a version of user-centred design that pays more attention to the user. This is true but in the author's view the emphasis in user-centred design is on employing users to evaluate interface designs and can be used in practice, and it is acknowledged that this happened in the case of one of the exemplar interfaces discussed in this chapter, to enhance, and eliminate the problems in, a preconceived design. It is argued here that User Sensitive Inclusive Design places the emphasis in the process on the user rather than the design.

6 The familiar technology approach for older adults

6.1 The voice access booking system (VABS)

A second design approach involves computer interaction using familiar pervasive telephone technology. Most homes have telephones and the technology is so familiar that many people would not consider it to be technology at all. The new solution put forward here utilises XML-based technology through Voice XML to provide alternative forms of Web access over the telephone. Although this approach removes the need for older adults to learn how to use a standard desktop computer, the would-be dialogue user is nevertheless obliged to learn how to interact with a speech dialogue. The challenge of embedding context-sensitive help and instructions in dialogues is an important factor which affects usability of VoiceXML, and indeed all computerised speech, dialogues for older adults.

An exemplar is provided by the Voice Access Booking System (VABS) built for Age Concern Oxfordshire, and based upon a Web-accessible database that holds the bookings for IT taster sessions at their Age Resource Desk. Using the VABS the session organiser can interact with the database of appointments using a standard XML-based graphical interface and during office hours clients can book, cancel or reschedule a session, which the organiser records on the database. A useful feature of the system is that it can also be programmed to initialise an automatic telephone call to the clients to remind them that they have an appointment on the next day. However, the main feature reported here is that clients can also phone up the database and make their own bookings using a VoiceXML dialogue that interacts with the database.

VoiceXML http://www.w3.org/TR/voicexml20/ is a new technology, which is only a couple of years old. It offers the dialogue builder simple building blocks known as form and menu, and a set of grammars. The challenge for the dialogue builder is to use these components to construct a successful dialogue, which older adults will be able to use unaided in their own homes to organise their own taster session appointments.

The system allows users to complete the following tasks:

- book a taster session with a reminder call;
- book a taster session without a reminder call;
- cancel a taster session;
- notify the database if they are going to be late.

6.2 Usability features in dialogue design

A major challenge for the dialogue designer is to provide context-sensitive help and instructions to help the older adult to use the dialogue, together with keeping output messages as short as possible, and providing positive feedback to users. The solution is to provide ubiquitous help where older adults are able at any time to say "help" and the system would jump to help instructions. Details of the contents of the help messages can be found in Zajicek et al. (2003).

The complete VABS dialogue is complex and cannot be covered in detail in this chapter. However, the fragment comprising the dialogue for the call reminder task, shown in Figure 2 serves to illustrate the usability issues under discussion. The call reminder dialogue allows clients to set themselves a reminder that they have an appointment at a time of choice on the day before their appointment.

An issue in this fragment of dialogue is how to let the user know that call reminders can only be set using the twenty-four-hour clock and are possible only on the hour. This information is treated as help information, which is embedded in the error recovery loop to avoid lengthy introductory messages. In effect the user is prompted through the dialogue. One client at Age Concern Oxfordshire commented that "the dialogue takes what you have given and then prompts for the gaps".

The dialogue fragment in Figure 1 also features the use of the default message, "Unable to determine a time for a reminder call. Would 7 pm be OK?" which offers a possible retrieval of the task by offering a default booking time for a call rather than allowing the user to leave the dialogue without having completed the task. This approach contrasts with that of a standard telephone answering system in which users often have to start the call all over again if they make an error or forget something.

To ensure that users feel in control and confident during interaction confirmatory sentences were used. For example, "Please confirm that you want a call reminder at <time>", or "Thank you. You will receive a call at your registered number at <time> the day before your session". Defaults and confirmatory sentences provide positive reinforcement for older adults.

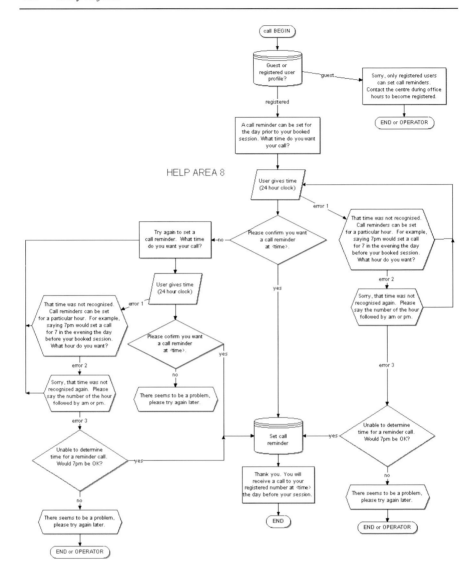

Fig. 2. Dialogue for the call reminder task in the Voice Access Booking System

6.3 Dialogue evaluation

The VABS dialogue was tested with six older adult users at Age Concern Oxfordshire. The set of tasks for the whole system was identified and the optimum and worst potential routes traced. A route includes system output, user input and error cycles. Fatal errors that return the user to the main menu or the operator are denoted by an ^{F}, one for each potential error.

Table 1. Optimum and worst case number of steps for each task.

Task	Optimum	Worst
1. Guest Main Menu.	9	18^F
2. Registered Main Menu.	5	14^F
3. Guest booking, yes to call.	6 + 1	$16^{FF} + 1$
4. Registered booking, yes to call.	6 + 4	$16^{FF} + 9^F$
5. Guest booking, no to call.	6	16^{FF}
6. Registered booking, no to call.	6	16^{FF}
7. Guest cancellation.	7	12^{FFF}
8. Registered cancellation.	1 - 4	$1 - \infty$
9. Guest late.	1	1
10. Registered late.	4	6

Table 1 shows the optimum and worst-case number of steps for each VABS task. The figures in the table indicate that some tasks are better supported by the dialogue than others. Task 9: Guest late, for example, is supported to such an extent that the user can carry it out in one step and cannot go wrong. Whereas with Task 8: Registered cancellation, the user could remain in a continuous loop. However, Table 2 which sets out the actual number of steps taken by older adults, shows that the two users who tried Task 8 both carried it out in four steps. This demonstrates that the number of possible steps in a dialogue cannot be taken in isolation as a usability measure. The quality and positioning of messages appears to also play an important part in helping users to avoid the continuous loop situation. The designer's aim is to reduce the number of potential steps and ultimately make them the same as the optimum path. This is particularly challenging for data entry tasks where input recognition quality is not easy to predict or control.

The user tests were recorded on video camera and the script file from the simulation software stored for analysis. Table 2 details the tasks taken by each user and the number of nodes on the route visited to successfully complete the task, thus enabling easy inspection to see which dialogues are most successful in terms of the number of user steps.

Table 2. Number of steps for each user by task.

Task	User1	User2	User3	User4	User5	User6
1. Guest Main Menu.						9
2. Registered Main Menu.	7	5	7	7	5	
3. Guest booking, yes to call.						10+1
4. Registered booking, yes to call.	11+6^F	11+9	13+5		13+7	
5. Guest booking, no to call.						
6. Registered booking, no to call.				16		
7. Guest cancellation.						12
8. Registered cancellation.		4	4			
9. Guest late.						1
10. Registered late.		5				

Table 2 shows that no user filled in the booking form in the optimum number of steps, and only one fatal error was encountered throughout the tests which was due to a misunderstanding by the recognition engine of the desired time for a call reminder. Only one user asked for help and then proceeded to answer the next prompt successfully.

Task 3: Guest booking, yes to call, and Task 4: Registered booking, yes to call, both also shown in Figure 2, were the most problematic because they rely on voice recognition for data entry. The user paths for those tasks that did not involve data entry were much nearer to the optimum score.

The data in Table 2 show that most tasks were completed in near to the optimum number of steps and users were able to use the entire dialogue to complete their tasks. The tasks requiring voice input data entry proved to be the most problematic. This can be improved by using a yes, no type of dialogue, which will in effect perform binary chops on the possible entry data. For example, when a time for a reminder call is required instead of being asked to enter the time, the user would be asked, "Would you like your reminder call in the morning or afternoon?" as normally occurs when the session organiser sets up the reminder call. If the answer is morning the system would then respond, "Before eleven o'clock or after?" The dialogue would continue to halve the search area until a time is found. This form of data entry is less cognitively demanding for older adults and proves to be a successful method for handling data entry.

7 Reflections on design for older adults

This section addresses the important drivers for interface design for older adults. Firstly, however, we must deal with the question of whether we should treat older adults as a separate and different user group or simply as a more extreme version of the standard user. Dulude (2002) performed experiments with this question in mind and showed that performance on interactive voice response systems was worse for older adults than younger users, but this was because older adults were simply responding more negatively to design problems that made their interaction difficult whereas younger people were more flexible and able to work around the problem. The inference here is that features that are specially designed to make interaction easier for older adults will be useful for everybody. We should therefore be designing for older adults as an integrated element of the user group to promote the design of systems that are easier for everybody to use. When interface designers explicitly seek out diversity in their proposed user group and apply User Sensitive Inclusive Design principles they will be able to identify those areas of their design which entail difficulties for certain extreme users in the group, to which other users are managing to adapt. Redesigning these problem areas will therefore lead to greater universal usability.

The exemplar systems described in Sections 5 and 6 demonstrate that dynamic diversity in the user group can be successfully incorporated into interface design and that designing for older adults, as part of the dynamic and varied user group need not compromise usability for any other group.

The challenge then is to design for older adults as an integrated subset of a dynamic user group. We can identify three key drivers for success in interface design for older adults: the use of context-sensitive help, the need to encapsulate good interface design for older adults in a way that is accessible to inexperienced designers and the potentially invaluable use of computer systems to support memory.

7.1 Context-sensitive help

Both of the exemplar systems described in Sections 5 and 6 demonstrated the use of context-sensitive help, which promises to provide valuable support for all users. Older adults are faced today with an increasing range of interactive electronic devices, which could be potentially useful to them, and whose mode of interaction shows many similarities with our exemplar systems in that they are complex and require some form of instruction in order to use them, and also require the user to develop strategies in order to learn how they work, that is, I did A last time and B happened.

Thus electronic devices, such as video recorders and interactive TV, would benefit considerably from helpful spoken output, especially if the output is timed to be useful for the function the user is currently engaged in (i.e., is context sensitive). Imagine, for example, an older adult trying to program a video recorder to record a particular programme. Think how helpful it would be if a spoken message, describing how to record a start time, for example, cut in at that point in the interaction, especially if it happens just at the point when he is beginning to feel confused.

Context-sensitive help should be available at exactly the moment that it is needed, and if, for example, it is programmed to cut in when a delay of a certain time is detected it will not irritate those who are confident and proficient and work through their interaction without a delay. The delay algorithm, however, creates challenges when, for example, experienced users pause, not because they do not know what to do, but perhaps because they broke off their interaction to answer the telephone. Luckily the user who is unintentionally provided with help in this instance is the very user who can best adjust to unexpected features in the interaction. Here the conceptual load is removed from those who find interaction difficult to those who find it easy.

As modes of interaction with interactive products become more complex research questions arise such as, when should help be activated? Should the system learn about particular users and learn how to help them? Should it be set to detect the point when users take a set of wrong paths in their interaction, or simply kick in when a non-optimal path through the interaction is detected?

Older people often experience difficulty working out how to use interactive gadgets and can be excluded from using many useful products such as automated chair lifts and home alarm systems as a result. Spoken help to guide them through their interaction with these types of products could significantly increase the length of time that older adults are able to live independently and enable them to enjoy the benefits of the information society.

7.2 Encapsulating exemplars of good design for older adults

Given that we wish to design for a diverse user group with varying abilities, the designer must be vigilant that every aspect of the design satisfies this requirement. The instances of design for dynamic diversity provided by our exemplar systems evolved over time and arose from a considerable body of research work. These findings should be made available to the interface design community in a structured manner as the requirement to address interface design for older adults becomes more pervasive.

The patterns approach outlined in Section 4.3 provides a powerful and acceptable means of presenting knowledge concerning the design requirements of older adults, where examples of good design and reasons for using it are presented in an easy-to-use way. These are early days for the use of patterns for interface design; they embody a sense of value concerning interface design but they do not represent the definite answer. Alexander's work also encourages a design community to find its own patterns and use them selectively for individual problems. Their purpose is to educate, and to stimulate discussion between designers and ideally would include users in the discussion. A further aim is to develop a pattern language, which would indicate how particular patterns should be used together to maximise usability. The existence of several formats for interface design patterns (Fincher 2003a) is also problematic although a full day workshop, "Perspectives on HCI Patterns: Concepts and Tools" at CHI 2003 was attended by several of the pattern developers referenced above, where they formulated the Pattern Language Markup Language (PLML) (Fincher 2003b) which promises to provide an easy-to-use generic pattern format.

7.3 Memory support

The ability to set up pretimed telephone-based reminders is a particularly powerful aspect of VoiceXML technology, and can be usefully extended to include preprogrammed reminders that place telephone calls to remind an older adult to take medicine, switch on the heating or remember that a particular person will be visiting. Potentially then a remote carer can populate a database with reminders, which will prompt telephone calls to care recipients at prearranged times, a useful development for people trying to organise the lives of elderly parents who are still living independently, for example.

We can envisage the possibility of effective asynchronous communication between care provider and care recipient, where reminders are set in prerecorded or synthetic speech and the system is able to confirm to the care provider whether they have been acted upon. There is a considerable amount of work to be done in this area concerning acceptability of such systems, and how they will fit into people's lives, but if these issues can be resolved they also have potential to enable older adults to live independently for longer.

8 The future is bright!

With context-sensitive help, and memory support systems fully developed, and an effective mechanism for sharing design for dynamic diversity solutions in place, we will see older adults integrated into the information age accessing information in a manner that suits their needs. Speech systems that can be used without a computer will play an important role and speech dialogues will be developed to support easy interaction for Web access with a variety of applications. We can envisage older adults making their own doctor appointments over the Web or sending biometric data such as blood pressure in for interpretation by doctors who will if necessary suggest, also via the Web, a new regime. This flow of data will remove the need for travel to and from hospital for face-to-face appointments. It is also important to note that while seeking to speed up the efficiency of data flow the value of social contact should also be recognised. User Sensitive Inclusive Design focusing as it does on sensitive consultation with a diverse user group is particularly useful in this regard so that a sound balance in provision can be achieved.

It is hoped that we will also see a fairer distribution of programming effort. The debate concerning who has right of access to information has recently been extended, mainly as a result of legislation, to who should have the ability of right of access promoting concepts of universal access, which also has an impact on the availability of programming resources. Current PC-based systems have been developed mainly for people with good memories who can see small buttons on a crowded screen, can multitask, build strategies on the fly and work round poor interface design. We can envisage a world where the distribution of programming resources as with other resources is debated in ethical terms and where interface design follows egalitarian principles. Interface customisation, instead of being provided for older people who find it difficult to set up and use, could be better provided for those who find it easy. Rather than those who have special needs being required to customise standard, complex, multifunctional difficult-to-use interfaces for their specific requirements for large buttons etc., we will see simple interfaces for those in most need of interface support built as standard and those who are more able to be flexible who would like to speed up their interaction with multifunctional multitasking interfaces will be required to customise a simple standard system to their more complex needs.

When the information society has matured sufficiently to be called a civilised society, one that provides and cares for the special needs of all its members, universal usability will become a societal goal. In interface design terms this means that more able users will be required to carry a cognitive burden to lessen the load borne by those who find computer use more difficult and thereby society's resources will be more fairly shared.

References

Alexander C (1979) The Timeless Way of Building. Oxford University Press
Alexander C, Ishikawa S, Silverstein M (1977) A Pattern Language: Towns, Buildings, Construction. Oxford University Press
Alm N (1994) Ethical issues in AAC research. In: Brodin J, Ajessibm EB (eds) Methodological Issues in Research in Augmentative and Alternative Communication. Proc. Third ISAAC Research Symposium. Jönköping, Universty Press, Sweden, pp 98-104
Americans with Disabilities Act of 1990. (1990). US Public Law, pp 101-336
Balandin S, Raghavendra P (1999) Challenging oppression: Augmented communicators' involvement in AAC Research. In: Loncke FT, Clibbens J, Arvidson HH, Lloyd LL (eds) Augmentative and Alternative Communication, New Directions in Research and Practice. Whurr, London, pp 262-277
Bruce I, McKennell A, Walker E (1991) Blind and Partially Sighted Adults in Britain: The RNIB Survey. Vol 1, HMSO, London
Buhler C (2002) eEurope - eAccessibility - user participation: participation of people with disabilities and older people in the information society. In: Miesenberger K, Klaus J, Zagler W (eds) Computers Helping People with Special Needs. LNCS 2398, Berlin Heidelberg New York, pp 3-5
Czaja S (1996) Interface design for older adults. In: Ozok AF, Salvendy G (eds) Advances in Applied Ergonomics. USA Publishing, pp 262-266
Dewsbury G, Edge H (2000) Designing the home to meet the needs of tomorrow...today: Deconstructing and rebuilding the home for life. Paper presented at the ENHR 2000 Conference, June 26-30, Gävle
Dulude L (2002) Automated telephone answering systems and aging. Behaviour Information Technology 21(3):171-184

Eisma R, Dickinson A, Goodman J, Mival O, Syme A, Tiwari L (2003) Mutual inspiration in the development of new technology for older people. Proc. Include 2003 conference, London

Fincher S (2003a) HCI Pattern-Form Gallery. Retrieved January 18, 2004, from http://www.cs.ukc.ac.uk/people/staff/saf/patterns/gallery.htm

Fincher S (2003b). CHI 2003, workshop report. Interfaces 56, Journal of the BCS HCI Group

Foresight Ageing Population Panel. Finance. (2000). Office of Science and Technology

Gregor P, Newell AF (1999) The application of computing technology to interpersonal communication at the University of Dundee's Department of Applied Computing. Technology and Disability 10:107-113

Gregor P, Newell AF, Zajicek M (2002) Designing for dynamic diversity - interfaces for older people. In: Jacko J (ed) ASSETS 2002 (The Fifth International ACM Conference on Assistive Technologies, 8-10 July, Edinburgh, Scotland). ACM, pp 151-156

Hawthorn D (2000) Possible implications of ageing for interface designers. Interacting with Computers 12:507-528

Help the Aged (2002a) Nothing Personal: Rationing Social Care for Older People. Retrieved January 18, 2004, from http://www.helptheaged.org.uk/Viewpoint/Research/_default.htm

Help the Aged (2002b) The Older Population. Retrieved January 18, 2004, from http://www.helptheaged.org.uk/AdviceInfo/InfoPoint/_default.htm

Inglis E, Szymkowiak A, Gregor P, Newell AF, Hine N, Wilson BA, Evans J (2002) Issues surrounding the user centred development of a new interactive memory aid. In: Proceedings of the Cambridge Workshop Series on Universal Access & Assistive Technology (CWUAAT). pp 171-178

Keates S, Clarkson PJ (2003) Countering Design Exclusion: An Introduction to Inclusive Design. Springer-Verlag, London, UK

Keates S, Lebbon C, Clarkson PJ (2000) Investigating industry attitudes to universal design. In: RESNA 2000. Orlando, USA, pp 276-278

Kirakawski J (1997) Methods for user-orientated requirements specification. Telematics Applications Project TE2010. Retrieved January 18, 2004, from http://www.ejeisa.com/nectar/respect/3.2/index.htm

Lines L, Hone K (2002) Research methods for older adults. Presented at the workshop "A New Research Agenda for Older Adults" at HCI 2002

McGregor A (1995) A voice for the future. In: Proceedings of the European Conference on the Advancement of Rehabilitation Technology (ECART '95), 10-13 October 1995, Lisbon. National Secretariat of Rehabilitation, Lisbon, Portugal, pp 127-129

Morris J (1994) User interface design for older adults. Interacting with Computers 6(4):373-393

Morrow D, Leirer V (1997) Ageing, pilot performance and expertise. In: Fisk A, Rogers W (eds) Handbook of Human Factors and the Older Adult. Academic Press, pp 199-230

Myatt ED, Essa I, Rogers W (2000) Increasing the opportunities for ageing in place. In: Proceedings of the ACM Conference on Universal Usability. Washington DC, ACM Press, New York, pp 39-44

Nielsen J (1993) Usability Engineering. Academic Press, London

Sutcliffe AG, Carroll JM (1999) Designing claims for reuse in interactive systems design. International Journal of Human Computer Studies 50(3):213-242

Sutherland S (1999) With Respect to Old Age: Long Term Care - Rights and Responsibilities. A Report by The Royal Commission on Long Term Care. The Stationery Office

The Disability Discrimination Act - Chapter 50. (1995). Department for Education and Employment, UK

Tidwell J (2002) UI Patterns and Techniques. Retrieved January 18, 2004, from http://time-tripper.com/uipatterns/about-patterns.html

Trewin S (2000) Configuration Agents, Control and Privacy. Proceedings of the ACM Conference on Universal Usability. Washington, DC

Trewin S, Pain H (1999) Keyboard and mouse errors due to motor disabilities. International Journal of Human-Computer Studies 50:109–144

van Welie M (2002) Interaction Design Patterns. Retrieved January 18, 2004, from http://www.welie.com/patterns/index.html

Zajicek M (2003) Patterns for encapsulating speech interface design solutions for older adults. Proceedings of the second ACM SIGCHI & SIGCAPH Conference Computersand Universal Usability, CUU 2003. ACM Press, Vancouver, pp 54- 60

Zajicek M, Arnold A (1999) The "Technology Push" and The user tailored information environment. Fifth European Research Consortium for Informatics and Mathematics, Workshop on "User interfaces for all". Dagstuhl, Germany, pp 5-12

Zajicek M, Hall S (2000) Solutions for elderly visually impaired people using the Internet. HCI 2000, Sunderland, pp 299-307

Zajicek M, Lee A, Wales R (2003) Voice XML: A new opportunity for older adults. Proceedings of HCI International 2003, pp 912-916

Zajicek M, Morrissey W (2001a) Speech output for older visually impaired adults. In: Blandford A, Vanderdonckt L, Grat P (eds) Interaction Without Frontiers. Joint Proceedings of HCI 2002 and IHM 2001, pp 503-513

Zajicek M, Morrissey W (2001b) Spoken message length for older adults. Proceedings of INTERACT'2001, pp 789-790

Zajicek M, Morrissey W (2003) Multimodality and interactional differences in older adults, Special Issue "Multimodality: A Step Towards Universal Access" of Universal Access in the Information Society. (ed Carbonell N) Springer, vol 2/2, pp 125-133

Zajicek M, Powell C, Reeves C (1998a) A Web navigation tool for the blind. Proceedings of the third ACM/SIGAPH on Assistive Technologies, California, pp 204-206

Zajicek M, Wheatley B, Winstone-Partridge C (1998b) Improving the performance of the tourism and hospitality industry in the Thames Valley. Technical report no. CMS-TR-99-04. School of Computing and Mathematical Sciences, Oxford Brookes University

Society of mixtangibles

Michael Thomsen

Interactive Institute AB
Kastrup
Denmark
michael.thomsen@tii.se

Abstract

We are facing an inevitable invasion of digital computation in our surroundings
and in everyday objects such as toys, teapots and t-shirts. At this point in time we
have no way of knowing what this invasion will mean to us and to our daily lives.
We know that it will happen, however, and we know that we will have to deal
with this exponential growth in computational complexity – both in our daily lives
and in all the various disciplines involved in the development of our everyday
surroundings. Once imbued with the capacity to communicate and to compute, our
teapots may never be the same again. Certainly the task of designing such
everyday artefacts will be a very different and much more complex task than
design schools ever envisioned.

This chapter provides an overview of some of the design challenges associated
with this development. Through the introduction of a simple functional taxonomy
it is shown that the ever-increasing complexity of artefacts requires an expansion
of the notion of design to cover disciplines ranging from political science to
software engineering. Furthermore, only a concerted effort among these
disciplines can aspire to create a worthwhile and sound world of communicating
computational artefacts.

The chapter claims that the complexity must be dealt with in a controlled
bottom-up fashion. The ideals and ideas of self-organising systems built on basic
rules and guidelines must be applied to computational artefacts in order for them
to be able to cope with their peers and serve their creators. But the choice of rules
and regulations is crucial on many levels including the social and political. These
choices determine the range of behaviours and the types of social constructs
exhibited by communities of people and computational artefacts. The bottom-up
development must therefore be strongly coupled with a vision of the kind of
society we wish to create and what role computational artefacts will play in that
society.

This means that design is both a question of responsible social intervention and
of facilitating the unexpected. This chapter thus argues for a very broad concept of

interaction design as well as for the creation of structures and environments in which this broad design discussion and practice can take place.

1 Introducing mixtangibles

...humans will, in an Ambient Intelligent Environment, be surrounded by intelligent interfaces supported by computing and networking technology that is embedded in everyday objects such as furniture, clothes, vehicles, roads and smart materials – even particles of decorative substances like paint. AmI (Ambient Intelligence - ed) implies a seamless environment of computing, advanced networking technology and specific interfaces. This environment should be aware of the specific characteristics of human presence and personalities; adapt to the needs of users; be capable of responding intelligently to spoken or gestured indications of desire; and even result in systems that are capable of engaging in intelligent dialogue. Ambient Intelligence should also be unobtrusive – interaction should be relaxing and enjoyable for the citizen, and not involve a steep learning curve. (ISTAG 2003)

The future of interaction design will provide a wide variety of challenges, but none as interesting as the ones presented by the appearance of multitudes of functionally enhanced, networked everyday artefacts. The large EU Ambient Intelligence initiative together with the numerous ubiquitous, pervasive, transparent and ambient computing conferences that abound indicate, that we are rapidly entering a time where virtually every object in our surroundings and on our bodies will be capable of computation and communication. We are presented with visions requiring very sophisticated sense-making and networking capabilities of even the simplest artefacts. A plethora of articles on the subject discuss the technical, social or design aspects of this development, but have we really grasped the magnitude of the design challenge facing us? Do we realise what it takes for large numbers of computational artefacts from different manufacturers and different design traditions to exist together and to collaborate in order to provide us with worthwhile services? Is it safe to assume that interaction design is the answer to these questions? To start addressing these questions we must examine the notion of design as it relates to the development of artefacts of ever-increasing complexity.[1]

The design of artefacts has always been concerned with both aesthetics and use. It is never pure aesthetics, because design is always concerned with function or purpose. A large part of design practice deals with the correspondence between form and function, that is, how to make artefacts communicate and facilitate their message or functionality in the most intuitive and efficient way.

Artefacts have numerous functions and purposes. In order to see the design challenges introduced with the penetration of computation and communication into every aspect of daily life we will introduce a simple taxonomy of artefacts in terms of their functionality.

---

[1] For a slightly different, but excellent perspective on the history and character of design in the digital domain, see Rettig (2003).

1.1 Static objects

The vast majority of everyday objects are simple tools or artefacts that do not perform any kind of work by themselves. A traditional cup affords drinking, but does not perform any active service. Its functionality is straightforward, and we have a fairly fixed concept of cups, which allows us to recognise and use virtually any cup anywhere.

The design of static objects therefore is mainly one of aesthetics, simple functionality and of creating and communicating affordance in a physical form.

1.2 Machines

A machine can be defined as an apparatus, which takes an input and transforms it to produce some form of output. It thus differs from simple tools in that it contains some form of active mechanism of transformation. Machines can have a complex and hidden functionality, but in general classical machines have a fairly straightforward and constant mapping between input and output. We do not usually attribute intention or autonomy to machines. They are simply mechanical extensions of our bodies and perform functions (it is hoped) in accordance with our expectations. A good example of a classical machine is the automobile. It is a complex piece of machinery with considerable hidden functionality, but the mapping between driver and driving is rather simple and has been fairly fixed and universal for almost 100 years.

Machines, however, with their input-output mechanisms introduce the notion of interface to design at several levels. In their normal use, machines must communicate their affordance without necessarily revealing their functionality. They must, however, also lend themselves to repair and maintenance. The design of machines is thus much more complex than the design of simple artefacts. Here we start to see the division between the design of the mechanistic functionality and the design of the interface, that is, of engineering and industrial design.

1.3 Computers

As described by Alan Turing (1936) computers are also basically just machines, and in many cases they just add to the functionality of existing machinery. Computation, however, introduces complex and dynamic functionality and thus dramatically increases the design challenge. We are still dealing with input-output phenomena, but suddenly design can be implemented as purely abstract functionality communicated through, for example, dynamic screens, and thus interface design takes on a whole new dimension. Initially we still see the computer as simply a machine, but whereas mechanical machines are physical extensions of our capabilities the computer also represents a mental extension, and design now clearly becomes a matter of choosing perspectives and metaphors. As noted by Susanne Bødker (1987) the computer can be seen as a tool, a system, a dialogue partner or a medium, and within each of these metaphors any number of design perspectives can be chosen.

Systems design and interface design become highly interdependent disciplines, and it is interesting to observe the changing view of the computer as reflected in the development of programming paradigms. The first programming languages, which dominated for at least thirty years, were procedural: they view the machine as performing a temporal sequence of logic steps. Functional programming, which appeared in the fifties and has lived a fairly quiet life in academic circles, sees the computer as a mathematical number cruncher, whilst the dominant programming paradigm of the last fifteen years, object-oriented programming, sees programs as collections of inherently passive objects that can respond to external stimuli.

The different paradigms do not require different computers, and they can to a certain degree be mixed together, but they signify clearly different perspectives on the character of the machine (and of the world) and can lead to very different design results – both in terms of basic functionality and of user interface. What they all have in common is that they inherently treat the computer as a machine; that is, it is perceived as a mechanical slave that just happens to be able to do complex calculations, execute a series of instructions and interact with its surrounding through various input-output devices. None of the paradigms attempt to treat the computer as an organic rather than a mechanical device (or, in other words, as a living subject rather than a constructed object). Throughout the history of computer science there have been attempts to use more organic models, but, as witnessed in both systems and industrial computer design, we have continued to view the digital technology as an extension of the industrial paradigm. It may be claimed that object-oriented programming is fully sufficient for dealing with dynamic and intentional computational artefacts, but programming paradigms shape the way we think about computers and directly influence the systems we develop.

As computers have entered into our workplace and our homes we have seen an increasing focus on design issues, and gradually the whole concept of design in this area has become very hard to define. In fact, the only ones left out of the design process in the development of computers up until the nineties seem to have been the traditional designers. The design of computer systems became a matter of systems design, interface design, organisational design etc., and by the mid-eighties a systems designer had to be somewhat of a jack-of-all-design-trades. As the field started to mature, however, it became clear that what was needed were multidisciplinary teams rather than multidisciplinary people.[2]

---

[2] For proof of this all you need to do is to look to the computer games industry, where the task of design and implementation is divided amongst a large number of disciplines – all of which have an effect on the design and usability of the final product.

1.4 Mixtangibles

Computation has been used in industrial control mechanisms for decades, but during recent years computation has started to enter into everyday artefacts such as cars, phones, and the proverbial coffee mug. In many cases this transition has been possible without a change in the basic use pattern, since computation has added invisible or extensive functionality to an already established use. Increasingly, however, the design discipline is faced with a multitude of new possibilities in the realm of tangible artefacts with computational properties. The challenge is one of form as well as function, but more than anything else it is a conceptual challenge to develop a new understanding of artefacts that includes the concept of dynamic and behavioural functionality.

Examples, like the smart coffee mug and the smart house, exist in abundance, but so far very few interesting or useful artefacts have been created, and one suspects that we are simply lacking a conceptual grasp of this new domain. We are so used to thinking of artefacts as passive and unresponsive that we lack the imagination to think of a world containing responsive and intentional artefacts.

Tangible artefacts with computational properties have become an increasingly important area of study and design in recent years, and today the field is known under headings such as ubiquitous computing (see, e.g., Weiser 1991), pervasive computing, ambient intelligence (Ambient 2002) and tangible media (Tangible 2003). Unfortunately these terms are all based on the notion of artefacts and environments as interfaces to computation and communication rather than on computation as an integral part of the artefact. In other words these terms basically start and end in computer science or media studies, and thus they fail to describe the true integration of the physical and the virtual. In particular they fail to address the issue of computational artefacts in use. The Disappearing Computer Initiative from the EU IST programme comes closer to integrating the two in its mission to

...see how information technology can be diffused into everyday objects and settings, and to see how this can lead to new ways of supporting and enhancing people's lives that go above and beyond what is possible with the computer today. (Disappearing 2003)

but the initiative's use of the term "information artefacts" once again points to an excessive focus on the information or computation aspects.

In the spirit of Johan Redström, who in his Ph.D. thesis (2001) discusses computation as just another design material, Caroline Søeborg Ohlsen and I have introduced the term "mixtangibles" to denote what Redström calls computational things, that is, physical artefacts with computational properties.

As the computer disappears into everyday objects, human-computer interaction starts to lose its meaning, and a new discipline emerges: interaction design. As a sort of hybrid amongst systems design, graphical design and industrial design, interaction design tries to take centre stage as the solution to the new design challenges, and one fears that another jack-of-all-trades is invoked. It should be remembered that we are now dealing with a very complex design challenge requiring advanced skills from several different professions ranging from social sciences through industrial design to hard-core computer science and hardware engineering. Moreover, it requires understanding and respect between the different disciplines, because they each add unique skills and insight to the design process. The history of the PC and of several other digital products shows us the perils of technology-led development, and there is no reason to believe that a design process driven by people with limited or no understanding of the complexity and possibilities afforded by digital technology will fare any better. An integrated and multidisciplinary approach such as the one found in the computer games industry is clearly needed.

1.5 Communicating mixtangibles

The challenge becomes even more interesting when the mixtangibles start talking to each other and start to actively affect the external world. A lonely coffee mug desperately longing for hot coffee is one thing. It is another thing entirely when that coffee mug starts complaining about its owner to its peers or perhaps to the world at large – or even calls out to a coffee machine willing to respond to its desires. What happens when two entirely different mixtangibles with different structures and worldviews meet each other for the first time? What happens when our surroundings are filled with mixtangibles that try to make sense of each other in their Asimovic[3] attempt to please their owner? How do we make sense of mixtangibles when they present themselves to us amidst a plethora of voices vying for our attention?

We must expect from these artefacts that they handle a lot of the sense making on their own. They are no longer solitary tools just waiting to be used, but part of a society of mixtangibles working actively to serve their masters. The responsibility for negotiating, merging and presenting their capabilities to us must rest largely on their mixtangible shoulders. We must also expect the societies of artefacts to present themselves to humans in a form that makes them comprehensible and useful for the task at hand. In everyday use our focus should be on the task, not the artefact. Considering industry's limited success in making desktop computers or even simpler machines like coffee machines fulfil this promise, one can imagine the problems we face when attempting to design complex and communicating mixtangibles that are not only to make sense to us, but also make sense to each other.

At least one order of complexity is added to the design challenge. First of all communicating mixtangibles are no longer passive artefacts, but active participants, and thus need to be viewed from a much more organic perspective than previous computational objects. This requires new software paradigms allowing for the embodiment of such aspects as intentionality and self-awareness.

---

[3] Isaac Asimov during the 1940s created the Three Laws of Robotics:
1. Robots must never harm human beings or, through inaction, allow a human being to come to harm.
2. Robots must follow instructions from humans without violating rule 1.
3. Robots must protect themselves without violating the other rules.

Secondly they will need to take part in a heterogeneous community of mixtangibles in which they will continuously encounter and need to collaborate with new species speaking unknown tongues and performing hitherto unseen tasks. In order to do so, they will need a higher-level understanding and openness toward the unknown. They will need the ability to collaborate to create aggregate or emergent functionality, and they will need the ability to negotiate and delegate interface responsibility to other mixtangibles.

The technical challenges in this are immense and will need the attention of hoards of engineers for decades to come. The conceptual challenges are no less demanding, and it seems clear that new design approaches and entirely new perspectives on functionality will be needed. When the artefacts in our world are no longer passive solitary objects, we can no longer treat them as singular passive entities. Instead we must focus considerable design attention on the characteristics of a dynamic, unpredictable society of semi-autonomous mixtangibles and its consequences for our everyday lives and interaction with each other and with our environment.

2 Designing for the society of mixtangibles

As indicated above, the design challenge of communicating mixtangibles is extremely complex and requires considerable knowledge and development within a variety of disciplines. The following sections briefly outline some of the central elements in this challenge and discuss how they can be related in a more concerted effort.

Figure 1 describes the complexity of the design challenge when technology is seen through the media use within a social context.

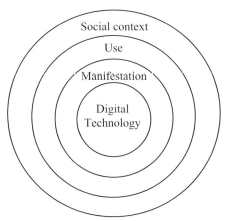

Fig. 1. Digital technology in the context of use

Digital technology carries with it all the technical design challenges, but it has no relevance whatsoever unless it manifests itself in media artefacts which again only obtain meaning in a context of use. The manifestation of and interaction with digital technology is primarily an interaction design challenge, which in itself involves a number of skills and disciplines. However, when digital technology with all its aspects of information, computation and communication becomes pervasive, the implications reach far beyond the individual use situation. The development must thus be viewed in a social context and shaped by social deliberations and decisions.

We arc thus basically faced with three design challenges: a technical design, an interaction design and a social design. The following sections discuss each of these challenges, and thus attempt to paint an overall picture of the complexity and integrated nature of the design challenge in societies of mixtangibles.

2.1 The technical design challenge

History tells us that heterogeneous and dynamic environments are very difficult to design top-down. Centralised systems simply are too vulnerable to disruptive change and to new entrants that do not follow the established rules. In contained, centrally controlled systems, such as a car, it is possible to control the parts and their interoperability. When communicating mixtangibles are let loose in society at large, however, they must be designed for the unexpected, and they must collaborate to offer aggregate services and interfaces to their surroundings. So, how does one design for the unexpected and how does one design for emergent functionality?

Nature with its adaptable systems is a wonderful example, but it is the result of a slow, evolutionary and rather barbaric process, which, although inspirational, is hardly practical. A more pragmatic example to learn from, albeit from a more static and controlled domain, is the LEGO brick. A LEGO brick is a self-contained object designed with two primary objectives in mind: it has to fulfil a normally fairly static function and it has to be able to connect to every other LEGO brick it might meet when subjected to the fantasy of a child at play. When creating a new LEGO brick the designer must therefore not only consider the specific need at hand, but must also adhere to some very strict syntactic principles and carefully contemplate the general applicability of the brick. Designers should never indiscriminately add new bricks to the vocabulary, and they should always bear in mind that a brick will not exist for many minutes before being exposed to unanticipated use. A wonderful side effect of this approach is that new functionality emerges when bricks are connected to form structures – without the need of a magic wand to imbue them with life.

It is a simple example, but it illustrates the need for a system of rules and for careful discriminate design focusing on the society of bricks, the user and the unexpected use. When dealing with communicating mixtangibles, as with the case of the LEGO brick, we must focus on open-ended systems and give as much attention to the generic as to the specific and as much attention to connections as to functions.

Dealing with fairly static artefacts, where connections consist of standardised studs and tubes is a far cry from trying to cope with dynamic, intentional and heterogeneous mixtangibles entering the world from virtually every industry each with their specific objectives and functionality. We should, however, be able to learn some basic rules by studying atomary systems such as nature, alphabetic languages and LEGO bricks and then apply them on not only a technical, but also a conceptual, level.

One way to be inspired is by performing a little thought experiment. Imagine that all the LEGO bricks were living creatures, sharing a common language, and intent on finding and fulfilling their purpose in life (in order to stay fairly close to the anticipated world of mixtangibles we will not imbue them with the capability of motion). What would they want to do? What would be the characteristics of their language, and about what would they be communicating?

Let's start with the fundamental 2 by 4 brick. It is very generic and would of course have a very broad and sketchy concept of individual purpose compared to the golden crown brick, which would always be yearning for a king's head upon which to rest. Yet, left to its own devices a 2 by 4 brick would search deeply within its industrial roots and would discover the image of a Danish quaint brick house It would see itself as an indispensable part of a wall holding up some grand structure – a symbol of Cartesian beauty and material wealth; and it would wish to find other, like-minded 2 by 4s with which to share its sense of purpose. Without other bricks it is nothing, and it would therefore need to be able to identify and share possibilities and sense of purpose with other bricks that it might meet between the hands of a child. It would need to know some basics about structural integrity and about where 2 by 4s do and do not fit.

But, perhaps it doesn't know about houses. Perhaps it just has a concept of self and has some vague notion about belonging, and it just roams around looking for connections. It could have an affinity towards certain types of connections, and it could have yearnings for stability, structure and perhaps even aesthetics. Yet, in order for a model built from bricks to make sense to its surroundings, some design principles must ensure that the aggregate structure communicates to the surroundings as an entity rather than as an incomprehensible murmur of a thousand more or less satisfied bricks. This entity can only appear as an aggregate of the individual bricks – no matter whether they have organised themselves in a hierarchy, a network or a hive.

What is the purpose of all this? The possibilities are endless, and just about any engineer can come up with numerous useful examples, but it is very easy to lose track of the fact that LEGO bricks are actually supposed to be fun toys that scaffold creativity in children. The sobering question remains: do the children really want mixtangibles, and can we really provide them with mixtangibles that enhance their creativity in a better way than dumb plastic bricks?[4]

---

[4] In fact this is also a sobering thought for the whole area of mixtangibles. The development of societies of mixtangibles is inevitable, but whether they will be of real value to human society is very much an open question, which is unfortunately virtually impossible to address due to the complexity of the issue and the speed of development.

Nevertheless, the example points to some very important design principles. If communicating mixtangibles are to be able to participate in an ordered society of mixtangibles, be prepared for the unexpected encounter and be able to collaborate with other mixtangibles to form and communicate aggregate functionality, they must at least:

1. Be fundamentally designed within a syntactically simple but semantically rich structure of communication and collaboration,[5]
2. Be imbued with some form of self-awareness and sense of purpose,
3. Be adaptable within an ever-changing social setting and a fairly stable set of ground rules, and
4. Be able to work as peers, but also to subordinate themselves or take charge as the situation requires.

These are formidable challenges, but from the point of view of software design they are not insurmountable. Open standards for communication and collaboration exist and are continuously being refined, and issues such as flexibility, adaptability, rule following and collaboration are being addressed within a number of research areas such as artificial life, neural networks and software agents. Unfortunately all of these efforts have so far only provided some basic and mostly application-specific building blocks, and the crucial issues remain at a much higher level of abstraction. When discussing the OSI model[6] in conjunction with communicating mixtangibles, researchers tend to agree that the lower five layers dealing with establishing networks and conducting communication can be handled, but as soon as the discussion turns to the presentation and application layers a number of major conceptual problems appear. This observation clearly points to the fact, that, although we may be able to solve the issues of making mixtangibles communicate with each other, our technical design work gives us virtually no clues as to how the mixtangibles could or should communicate with us.

2.2 The interaction design challenge

2.2.1 Designing individual mixtangibles

Designing mixtangibles is a different and more complicated task than designing simple artefacts or interfaces for standard computers. A mixtangible must speak to

---

[5] Proponents of a-life systems would argue that this structure would need to be adaptable in order not to limit the fundamental system to the visions of its designers. The system of LEGO bricks with its inherently discrete and Cartesian structure and limitations provides a very good example of the limits of a fixed set of rules. It should, however, be noted, that the requirement does not state anything about the level of abstraction or the dynamism of the rule set, and I consider this discussion beyond the scope of this chapter.

[6] The OSI (Open Systems Interconnect) model from ISO is the seven-layer standard for creating connections and communications between systems. See www.iso.org.

its user through its physical form just like any other designed object, but how does one communicate complex and dynamic functionality through physical form?

The most ubiquitous mixtangible today is probably the mobile phone. It started more or less as a normal phone, which just happened to be connected to a big, semi-portable box rather than to a wall socket, and most mobile phones today still resemble normal phones with their keypads and overall shape. In terms of functionality, however, they have become increasingly complex, and today a mobile phone can fulfil a large variety of functions: PDA, messenger, alarm clock, game machine, MP3 player, camera, memo recorder and even remote control. The result is that we today have phones such as the Ericsson P800, which is very powerful, yet remarkably difficult to use for its original purpose – making and answering a phone call! It does not look or handle much like a clock or a music device either, and one might wonder how it had looked, if it had grown out of a "disc man" instead of out of a phone.[7]

The issue is always one of choosing or striking a balance between extending well known metaphors such as the phone or the wrist watch or creating completely new ones, such as for instance the C-Pen.

Fig. 2. The C-Pen from C Technologies AB (Courtesy of CPEN 2003)

Traditional metaphors allow for immediate recognition, but tend to lock people into established expectations and behaviour patterns, whereas completely new

---

[7] An interesting example of recent attempts in breaking away from tradition is the Nokia N-Gage, which has been created almost entirely as a game machine and has virtually no visible phone identity (see Nokia 2003).

metaphors, though potentially more powerful, are much harder to develop, design and communicate through design.

So how do we come up with these new metaphors? The only way to do this is to break the boundaries of traditional thinking. Unfortunately, the likelihood of this happening within already established disciplines is low. In my experience, boundaries are best broken when different disciplines and perspectives are confronted with each other in the pursuit of a joint task. I will thus once again point to the necessity of mixing a variety of disciplines to address these new design challenges.

2.2.2 Designing societies of mixtangibles

The notion of ambient intelligence as described in the ambient intelligence vision quoted above and in the Scenarios for Ambient Intelligence 2010 (Ambient 2002) envisions scenarios in which our surroundings have acquired not only intelligence but also the ability to dynamically aggregate the functionality of large numbers of computational devices into a seamless and coherent interface between people and environment. As described above, creating such an ad hoc, aggregate interface from an unpredictable and dynamic combination of mixtangibles is a vast technical challenge, but it is an even greater interaction design challenge, as the desired interaction with a smart environment is entirely unclear. Throughout the last thirty years we have been living with largely engineering-driven visions of the smart house, the smart meeting room, the smart office etc., but none of these visions have found their way into reality. Engineers have a great track record of coming up with specific useful devices, but when it comes to creating a larger vision of human life in the future, they have tended to fail dismally. Engineering visions tend to be overly simplistic and mechanistic with little understanding of the complexity of social life. They fail to recognise that we do not organise our lives in accordance with technology – we appropriate technology into our lives and invariably use it in ways for which it was never intended. Therefore, there is no room for these grand technology-driven visions, and quite possibly not for grand visions driven from other disciplines either.

It is one thing to imagine specific functionality such as your PDA recognising and creating an interface to the projector in a meeting room. It is an entirely different issue to design for heterogeneous dynamic environments. Should one device take control and be the interface to all the others? Should there be a central system with a specific intelligent environment or does the intelligent environment emerge as a result of a negotiation between independent services? In fact do we really have any idea of how to design emergent environments?

These are all relevant interaction design challenges in terms of aesthetics, affordances and functionality, but they all depend on both higher-level choices and lower-level systems design. There is simply no way they can be handled in isolation without close collaboration with both social and technical design.

At this point in time we have many more questions than answers, and I believe it is only possible to give very general guidelines that might help us to start to explore the area.

First of all, grand visions must be replaced with open-ended designs and systems of communication, but secondly we must create an acute awareness of the implications of our choices. The interaction design challenge within societies of mixtangibles will thus be highly dependent on our answers to both the technical and social design challenges. An important implication of this is that we cannot assume that an extension of industrial design into interaction design will be a sufficient solution to the design challenge at hand.

2.3 The social design challenge

Mixtangibles will change the way we live, as indicated by the numerous scenarios created (mainly by technologists) for research planning (see, e.g., Ambient 2002; Pervasive 2003). Our surroundings can become responsive in new ways, we can be in communication at all times and both we and the objects around us can be continuously tracked. Great opportunities open up, but there are also new threats and perils to face. What happens to our personal freedom? Will we want to have chips implanted in the bodies of our children in order to be able to track them at all times? Will they then be the subjects of abductions and mutilations for the purpose of identity theft? Do we wish to eliminate the distinction between work and leisure, between public and private?

It seems obvious that we should start with visions of how we wish to live in the future but is this a design challenge? The artefacts we create shape our lives, and the designer is thus an agent of social change. Without social responsibility design becomes empty, and the design of communicating mixtangibles without consideration of the social consequences can be downright dangerous.

But how can we possibly hope to shape society through the design of communicating mixtangibles when, as we have already noted, it is virtually impossible to design such complex systems top-down, and when we will only be able to control the development of a fraction of the society of mixtangibles anyway? Experience tells us that technology affects our social world in unexpected ways, so how do we address the issue of value-based design when dealing with a complex unknown?

One way of doing so is by setting the ground rules properly. As a society can be governed by a constitution and a set of social constructs, the society of mixtangibles can be created and governed by a set of design rules that are very similar to our own laws and regulations. These laws must allow for a great degree of freedom of design, expression and functionality of each mixtangible but under adherence to a set of rules and a language of communication and negotiation.

The task of implementing rules and language is largely a technical one, but the consequences reach beyond technology in ways we have not seen before, and the foundation must be based in value systems resembling those we find in political and social theory. Choosing between hierarchies and peer networks, for instance, will have huge implications on every level, and we can draw important lessons from historical examples.

Consider for instance the mobile phone. Phones were created to facilitate communication; yet they are not able to communicate with each other. If you are in a city your phone will be within direct reach of hundreds of mobile phones, yet it cannot communicate with them without the aid of a phone company and a hierarchy of relay systems. Currently, all business models found in the established communications industry are based on this model, which is beyond doubt stifling to creativity, innovation AND communication.

Daniel Siewiorek (2003) writes that "the goal of the merger of ubiquitous and wearable computing should be to provide 'the right information to the right person at the right time'", but is it really that simple? If the mobile phones were actually able to talk directly to each other and to other computational devices, mobile communication between people could of course be virtually free. The machine-to-machine communication aspect is also interesting. About what would they be talking to each other? Would it all be directed at providing information to their owners, or would they lend themselves, for example, to other phones to act as relay stations. Would they form clusters of interest and information, provide information to a stationary system directing traffic, or perhaps engage in improving their neural network-based backgammon game by engaging in city-wide tournaments? All these activities have little meaning to us, unless they result in some information to someone at some time, but the implications seem to be much bigger than those concerned with the individual user or the individual artefact.

A number of examples of ad hoc peer-to-peer networks have begun to appear. The rapid grass roots development of wireless ad hoc networking with both local and global implications[8] gives hope to the idea that future developments will be based on a social model of free communication among peers rather than communication hierarchies controlled by large corporations. This development was started with the advent of the Internet, and it is by far the most interesting social agenda to be following and pursuing in the development of societies of mixtangibles.

3 Conclusion

A quick and rather superficial tour de force of the society of mixtangibles has revealed a wealth of design challenges involving numerous disciplines. Yet, virtually none of these challenges can be addressed independently of the others.

In order to create a reality of dynamic societies of heterogeneous mixtangibles we must come up with ground rules and with an open architecture that allows for maximum freedom of expression and innovation under the responsibility of adhering to ground rules.

---

[8] See for instance Picopeer (2003), which is an agreement by which wireless networks can automatically join up to form aggregate networks.

Viable societies of mixtangibles, however, can only be created if the individual mixtangibles can act as responsible citizens, and they can only serve us mere mortals if they can create affordance from complexity. We must in other words treat the society of mixtangibles in much the same way as we treat the society of humans – designing for diversity, disruption and freedom of expression.

None of these things can happen without some serious software engineering, but if we start at the bottom without considering at least some central aspects of what kind of societies (human and mixtangible) we wish to create, we do so at our own peril. This is also the case if we let ourselves be driven by technical visions of smart environments rather than social visions of a better life.

The ISTAG Report on Ambient Intelligence (2003) takes a first step in the right direction with its formulation of a social agenda for the development of ubiquitous digital technology. In order to turn words into action, however, our main challenge in the near future will be to create open environments in which the necessary social, technical and aesthetic discussions can take place and be turned into a collaborative design practice. Around the world several attempts in this direction are being made, but unfortunately strong traditions separate the fields, and most of the initiatives show a bias towards design, engineering or academic reflection.

A new notion of computation as just another, albeit complex, material for design must be developed in order to put the technology in its right place, and design must be seen as social intervention driven by social visions. This broad view of design as a technical, interaction-oriented and social endeavour does not imply the invocation of the Renaissance man. It requires the involvement of people from a variety of disciplines, and it requires organisations, processes and methods in which they can meet as equals in respect of each skill and perspective and with an understanding of the necessity of the multidisciplinary discourse and design challenge.

References

Ambient. (2002). European Commission, Community Research, User-friendly Information Society, ISTAG, Scenarios for Ambient Intelligence 2010.
    ftp://ftp.cordis.lu/pub/ist/docs/istagscenarios2010.pdf
Bødker S (1987) Through the Interface – A Human Activity Approach to User Interface Design. Ph.D. thesis, Århus, DAIMI PB – 224
CPEN. (2003). Retrieved October, 2003, from http://www.cpen.com/
Disappearing. (2003). Retrieved November, 2003, from http://www.disappearing-computer.net/
ISTAG. (2003). IST Advisory Group, Ambient Intelligence: from vision to reality, Draft Report. Retrieved November, 2003, from ftp://ftp.cordis.lu/pub/ist/docs/istag-ist2003_draft_consolidated_report.pdf
Nokia. (2003). Retrieved November, 2003, from www.n-gage.com
Pervasive. (2003). Teknologisk Fremsyn, Ministeriet for Viden, Teknik og Udvikling, Pervasive Computing, Copenhagen. From
    http://www.teknologiskfremsyn.dk/html/docs/ikt_hovedrapport.pdf

Picopeer. (2003). Retrieved November, 2003, from
http://www.picopeer.net/wiki/index.php/PicoPeeringAgreement
Redström J (2001) Design of Everyday Computational Things. Ph.D. thesis, Gothenburg
Studies in Informatics. (Report 20, ISSN 1400-741X, Gothenburg). Retrieved
November, 2003, from http://www.math.chalmers.se/~redstrom/thesis/index.html
Rettig M (2003): Interaction Design History in a Teeny Little Nutshell. Retrieved
December, 2003, from
http://www.marcrettig.com/writings/rettig.interactionDesignHistory.2.03.pdf
Siewiorek DP (2003) New frontiers in application design. Communications of the ACM
45(12)
Tangible. (2003). Retrieved November, 2003, from http://tangible.media.mit.edu/
Turing A (1936) On computable numbers, with an application to the
Entscheidungsproblem. Proceedings of the London Mathematical Society, series 2, vol
42. Retrieved November, 2003, from
http://www.cs.umass.edu/~immerman/cs601/turingReference.html
Weiser M (1991) The computer for the 21st century. Scientific American 265(3):94-104

Digital jewellery as experience

Jayne Wallace[1], Andrew Dearden[2]

[1]Art & Design Research Centre, Sheffield Hallam University
UK
jswallac@athena.shu.ac.uk

[2]Computing Research Centre, Sheffield Hallam University
UK
a.m.dearden@shu.ac.uk

Abstract

When designing interactive devices or environments the role of human experience is crucial to the depth and sensitivity of that interaction. Increasing attention is being paid within the fields of HCI and Interaction Design to the importance of human experience, how we can learn to gain an understanding of experience and how to use this to inform the creation of environments for positive technological interactions. As computing and technology become more ubiquitous in their conception, designers are looking for methods of bridging technology with the human form.

In this chapter we explore our different perspectives as a contemporary jeweller and an interaction designer focusing on a framework, which has supported and enabled a dialogue of our respective and collective understandings of experience in the area of wearable interactive devices and contemporary jewellery. We use the framework to explore our experience of existing designs of contemporary jewellery and also of interactive jewellery proposals, which lead us to suggest possible ways forward in the design of wearable artefacts, which can truly be described as digital jewellery.

1 Introduction

Designing for the full range of human experience may well be the theme for the next generation of discourse about software design. (Winograd 1996, p. xix)

The design of any interactive device requires sensitivity to multiple disciplines and typically involves input from different people with a range of training and expertise. Psychologists, sociologists, industrial designers, artists and communications theorists are already widely recognised as important contributors to interactive systems design. As our devices become smaller and lighter, they are increasingly worn and carried, as well as being used. Additionally, there is a growing interest within HCI in emotional aspects of our relationships with technology (Monk et al. 2002; Blythe et al. 2003; Norman 2004; Taylor and Harper 2002). These trends suggest the need for a dialogue with disciplines such as jewellery design, which is centrally concerned with the design of objects that are worn, and with issues of the emotional meanings that we attach to physical objects.

In this chapter, from our different perspectives as a contemporary jeweller and an interaction designer, we explore what our disciplines can learn from each other, and reflect on a framework that has supported our mutual understandings of experience. Based on our investigations we suggest some routes forward to digital artefacts that can truly qualify as jewellery.

In the next section, we present a brief introduction to contemporary jewellery, illustrate how contemporary jewellers seek to imbue objects with emotional meaning and use these objects to communicate with wearers and viewers. This understanding of jewellery can be related to design for experience. In Section 3, we examine Wright, McCarthy and Meekison's (2003) proposed framework for the analysis of experience, and relate it to examples of contemporary jewellery. In Section 4, we examine some recent projects and proposals that explore the concept of digital jewellery, based on the framework, and discuss the successes and limitations of such work. We are concerned with the potential of these projects to establish the emotional quality of relationship between a wearer and an object that we would expect from great jewellery. In Section 5, we examine a number of efforts that indicate possible routes towards the realisation of digital artefacts that truly qualify as jewellery. From our experience, we conclude that the proposed framework is a valuable tool to enable a dialogue between HCI and jewellery, and to support design that can surpass user expectations and create opportunities for rich experience.

2 An introduction to contemporary jewellery

2.1 Beyond jewellery as social signifier

In the context of studies of Upper Palaeolithic societies White observes:

What people wear, and what they do to and with their bodies in general, forms an important part of the flow of information – establishing, modifying, and commenting on major social categories. (White 2002)

Traditionally jewellery has been used to symbolise wealth, social status and cultural positioning, and has focused on the use of rare materials. In the past century, the power an object has, especially one worn on the body, to exemplify and express broader concepts, has advanced jewellery beyond this traditional role.

In the post-war period, the modernist movement, with its promotion of technology, machine industrialisation and a distinct aesthetic, led many jewellers to reappraise the methods and materials they used. The *New Jewellery* movement heralded a radical departure in the period from the mid 1960s to the early 1970s. Emmy Van Leersum and Gijs Bakker went far to establish the basis of how we perceive the breadth of the potential role of jewellery today. They protested against the use of expensive materials, the limited translation of the meanings jewellery could represent and conservatism in the form and placement on the body. Their work deliberately questioned the social and cultural politics of jewellery consumption and pushed the perimeters of what is accepted as jewellery. The influences of an industrial aesthetic are clear; the pieces reflect a feeling of the "future", technological accomplishment and possibility (Figure 1). The forms were minimal and the scale was often challenging.

Fig. 1. *Large Collar* 1967. Aluminium. Gijs Bakker. From http://www.gijsbakker.com

Following the work of these early pioneers, public conception of jewellery has moved significantly in the past four decades, accepting a much broader range of forms and materials.

2.2 Jewellery as comment

A controversial phenomenon from the early 1970s is *Conceptual Jewellery*.

(Conceptual Jewellers)…don't necessarily consider jewellery an adornment, but rather a message mediator. (Riklin-Schelbert 1999, p. 111)

The value of this type of jewellery is perceived to be in the thought process or concept of a piece, rather than in the materials used or the form. The intended site of these pieces was often the gallery rather than the street. For conceptual jewellers, the intention of a piece is to provoke and stimulate reactions from wearers and viewers.

Otto Künzli extended this approach, using jewellery to make direct social or political comment. One piece (Figure 2) titled *Gold Makes Blind* consisted of a black rubber armband completely concealing a gold ball. The piece challenges us as viewer in a number of ways. We must consider whether or not there is a gold ball within the piece. If we accept this, do we perceive the piece to be of greater value because of the gold even though it is not visible? The piece also invites us to consider the way gold bullion is stored in underground vaults, protecting the world economy and to reflect on the importance of South Africa in gold production (where apartheid was still in operation), and question our willingness to use the products of such regimes.

British jeweller Hazel White has produced a number of pieces that comment on modern gender power relationships, for example, *Defence Mechanism #4* (Figure 3).

The aim of these pieces is not adornment, but to engage the viewer intellectually and emotionally. McCarthy and Wright (2003) examine the notion of enchantment, the sense of personal captivation in an experience. These conceptual pieces aim to enchant the wearer or viewer and through that enchantment, stimulate the viewer towards a new awareness of the issues the jeweller addresses.

2.3 The emotional content of jewellery

Whilst jewellery has departed from the notion of value based on the rarity of the materials used, many of the forms used in contemporary jewellery reflect a concern with preciousness. The fact that jewellery is worn close to the body, within the wearer's personal space, gives it a particular intimacy that may be absent from other tools or devices that a user encounters. There is a further reflection of intimacy through the symbolism used in some pieces where the maker handles personally significant subject matter.

Since the anticipation of the Millennium and beyond many jewellers have been exploring issues of identity, memory and notions of presence and absence. The jewellery of Iris Eichenberg reflects many of these issues (Figure 4).

Her work consists of small objects seeming to draw from memories and childhood, telling fragments of stories. For Eichenberg the elements of preciousness seem to be the memories she is working with and the connotations they bring to her work. Writer Louise Schouwenberg says of Eichenberg's work

At first they don't strike one as jewellery at all. (…) Iris Eichenberg is fascinated by invisible systems; there's a strong suggestion of machinery at work, but it remains concealed. Likewise the puzzling functioning of a human being captivates her. (…) Just as her jewellery objects can be read as a figurative language, all parts can be read as images loaded with references. (Schouwenberg 1998, p. 2)

Underneath its (the jewellery's) filmy skin a silent battle takes place in which all details matter, in which every single part carries its own specific meaning. (…) A knitted container is connected to a silver twig. Fruit trees are in full bloom, a child observes; the expectant energy flows back through the tiny twig. (Schouwenberg 1998, p. 2)

Fragments of memories are isolated by Eichenberg and then used in these pieces to create a piece of parts and a new interpretation from them. A memory is presented here not as a warm and cosy environment, but as a strange connection of remnants of events. They form a puzzle, a codification. The unease these pieces may present for a viewer could be viewed as a strength of the piece. They present a challenge, a provocation to find a way to interpret the piece personally where the narrative and structure are not easy to follow.

Jewellers Hiroko Ozeki (Figure 6) and Lin Cheung (Figure 5) have both used specific events from their own lives in their jewellery dealing with their feelings of loss and as a way to comment on the situation; the resulting pieces bring something beautiful and poetic from their experiences.

Both jewellers made mourning jewellery. Memoria is a neck hoop made by Cheung of which she says…

In memory of my Mother. Whilst sorting through her belongings, I came across several ear scrolls that did not belong to an earring. After putting her affairs in order, I gave the lost scrolls a meaning once more in the form of new jewellery. (Marzee 2001, p. 25)

These pieces are intended to evoke strong emotional responses from those who encounter them. These designers are not merely designing a form; they are seeking to design a rich experience for an audience. Enchantment, in the sense of McCarthy and Wright (2003) is as much a part of their trade as it is for the conceptual jewellers examined above.

2.4 Jewellery: A multilayered experience

Contemporary jewellery is a rich discipline that has extended the vocabulary of the three-dimensional language of form by embracing new materials, new inspirations and by challenging preconceptions of jewellery and its role in society. Jewellery is about positioning things: in a culture, in a space, on the body, in a time frame. Many jewellers characterise their work by describing it using the following layers; one layer is the object itself, the aesthetics and materials of the piece, which relate to the cultural, social and personal resonance of the jewellery. A second layer is the text or narrative accompanying the object, often in the form of a title. A further layer is how and where the piece is presented and a final layer is the mode of physical interaction, how it is worn, comfort and where it is placed on the body. Personal attention is paid by the jeweller to the significance of each of these elements in order to achieve the desired qualities. This translation of the production of jewellery objects as a desire to create a "complete" experience is about a dialogue. A dialogue firstly between maker and self through practice and self-expression resulting in the production of an object and then between maker and audience through this object. Contemporary jewellery is not about High Street fashion and accessories; that is the domain of commercial mass production jewellery, which acts to follow the ideas of fashion, rather than creating its own discourse. Jewellery as accessory, heirloom or symbol of social status is often how the non-specialist encounters it. In contrast contemporary jewellery explores relationships: between self and object, individuals, groups, maker and audience and maker and practice. As such it is part of human communication. The skilled contemporary jeweller is part of an ongoing conversation, using a rich vocabulary of forms, materials and concepts to enhance human experience.

3 Understanding jewellery as experience

As we have shown above, contemporary jewellery is not simply an issue of adornment or aesthetics. Rather, contemporary jewellers seek to communicate with their wearers and viewers. The concern of the jeweller becomes the potential experience of the viewer or wearer in response to the piece and its setting.

3.1 A vocabulary for analysing experience

Wright et al. (2003) suggest a framework for the analysis of "experience" exploring the ways in which users make sense of experience. Here, we draw upon one part of this framework to offer a vocabulary for discussing jewellery: namely the four "threads" of experience. These threads are each explained briefly by Wright et al., and below we offer a paraphrase of their descriptions, as we understand them.

- The *compositional* thread deals with the part-whole composition of the experience and the relations between components. In an interaction, the narrative structure, the options of action, notions of agency and explanations of cause and consequence of actions may be included. In our experience of a work of art or jewellery, examination of the juxtaposition, the setting and relationships between elements would be aspects of the compositional thread.
- The *sensual* thread explores the aesthetics and physical qualities of an event, encounter, object or image etc. This sensual thread is experienced through sensory perceptions: sight, sound, smell, taste and touch – our sensual engagement with the situation.
- The *emotional* thread covers the experience of different states of being through empathy. Wright et al. justify their distinction of emotion from sensation, giving the example of the way that control over sensations such as fear or anxiety may be used to support emotions of fulfillment, satisfaction or fun. Watching a horror movie or climbing a dangerous mountain peak highlight this distinction.

Fig. 2. *Gold Makes Blind* 1980. Armband. Rubber, gold. Otto Künzli

Fig. 3. *Defence Mechanism #4* 1995. Aluminium, body, C-type print. Hazel White
Image courtesy of artist.

Fig. 4. *Afbeelding Omslag* 1998. Brooch. Wool, silver. Iris Eichenberg
Image courtesy of Galerie Louise Smit, Amsterdam. Photographer Ron Zijlstra.

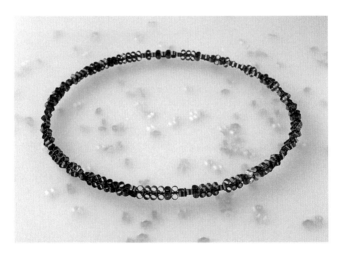

Fig. 5. *Memoria.* 1999. Neck hoop. Silver, gold. Lin Cheung
Image courtesy of Galerie Marzee, Netherlands. Photographer Michiel Heffels.

- The *spatiotemporal* thread relates to aspects of time and space, and our perceptions of them, within the experience. Our perception of the spatial and temporal qualities of an experience, of pace or proximity, can vary in response to emotional, sensual or compositional threads. Conversely, notions of public and private space, boundaries between self and other may have an impact upon the compositional, sensual or emotional threads.

It should be noted that Wright et al. present these threads as intertwined perspectives on a holistic concept, recognising both the conscious and unconscious aspects of experience, not as reductionist "components" to be considered in isolation. In what follows, we shall use these threads to provide a vocabulary for discussing existing approaches to digital device design, and tentative steps towards digital jewellery.

3.2 Examining Wright et al.'s framework in relation to examples of contemporary jewellery

How does contemporary jewellery attend to the four threads of experience as denoted by Wright et al.? Here we use four examples to illustrate the experiential dynamics at play. Think of your encounter with these pieces of jewellery as an experience.

Hiroko Ozeki's *Tear Collector* (Figure 6), made following the death of her father, is a silver representation of a rose petal, cupped in shape and small enough to fit in the palm.

Sensually, the piece is light in weight, similar to a real petal, and has a soft finish. The composition as a petal provides connotations of beauty. The piece is presented to us here away from the body, floating on a black background. This presentation is intentional, and composed with the title *Tear Collector*, it offers a narrative of solitude and sadness, contradicting the connotations of the rose. The black background suggests isolation and absence and along with the title leads to questions about the cause of the tears, or perhaps engages the viewer in an experience recalling their own tears. Thus the piece calls on the viewer to empathise with the maker, or communicates the maker's empathy to the viewer.

This empathy can offer a form of closure for the viewer of the piece, a way to gain a personal understanding of it. Brenda Laurel (1991) links empathy to the notion of catharsis in theatre. Catharsis and empathy therefore are vehicles through which we can connect with an experience, that is, a play, a piece of jewellery, or a piece of software in a personally significant emotional way. Catharsis allows us to identify with the experience and then to reinterpret it to fit it into and relate it to our own lives.

Eyelashes (Figure 7) and *Touch* (Figures 8 and 9) by co-author Jayne Wallace were made as part of a series of five pieces based on the individual. The pieces are worn by one person and involve individual experiences of the five senses. The communication experienced and commented on in these pieces is between the individual and his or her own body.

The eyelashes, made from silver and stainless steel, metals used medically with the body, are too heavy for the wearer to open her eyes once worn. The presentation and aesthetics of the piece offer a notion of femininity, of "dressing up", which suggests personal choice compositionally and sensually. Through the process of applying the eyelashes there is a sense of ceremony spatiotemporally, a private space, an intimacy, which is strengthened sensually because the objects feel gentle and fragile. The wearer found the eyelashes to be soporific. Although they mask a sense the eyelashes are very comfortable to wear and the silver quickly warms to the temperature of the body. The approach was to make quiet and theatrical, beautiful forms; by doing so the aim was to create an appearance of choice, not enforcement. The spatiotemporal and sensual qualities of the piece involve the sensations of wearing something in close proximity to the body which bars a sense. The sense of touch is often associated with intimacy and personal space, yet the sense of sight is often how we evaluate these phenomena. In excluding the sense of sight the wearer can exclude visual distractions and concentrate on the self. The main motivation of this collection of five pieces was to emotionally engage the wearer with the experience through self-reflection.

Touch are silver forms worn covering the pads of the fingers, made by casting a person's fingerprints. These pieces as with *Eyelashes* are presented on the body and offer a way of masking a sense. The compositional structure of the work suggests a gentle unity of form and body. Sensually the forms are cast from the body creating an intimacy through this personalisation. They have a satin surface texture akin to flesh and fit perfectly for one individual only, tracing the contours of the fingerprint and the nuances of the fleshy finger pads. The emotional thread is engaged with both through wearing the forms (the notion of hiding an element of identity is intensely personal) and through not wearing them. There is a transition from private to public space in removing the forms as this intimate element of an individual, the fingerprint, is then disclosed. In and after this act of revealing, spatiotemporally the physical marker can act as a visual memory, the memory of a touch or a trace of someone.

Christoph Zellweger's *Body Part VII* (Figure 10) is made from expanded polystyrene and chrome. The piece is presented to us on the naked human form indicating that this is its intended locus, or this is to what it relates.

These compositional qualities link to the spatiotemporal thread offering a very intimate location for the jewellery. The form is not only presented to us on the body, but it fits into the cavities shown in a specific way. This presentation of intimacy, physical "fit" to the body and the title of the piece give a strong idea that the jewellery is being absorbed into the human form in some way. This piece wouldn't "make sense" as a form alone without the compositional makeup of the presentation, or image. The aesthetics of the image, choice of material and form all strengthen the attention to the sensual and emotional threads. The expanded polystyrene is vastly different from a human body, yet at the same time the amorphous form and surface dimpling are evocative of human skin and inner organs. Most of us will have come into contact with expanded polystyrene; it is a throwaway material. The location of the material so intimately on the body may feel uneasy to the viewer, something so disposable and chemically produced depicted akin to body parts. However, polystyrene is a non-biodegradable material and therefore more lasting than gold. The material is used as a precious commodity in this work; its permanence and fragility provide juxtaposition to exploit. Zellweger understands this tension and uses references of chemically produced, manmade materials alongside the body to infer the sculpting and surgical implanting procedures we are increasingly turning to with our bodies. This idea of absorption of something inorganic into the human form illustrates one strand of comment making through his work.

These examples all illustrate how relatively complex pieces of contemporary jewellery relate to the four threads of experience. These examples are used here to open up the possibilities of what jewellery is and to explore and show how experientially rich an interaction with an object can be. The importance of our examples does not rely on the complexity of objects, however, in the attention to the different threads of experience. To illustrate this point, as a final example, we offer what is perhaps the most familiar form of jewellery: the wedding band. Compositionally it is made of one form, usually in a durable precious metal, seamless to represent a narrative of continuity. The wedding ceremony, the act of giving or placing the ring on the hand and the story of two people declaring their feelings for each other all act to strengthen the composition. The form of the ring is comfortable sensually, it is usually worn constantly and the physical act of placing the ring on the finger during the ceremony adds to the sensual thread. The ring is within our personal space constantly and acts as a representation of the event of marriage, the partner and the status of the wearer. This form of jewellery has a designated place on the body; it is important that it is worn on a particular finger which gives it a socially recognised meaning. Another interesting point spatiotemporally and sensually is that because the form is simple, non intrusive, comfortable and worn constantly, it can become part of us to the point that we forget we are wearing it. It is when we lose it or remove it that its presence is felt. Jeweller Lin Cheung reports:

I have made a discovery that I think comes much closer to my true feeling about the ring. After taking the band off, there is a very distinct ridge left on my finger. I find this more intimate and meaningful and closer to the real meaning of our union than that of the object that created it. But this impression would not appear without first the existence of the ring and the time it has taken to create it physically. (Cheung and Potter 2003, p. 6)

The wedding ring is one form of jewellery which is sometimes passed on through the generations connecting us to family histories. Compositionally and spatiotemporally this is a very strong form of jewellery, yet it is a paradox sensually and emotionally. It is one of the most emotionally laden forms of jewellery because of what it signifies; yet it is a common form, usually the simplest a ring can take. Its power emotionally and sensually is, initially, in what it represents, but over time the form grows into something different: a unique ring with scratches and marks indicative of the years of wear. The emotional thread is evident when someone chooses to wear the ring after the death of a partner as a constant reminder.

4 Existing approaches to digital jewellery

The increasing ubiquity of technology has led many design groups to consider the relationships between mobile digital technologies and jewellery. Organisations such as IBM, Philips Design and IDEO have all presented concepts that seek to combine technology with wearable jewellery. In this section, we shall consider some of these efforts, and assess the degree to which they offer rich multilayered experiences as sought by the makers of jewellery.

4.1 IBM's digital jewellery project

IBM research at their Almaden site has been working on the development of digital jewellery.

Cameron Miner, the founder of the design lab and lead scientist on the digital jewellery project states that

If you have something with you all the time, you might as well be able to wear it. (Miner, in Infoworld 2002)

The jewellery was created by Denise Chan, a graduate of mechanical engineering. The thinking behind digital jewellery is that as you push more functionality into pervasive devices, they are getting harder to use: smaller screens, tiny inputs, or just trying to talk and input at the same time; all these become a challenge. By taking the interface apart, putting it in the appropriate places, and allowing them to communicate wirelessly, IBM thinks it has a practical way to solve the problem. So we have a microphone on a pin or necklace, an earpiece on an earring or ear cuff, and a ring with a track point. There's a bracelet with text entry or dialling capability as well, or it might even have a small display. (Infoworld 2002)

This approach to design as "problem solving" with a focus on getting more functionality into pervasive devices to the neglect of the emotional, sensual, and playful potential in jewellery has resulted in commodities that are (in our opinion) no more challenging than some High Street jewellery. Turning to jewellery because "you might as well be able to wear it" offers a very narrow interpretation of what jewellery is, and naiveté in this case to the problems that may need solving.

In allowing function (voice communication) to lead the concept, the perceived issues or problems are potentially shallow and the resulting designs (again, in our opinion) echo this. The more important significant issues of why such devices should be made, or how such devices could enhance deeper levels of human communication are not evident in these pieces. The result is an experience for the wearer that may succeed in compositional and spatiotemporal terms, but is likely to provide little within the sensual and emotional threads of the experience.

Fig. 6. *Tear Collector* 2001. Silver. Hiroko Ozeki
Image courtesy of the artist

Fig. 7. *Eyelashes* 1999. Silver, steel. Jayne Wallace

Figs. 8 and 9. *Touch* 1999. Silver. Jayne Wallace

Fig. 10. *Body Part V11* 1997. Expanded polystyrene, chrome. Christoph Zellweger
Image courtesy of the artist

4.2 Phillips "New Nomads" concept

Research and Design at Philips has produced concepts for the integration of technology in our communities, homes and clothing. Philips is an example of a company with a number of approaches to the design of digital devices. They take a user-centred approach stating,

The traditional design disciplines are integrated with expertise from the human sciences and technology through a multi-disciplinary, research-based approach that makes it possible to create new solutions that satisfy and anticipate people's needs and aspirations. (Philips Corporate 2003)

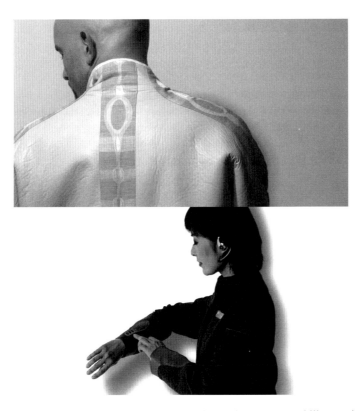

Figs. 11 and 12. *New Nomads*. Wearable Electronic Concepts. Philips Design
Images courtesy of Philips Design
http://www.design.philips.com/smartconnections/press/index.html

New Nomads (Figures 11 and 12) is an exploration of Wearable Electronics. Philips suggests that

As new technological developments advance they become better and smaller as we use refined, miniaturised technology. But there are limits to miniaturisation. It can help make products smaller and easier to use, but the ultimate dream is not to have easier tools: it is not to have to bother with tools at all! The step forward then is the integration of functions into objects that we do not feel clutter us, which are part of our life. (Philips Design 2003)

Philips' aim seems to be to create objects that are small enough to be unobtrusive, and worn within clothing, which are with us constantly in order to satisfy the need for ubiquitous connection. Their approach shows an openness to form and mode of interaction; their proposed devices often suggest playful ways of interacting with the systems and there is a tentative attempt to acknowledge the lack of sensory attention in current product design, by creating a "kimono"…

which is able to disperse an electrostatic charge via the fibres inside. The aim was to 'develop clothes that incorporate materials that help to de-stress the wearer.' (Philips Electronics 2000, pp. 125, 124)

Philips presents a pioneering spirit in their *New Nomads* concepts but the objects they propose lack intimacy. Consequently, they suggest an interesting offering only compositionally, sensually and spatiotemporally. The concept of integrating "de-stressing" functions into a garment that is enveloping and that may be associated with "serenity" suggests an attempt to address the emotional thread. However, it is not clear from the available images of this garment to what extent this has been achieved.

4.3 IDEO

Product Design Company IDEO has produced *Technojewelry*: proposals for wearable digital appliances, which intimate notions of jewellery. Figure 13 is an example called *GPS Toes* which are toe rings that act as signal transmitters, communicating to a GPS receiver kept in a bag or worn on a belt, which facilitates navigation around a city through the use of satellites.
    IDEO describes their use by stating,

Wearing one on each foot, the GPS Toes device will guide the wearer to a preset destination by vibrating and lighting up to signal upcoming direction changes. The left toe ring will indicate left turns and the right toe right turns, whether driving on the highway, walking on city streets, or hiking on the mountain trail. (IDEO Corporate Web site)

Technojewelry is part of IDEO's exploration of the relationship between people and wearable technology. The focuses of the appliances are the hands and feet described by IDEO as

… non intrusive locations for useful innovations, these concepts prove that new devices needn't look alien to your person and that we can make technology adapt to our lifestyles rather than the other way around." (IDEO Corporate Web site)

This proposal shows a more sensitive understanding of what it means to integrate an object into your appearance by wearing it. The attention to the spatiotemporal quality of the designs is strong, IDEO seem to recognise that the device needs to echo aspects of when and where it is going to be worn. The notions of someone wearing an object and someone using an object are considered in unison and yet we suggest that the *GPS Toes* do not offer such strong connections to the sensual, emotional and compositional threads of the experience they are creating. Compositionally and sensually the forms of the toe rings do not exploit the potential situation of being located on the foot. Although the notion of using the feet as receivers of information when walking is compositionally interesting, the devices are static forms, situated on the body, rather than acting with it, which do little to echo the organic shape and movement of the foot. There is an interesting element sensually and emotionally in the behaviour of the devices; how would it feel for toe rings to vibrate and flash to indicate direction? Sensually there is potential for enjoyment or irritation; emotionally there is the potential for playfulness or unease. The critique we offer is that these emotional and sensual qualities of the interaction are secondary to or a byproduct of the functionality and spatiotemporal aspects of the design.

It is evident in much wearable appliance design proposals that functionality and personal interaction with that function are explored intensively. However, what follows in terms of exploring the intricacies and opportunities of working with an object which is designed to be worn is limited and often naive. The fact that these considerations follow the functionality of a design is one key to the problem.

5 A new approach based on experience

How can we use the framework proposed by Wright et al. along with the specific perspective of contemporary jewellery to inform the conception and production of digital jewellery? What is the specific contribution of a contemporary jeweller to the design of wearable technology and digital jewellery?

Here we offer examples of progressive proposals for digital jewellery from product designers and contemporary jewellers. We suggest ways in which these proposals are contributing to a wider, more holistic approach to the conception and production of digital jewellery.

5.1 Progressive proposals from product design

The "Kiss Communicator" (Figure 14) by Heather Martin was developed as an RCA and IDEOlab research project with Duncan Kerr.

(Kiss Communicator)…is a hand held device which allows lovers to blow each other kisses across distance. It works by blowing into the central "mouth" of the object, where electronics translate the impulse into a series of randomly lit LEDs, which are then transmitted as a slow glow to your partner's equivalent device far away. (…) If picked up and squeezed, your partner's device will repeat the message in complementary colours, but if left untouched, the glowing message will fade quickly. (Myerson 2001, p. 120)

Kiss Communicator translates the idea of sending a message to someone through a very beautiful metaphor. Relating the Wright et al. framework to this piece we can suggest that the communicator relates strongly to the emotional thread of experience through the imagery of blowing a kiss to someone. The act of blowing into the device, or squeezing it to reciprocate the gesture of sending a kiss, provides a strong sensual element. Emotionally it is significant that the device reacts differently depending on the way in which the user blows the kiss. This opens the possibility of pairs of users each developing their own shared language. Spatiotemporally the form itself and the visual exchange of the act provide a substitute for the "other person", a physical representation of him or her. However, the spatiotemporal thread is weakened because there is no clear relationship between the object and the person blowing the kiss – where does the object reside or how is it carried when not in use? Compositionally the form does not echo a kiss. The form is a generic pod shape, which could be used to signify myriad ideas, but none specifically. The generic pod form lacks intimacy and individuality. However, it should be noted that Kiss Communicator was an early prototype, with a clearly pioneering concept exploring the exchange of emotional meaning between individuals through a behavioural ambiguous mode.

It aimed to explore new ways in which emotionally laden content could be exchanged via an intermediating technology when two people are separated by great distance. …This project sought to explore products that would facilitate new, more expressive, ways of communicating remotely. We asked the question: What would be the digital equivalent of a wave, a wink or a kiss? These are "messages" that are low on factual content, but laden with emotional value. (Heather Martin in www.interaction.rca.ac.uk/alumni/96-98/heather)

The compositional and spatiotemporal limitations of this design could be addressed effectively in further development, taking advantage of the fact that the size of the device could be significantly reduced using current technology.

The next examples from IDEO are the second of the *Technojewelry* concepts, *Ring Phone* (Figure 15).

Ring Phone is a concept for a mobile phone where the earpiece and mouthpiece telephony are embedded in finger jewellery. The cell phone rings unite an action of imitating a telephone with your hand with the actual function of the finger components. IDEO describes the use of the phones by stating

Calls can be initiated by raising the hand to the proper position, and voice-activated interaction will allow instant communication. The little-finger units will vibrate to indicate incoming calls and the thumb unit will beam the sound towards the ear when the hand is held in the listening position. (IDEO Corporate Website)

Emotionally the gestural quality of the concept is a strong element of the piece as it connects to play and childhood representations of the phone through mimicry signifying a phone. There is also a sensual quality to the gesture itself as the hand actually forms the structure of the phone in this intimate gesture. This affinity of function, the gestural representation of the phone and the way the rings are worn show a strong attention to the emotional, compositional, sensual and spatiotemporal threads. However, the forms of the rings as with the Kiss

Communicator do not reflect the concept, but they suggest a more imaginative interpretation of digital devices.

5.2 Progressive proposals from contemporary jewellery

Technology was used to express ideas of human communication by jeweller Nicole Gratiot Stöber (Figures 16 to 18). Her jewellery reacts to interaction between people using sensors and light sources, which illuminate when the forms are touched.

The body responds to the jewellery and the jewellery responds to the body. (Gilhooley and Costin 1997, p. 12)
   Stöber's work regards technology benignly, as a medium for communication and self expression. Transmitters and information interfaces operate without male gendered buttons. Switches and probes; clasps, sockets, chains and piercings are noticeably absent in works that pass by the sadistic baggage of jewellery and further blur the distinction between decorative and artistically autonomous objects. (Gilhooley and Costin 1997, p. 12)

The way the pieces react to the touch of an individual or collection of people shows a very human-centred handling of the technology used, reflecting all four threads of the framework. The focus of the pieces is human contact; they are about relationships and about touch.

A series of works that make visible an exchange of that which is normally not seen. Each brooch responds in different ways when touched by one person, and passed to another. (Description accompanying images, Daniel Gratiot 2004)

Compositionally the narrative structure reflects the notion of relationships in the way that the pieces "come to life" technologically through touch or through connection. The rings only illuminate when the two people wearing them hold hands.

Combining magnetic attraction, and warm red light, these rings individually are only forms. When the two wearers bring the bases into contact, they are attracted to each other, and form a circuit that activates the light in both rings. (Description accompanying images, Daniel Gratiot 2004)

Emotionally and spatiotemporally this is very strong; the private gesture of holding hands or physical contact is amplified by the illumination of the jewellery thus making a private gesture very public. The pieces highlight the thrill of a touch and also the potential embarrassment of the public display. The functionality of the work acts emotionally to echo how humans communicate to one another through touch. To touch is to be touched; in the glow of a light in response to this contact it is as if the object is returning your gesture. This is also reflected in the sensual quality of the pieces; the ambiguity of use invites playful exploration. Stöber stated of her own work:

My work with light invites reaction. If the light is directed, it may appear decorative as well as personal, or even indiscreet. Light itself can therefore underline or replace the personal touch. (Gilhooley and Costin 1997, p. 108)

5.3 A way forward

In the foregoing discussion, we have used the framework set by Wright et al. as a lens through which to explore experiences of various objects. One key element of our critique is that when we sense a proposal to be unsuccessful there is a failure to satisfy and entwine all of the four threads of the framework. This could be described as a sense of incompleteness in the work analysed. Some proposals offer strong compositional and spatiotemporal contributions, but neglect the sensual and emotional threads. Alternatively, when analysing non-digital pieces of jewellery many could be said to be "complete" in this way because they attend to and intertwine these four threads. This is not true for all contemporary jewellery, but many pieces do act to constitute environments rich in emotional content and do fulfil the criteria of the threads in this framework. We do not want to suggest that all four threads need to be equally strong to create an experientially rich interaction, but it is important that all four threads are acknowledged and considered. We are conducting further work using the four threads to inform our design in order to test this hypothesis.

As many of the previous examples illustrate, jewellers frequently emphasise the importance of details and layers of a piece. It may be that contemporary jewellers aim to envelop the viewer with their work, by paying attention to the nuances of the many layers of the jewellery object as "an experience". This viewpoint gives us a grasp of what it means to create an opportunity for emotionally, compositionally, sensually and spatiotemporally rich experience. It is not sufficient to simply meet needs and avoid interaction breakdowns; interaction design should seek to surpass expectations and elevate experience.

6 Conclusions

From our different perspectives as researchers in contemporary jewellery and in HCI, we have found that Wright et al.'s (2003) framework for the analysis of experience has offered us a way of describing digital objects and jewellery. It has acted as a translation tool, enabling us to discuss our differing interpretation of our experiences of three-dimensional forms. It allows us to discuss an analysis of our experience through different, but ever-connected elements and has formed the basis for a dialogue, in our situation, between different disciplines. In particular, it has allowed us to recognise aspects of our unconscious or tacit responses to objects and draw them into our conscious awareness in a way that may assist us in reflectively analysing our own design practice.

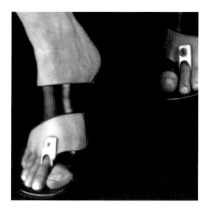

Figs. 13 and 15. Closeup. *Technojewelry*. 2002 Wearable Technology Concepts. IDEO
http://www.ideo.com

Fig. 14. Closeup. *Kiss Communicator*. 1996. Heather Martin.
Technology Concepts. IDEO lab research project with Duncan Kerr
http://www.ideo.com, http://www.interaction.rca.ac.uk/alumni/96-98/heather

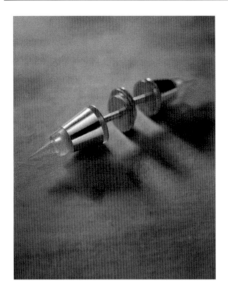

Figs. 16 and 17. *For Two Rings* 1994. Magnets, stainless steel, Perspex, LEDs with electronics. Nicole Gratiot Stöber © 1994 all rights reserved.
Photographer Christoph Grünig. Image courtesy Daniel Gratiot

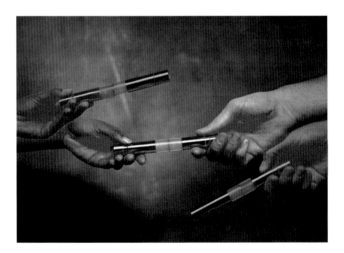

Fig. 18. *Light Brooches* 1994. stainless steel, plastic. LEDs with touch-sensitive electronics, magnets (for holding separate wire clothing pins).
Nicole Gratiot Stöber © 1994 all rights reserved.
Photographer Christoph Grünig. Image courtesy Daniel Gratiot

Through the formulation of a critique using the framework we have achieved a development of each of our individual criteria of what constitutes a successful enriching experience. The framework then enabled us to share not only the critique, but our personal criteria as well. This method of understanding the experiential components of an object along with the transparency of personal criteria constituting "completeness" of experience may enable an understanding of how to design experientially rich interactive objects. In the context of design, if design is a shared activity, then it becomes necessary to discuss our individual implicit criteria within experience and to do so we must be explicit. In the conception and design of digital jewellery this framework is a valuable tool, which we are incorporating into our practice as designers in different fields. Our experience leads us to recommend it to other interaction designers.

References

Blythe M, Monk A, Overbeeke K, Wright P (eds) (2003) Funology: From Usability to User Enjoyment. Kluwer, Dordrecht

Cheung L, Potter L (2003) Exhibition Catalogue. Treasure. Contemporary Notions of Sentimentality in Jewellery. The Pearoom Centre for Contemporary Craft

Gilhooley D, Costin C (1997) Unclasped: Contemporary British Jewellery. Black Dog Publishing

IDEO Corporate Web site. Retrieved February, 2004, http:www.ideo.com/portfolio/re.asp?x=50165

Infoworld (2002) Web site article detailing IBM's development of digital jewellery proposals. Retrieved March, 2003, from http://archive.infoworld.com/articles/op/xml/00/08/07/000807opwireless.xml

Laurel B (1991) Computers as Theatre. Addison-Wesley, Reading, MA

McCarthy J, Wright P (2003) The Enchantments of Technology. In: Blythe M, Monk A, Overbeeke C, Wright P (eds) Funology: From Usability to User Enjoyment. Kluwer, Dordrecht

Marzee Exhibition Catalogue 8 April-30 May 2001 Galerie Marzee, Netherlands

Monk A, Hassenzahl M, Blythe M, Reed D (2002) Funology: Designing Enjoyment. In: Proceedings of CHI 2002, extended abstracts, pp 924-925. ACM Press

Myerson, J (2001) IDEO: Masters of Innovation. Laurence King, London

Norman D (2004) Emotional Design: Why We Love (or Hate) Everyday Things. Basic Books, New York

Philips Electronics (2000) New Nomads: An Exploration of Wearable Electronics by Philips. Published by 010 2000

Philips Corporate Web site (2003) Retrieved January 2003, http://www.philips.com/InformationCenter/Global/FArticleSummary.asp?lNodeId=54 5&channel=545&channelId=N545A1659

Philips Design Web site (2003) Retrieved January 2003, http://www.design.philips.com/smartconnections/newnomads/index.html

Riklin-Schelbert A (1999) 20th Century Swiss Art Jewelry. VGS Verlagsgemeinschaft St. Gallen

Royal College of Art. Computer Related Design. Retrieved February, 2004,
http://www.interaction.rca.ac.uk/alumni/96-98/heather
Schouwenberg L (1998) The Secret Language of a Jewel: "Nieuw Werk" Exhibition
Catalogue Galerie Louise Smit. Amsterdam
Taylor AS, Harper R (2002) Age-old practices in the "New World": A study of gift-giving
between teenage mobile phone users. In: Proceedings of CHI 2002, CHI Letters 4(1).
ACM Press
White R (2002) BBC corporate Web site, science strand detailing palaeontology research
concerning jewellery. Retrieved July, 2002, from
http://www.bbc.co.uk/science/apeman/dig_deeper/article_2.shtml
Winograd T (1996) Bringing Design to Software. Addison-Wesley, Reading, MA
Wright P, McCarthy J, Meekison L (2003) Making sense of experience. In: Blythe M,
Monk A, Overbeeke C, Wright P (eds) Funology: From Usability to User Enjoyment.
Kluwer, Dordrecht, pp 43-53